I-Way Robbery

I-Way Robbery:
Crime on the Internet

William C. Boni, MBA, and
Dr. Gerald L. Kovacich, CFE, CPP, CISSP

BUTTERWORTH
HEINEMANN

Boston   Oxford   Auckland   Johannesburg   Melbourne   New Delhi

Butterworth–Heinemann supports the efforts of American Forests and the Global ReLeaf program in its campaign for the betterment of trees, forests, and our environment.

Library of Congress Cataloging-in-Publication Data

Boni, William.
    I-way robbery : crime on the Internet / William Boni and Gerald L. Kovacich.
        p. cm.
    Includes bibliographical references and index.
    ISBN 0-7506-7029-0 (paperback : alk. paper)
    1. Computer crimes.   2. Computer security.   3. Internet (Computer network)—Security measures.   I. Kovacich, Gerald L.   II. Title.
    HV6773.B66 1999
    364.16'8—dc21

                                                    99-11320
                                                         CIP

British Library Cataloguing-in-Publication Data
A catalogue record for this book is available from the British Library.

The publisher offers special discounts on bulk orders of this book.
For information, please contact:

> Manager of Special Sales
> Butterworth–Heinemann
> 225 Wildwood Avenue
> Woburn, MA 01801-2041
> Tel: 781-904-2500
> Fax: 781-904-2620

For information on all Butterworth–Heinemann publications available, contact our World Wide Web home page at: *http://www.bh.com*.

10 9 8 7 6 5 4 3 2 1

Printed in the United States of America

This book is dedicated to my wife, Charunee, who has supported me through every twist and turn of an evolving career, and to my children, who will travel the 21st-century I-Way to destinations undreamed of by their father!
William C. Boni

This book is dedicated to all the hackers, phreakers, crackers, nuts, weirdos, and associated other human beings who surf, spam, use, misuse, and abuse the I-Way. Because of their crazy personalities, criminal conduct, and all-around blatant disregard for rules, laws, and government controls, they have made all our lives more interesting, our work more challenging, and our information security market—and United States economy—growing!
Dr. Gerald L. Kovacich, CFE, CPP, CISSP

"Whatever man creates, should be controlled by man's character . . ."

Thomas Edison

"When we enter society at birth, we receive an inheritance from the people who lived before us. It is our responsibility to augment that inheritance for those who succeed us. I feel that all of us owe the world more than we received when we were born."

An Wang

"What do we live for if not to make life less difficult for each other?"

George Eliot

Contents

Foreword

The global Internet or "I-Way" is a worldwide network communications system having a profound impact on the way we conduct our personal relationships, international politics, and business with a multiple of innovations and benefits. However, there is an ominous downside of crimes and criminal enterprises exploiting the new technologies to commit crimes in new ways and totally new crimes. The exploits of hackers, phreakers, and crackers and increases in industrial and business fraud were widely publicized in the era before "I-Way" but what is happening today is quite different.

The "I-Way" is user friendly with many people from children and housewives in the home, students from elementary schools to colleges, corporate managers and farmers concerned about risks run when they use it. High governmental security officials have warned that most modern industrial nations are vulnerable to the ravages of techno-terrorists and cyber-criminals employing the "I-Way" to wreak havoc.

The book is timely because it will help the average user of the "I-Way" make the leap into "cyberspace." It makes this alien environment seem more understandable by the implied comparison to the nationwide highway system. The metaphor "I-Way" provides a useful way for framing the discussions of risks and protective measures for the average "John Q" citizen who uses the system. From beginning to end it will hold the reader's attention with such catchy chapter headings such as Dangerous Curves Ahead, I-Way Targets, and I-Way Robberies.

The authors are dedicated professionals with several decades of real world experience and research and both have international reputations for scholarly lectures.

This book is must reading for all new and regular users of the Internet.

John P. Kenney, Ph.D.
Professor Emeritus

Preface

The transformation of the global Internet, sometimes referred to as the "I-Way," from an academic research, communication and sometimes "techie playground," to a mainstream global communications medium, and baseline for the Global Information Infrastructure (GII), is one of the most significant developments in recent history. It is having a profound impact on all aspects of our civilization, and none more so than on the systems security administrators, law enforcement officers, and other security professionals who must defend their businesses' and government agencies' information assets against the "I-Way robbers," those miscreants and juvenile delinquents who use the I-Way for criminal, unethical, and immoral purposes.

One of the areas likely to change dramatically is the area of crimes and criminal enterprises exploiting the new I-Way technologies: both to commit old crimes in new ways, new crimes in old ways, and totally new crimes in new ways.

Already, newspapers and trade journals regularly document the exploits of hackers, phreakers, and crackers using the Internet to commit a wide range of computer frauds and crimes, computer-related crimes, and to support other criminal behavior. Many people from common users at home to corporate managers are concerned about the risks they run when they use the I-Way. To add to the concern, directors of both the FBI and the CIA have warned that most modern information age nations are vulnerable to the ravages of I-Way terrorists and other I-Way criminals exploiting this technology to wreak havoc on the United States' information infrastructure.

With everything being written and said about the topic of Internet crimes, criminals, pornography, scam artists, hackers, phreakers, crackers, techno-terrorists, economic espionage agents, information warriors, and the like, what basic information should the professional security person and law enforcement officer know about this topic? After all, it is his or her responsibility to protect the I-Way information and systems and/or investigate incidents, crimes, and frauds being perpetrated by the I-Way robbers.

Their problem seems to be that they are already burdened with other "priority" tasks; they don't understand the technology and don't have time to learn it; therefore, many of the problems and how to solve them default to consultants, information technology staff, and others. That delegation of authority, or outright abandonment of their responsibilities, may work, but it is *not* the right approach, unless the security professionals and/or law enforcement officers understand what they are abdicating both as part of the professional responsibilities and their inability to cope with such issues because they lack a basic understanding of what is involved.

It is the hope of the authors that this mostly nontechnical book on the topic provides these professionals with a basic foundation and understanding of the threats, vulnerabilities, risks, issues, problems, and maybe some possible solutions.

In this book, to help the average security and/or law enforcement professional make the leap into "cyberspace," we will refer to the Internet as simply the I-Way. This is a deliberate attempt to make this somewhat alien environment seem more understandable by the implied comparison to the nationwide highway system. This metaphor will also provide a useful vehicle for framing the discussion of risks and protective measures.

The authors hope that this book will serve as a primer that allows security and/or law enforcement professionals responsible for asset protection or investigation of I-Way wrongdoing to make informed judgments concerning the nature and extent of the new risks created by I-Way connectivity. It should also help them more completely understand their responsibilities to their customers and the public for providing a safe and secure I-Way environment.

This book is also designed to provide a foundation of basic information for protecting both corporations' and government agencies' assets from the new threats and risks posed by the Internet. One way to distinguish this book from other volumes discussing Internet security is to think of it as "driver's education manual" for new I-Way drivers.

This book is based on the nearly 50 years of combined "real world" operational experience of the authors, who together have been responsible for implementing information systems security and Internet-related protection programs. We have also conducted training for international and national corporations and United States and foreign government agencies ranging from military, law enforcement through intelligence services, as well as conducting or assisting in conducting national and international high-technology crime investigations related to the I-Way.

The authors have found that most of the existing books on the market concentrate on the technical aspects of Internet security, not on helping average security and law enforcement professional separate the hype and "sound bite" information from reality. This book provides accurate and timely information that tells the readers what they need to know and the steps they must take to protect themselves and their organizations as they make use of the I-Way. This book is written to provide the security and law enforcement professionals, as well as business managers, the information to help them understand the threats, vulnerabilities, and risks associated with the I-Way. It will also provide a general awareness of I-Way security issues for corporate managers or executives with interest in the Internet or formal responsibility for Internet projects.

This book is also well suited for university and college professors and their students as a textbook related to the study of information systems security, security management, and the criminal justice field.

The authors also believe that this book would be well worth reading by those home and small businesses who travel on the I-Way and who do not have the budget to employ full-time professional security personnel. Although they may lack security specialists, they do not want to suffer public embarrassment, so they don't call law enforcement professionals to investigate I-Way robberies. It is hoped that this book will enlighten them on some of the dangers they face and what they can do to manage their risks.

The unique aspect of this book is that it provides a basic foundation for dealing with the complex issues arising from access and use of the Internet. It begins with a brief explanation of the history and development of the Internet, its impact on organizations and individuals, and its expected growth to become one of the basic means of global communication and business in the early 21st century.

The book provides practical advice and insights into threats and protective measures, and packages these in the metaphor of the I-Way. With the blistering pace of technological change in this area and the focus on evolution of the Internet and fundamental protection measures, the authors have tried to present the information in such a manner as to help ensure it will not be outdated as soon as it is published.

Chapter One will describe the evolution of the Internet in the context of the "Three Waves" model presented by the Tofflers. Then follows a short history of Internet technology and its impact on contemporary organizations.

Chapter Two will discuss the impact of the Internet on organizations and individuals in both businesses and government agencies.

Chapter Three will provide a foreshadowing of the future risks associated with the Internet through a discussion of the evolution of technological crimes from the 1970s to the present.

Chapter Four will describe and frame the issues surrounding criminal acts and offenses associated with the Internet. Relevant U.S. and international laws and recent developments will be briefly discussed. Specific issues of popular concern will receive sufficient attention so the reader will understand the challenge of "policing" the Internet. The "new" problems of economic and industrial espionage, high-technology terrorism, and information warfare through use of the Internet will be briefly described.

Chapter Five will profile the various miscreants one may encounter while using the I-Way for business or government purposes.

Chapter Six discusses the assets which are typically targets and far too often accessible to the sophisticated Internet-based criminal.

Chapter Seven will discuss the tactics, tools, and techniques used to obtain information or other valuable property via the I-Way.

Chapter Eight will provide a series of reports drawn from the public domain which provide valuable insights into the incidents which have already happened.

Chapter Nine will build on the incidents presented in Chapter Eight and describe the factors that have contributed to the risks of using the I-Way.

Chapter Ten will describe the techniques and technologies that are essential to safe travel on the I-Way for the business or government agency.

Chapter Eleven will provide a summary and conclusions, as well as a look into the future and will discuss the likely challenges to the security and law enforcement professionals in the early 21st century.

We hope this book's format and choice of topics will make a contribution to the successful and secure use of the Internet.

William C. Boni
Simi Valley, California
Dr. Gerald L. Kovacich, CFE, CPP, CISSP
An Island in Washington State

Acknowledgments

To take on a project such as this takes more than just the authors. It takes friends, professional associates, and peers who unselfishly give of their time and effort to help make this book worth publishing.

We are very grateful to all and to a special group who have helped us over the years and again with this project, to include: Motomu Akashi, Industrial Security Expert (retired); Jerry Swick, High Technology Crime Investigations Expert, MCI; Paul Zavidniak, InfoWar Specialist, Logicon Corporation; Professor James Chandler, George Washington University; and a special thanks to Ken Cutler, Managing Director, Information Security Institute, MIS Training Institute, for the "ISI Swiss Army Knife" and his support over the years.

We must also acknowledge the staff of Butterworth–Heinemann, especially Laurel A. DeWolf, Maura Kelly, and Rita Lombard, for their time, effort, and support in making this book a reality. Without their support and guidance, this book truly could not have been written.

What Is the I-Way?

1

CHAPTER OBJECTIVE

The objective of this chapter is to discuss (1) the evolution of the Internet, known as the I-Way, and (2) the implications it has for both law enforcement and security professionals as well as potential criminals—the I-Way robbers.

HOW DID WE GET FROM ADAM TO INTERNET?

The use of the Tofflers' model of technological evolution provides a useful framework for discussing changes arising from the impact of technology generally, and the Internet specifically. The model begins by describing the Agricultural Age that lasted from about the time of Adam until about 1745 in the United States.[1] Manual labor and a focus on accumulating a minimum food surplus to allow for governance characterized this long period. During this time, technological progress was very limited, slow, and laborious. The major lack of understanding of even the most basic concepts of science impeded progress. Warfare, although common, was generally short in duration and decided often by major battles or campaigns lasting less than a year. Although large armies were possible (at one point the Roman Empire fielded over 700,000 soldiers) there were limited and relatively ineffective methods for communicating and controlling more than a small percentage of these forces. Runners, horse-borne message couriers supplemented by flags and other visual media, were the major methods of remote communication.

The Industrial Age, in the United States, lasted a much shorter time, only from approximately 1745 until about 1955.[2] The defining event of the Industrial Age was the introduction of the steam engine that allowed mechanical equipment to replace muscle powered efforts of both humans and animals. These devices introduced a new and much accelerated pace of technical innovation. During this 200-year period, there was a dramatic expansion of human knowledge and understanding of the basic principles of physical science. Enhanced agriculture allowed nations to accumulate huge food surpluses. Upon the food surplus foundation, nation-states increased their power by developing mass production. Mass production of weapons and the mass slaughter of both combatants and noncombatants characterized the conflicts of this period.

Communications technology evolved from primitive signaling involving lanterns and reflected lights (heliograph) to supplement the continued use of human couriers whether riding horses, trains, or water-borne craft. The inventions of the telegraph in the early 1800s, followed in the late 1890s by the telephone, and then by wireless radio in the early 1900s were essential evolutionary steps towards today's telecommunications infrastructure.

The Information Age in the United States, according to the Tofflers, began about 1955, which is the first year that white-collar employees exceeded blue-collar production jobs. This has been the era with the most explosive growth in human knowledge. More has been discovered in the past 50 years in both science and engineering than in the thousands of years of recorded human history. In the Information Age, knowledge is growing exponentially.

The pace of evolution in communications and other technologies accelerated (see Figure 1–1) during the early years of the Information Age with the advent of satellites, fiber optics connections, and other high-speed and high bandwidth telecommunications technologies.

It is in the context of this phenomenal growth of technology and human knowledge that the I-Way arises as one of the mechanisms to facilitate sharing of information and as a medium that encourages global communications. According to the United States General Accounting Office in a report to Congress,[3] the rapid developments of telecommunications infrastructure in the United States resulted in the creation of three separate and frequently incompatible communications networks including:

Wire-based voice and data telephone networks;

Cable-based video networks; and

Wireless voice, data, and video networks.

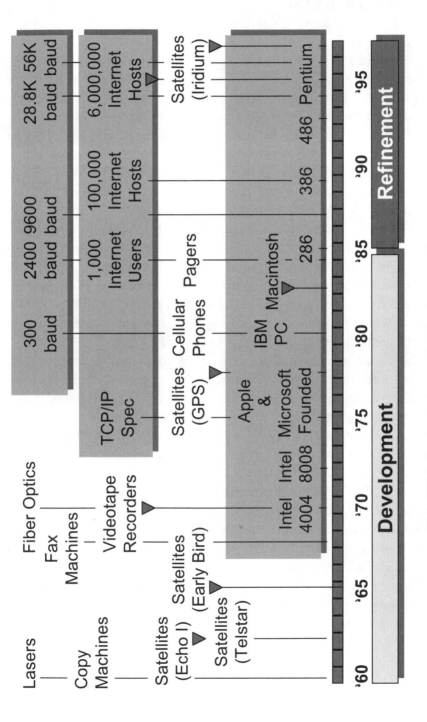

FIGURE 1–1   The Evolution of Technology over the Past 30 Years

BIRTH OF THE I-WAY

The global collection of networks that have evolved in the late 20th century to become the I-Way represent what could be described as a "global nervous system" transmitting facts, opinions, and opportunity from anywhere to anywhere else. However, when most security and law enforcement professionals think of the I-Way, it seems to be something either vaguely sinister or of such complexity that it makes it difficult to understand. Popular culture, as manifested by Hollywood and network television programs, does little to dispel this impression of danger and out-of-control complexity.

The I-Way arose out of projects sponsored by the Advanced Research Project Agency (ARPA) in the United States in the 1960s. It is perhaps one of the most exciting legacy developments of that era. Originally an effort to facilitate sharing of expensive computer resources and enhance military communications, it has over the ten-plus years from about 1988 until 1999 rapidly evolved from its scientific and military roots into one of the premier *commercial* communications media. The I-Way, which is described as a global metanetwork, or network of networks,[4] provides the foundation upon which the global information superhighway will be built.

However, it was not until the early 1990s that I-Way communication technologies became easily accessible to the average person. Prior to that time, I-Way accesses required mastery of many arcane and difficult to remember programming language codes. However, the combination of declining microcomputer prices, enhanced microcomputer performance, and the advent of easy to use *browser*[5] software, were key enabling technologies that created the foundation for mass I-Way activity. When these variables aligned with the developing global telecommunications infrastructure, they allowed a benign convergence of capability. It has now become a simple matter for average people, even those who had trouble programming their VCRs, to obtain access to the global I-Way, and with the access search the huge volume of information it contains. In the United States alone, tens of millions of people are accessing the I-Way on a regular basis. Millions of others around the world are logging in, creating a vast environment often referred to as *cyberspace* and the Global Information Infrastructure (GII), which has been described as the virtual, on-line, computer-enabled environment, and distinct from the physical reality of "real life." The most commonly accessed application on the I-Way is the World Wide Web (Web). Originally developed in Switzerland, the Web was envisioned by its inventor as a way to help share information. The ability to find information concerning virtually any topic via search engines, such as Alta Vista, HotBot, Lycos, InfoSeek, or others, from among the rapidly growing array of Web servers is an amazing example of how the I-Way increases the information available to nearly everyone. One gains some sense of how fast and pervasive the I-Way has become as more TV, radio, and print advertisements direct prospective customers to visit their business or government agency Web sites. Such sites are typically named www.companyname.com for businesses or www.governmentagency.gov for government agencies.

By the year 2000, worldwide revenues via I-Way commerce are expected to reach perhaps hundreds of billions of dollars, an unparalleled growth rate for a technology that was effected only since the early 1990s! The electronic commerce of the early 21st century is expected to include everything from on-line information concerning products, purchases, and services, to the development of entirely new business activities (e.g., I-Way enabled banking).

An important fact to understand, and one of supreme importance for security and law enforcement professionals, is that the Web is truly global in scope. Physical borders as well as geographical distance are almost meaningless in cyberspace; the distant target is as easily attacked as a local one. This is an important concept for security and law enforcement professionals to understand, as it will impact their capability to successfully do their jobs. The annihilation of time and space makes the I-Way an almost perfect environment for the I-Way robbers. When finding a desired server located on the other side of the planet is as easy and convenient as calling directory assistance to find a local telephone number, I-Way robbers have the potential to act in ways that we can only begin to imagine. Undeterred by distance, borders, time, or season, the potential bonanza awaiting the I-Way robber is a chilling prospect for those who are responsible for safeguarding the assets of a business or government agency.

FUTURE SHOCK

With appreciation for Toffler's book, *Future Shock*, the reaction of people and organizations to the dizzying pace of I-Way "progress" has been mixed. Although some technologically sophisticated individuals and organizations have been very quick to exploit the potential of this new technology, many have been slower, adopting more of a wait and see posture. The rapid pace of evolution of the I-Way does raise some questions as to how much a society can absorb, how much can actually be used to benefit organizations in such a compressed time frame. Sometimes lost in the technological hype concerning the physical speed of I-Way enabled communications or the new technologies that are making it easier to display commercial content is the fact that the I-Way's greatest impact ultimately is in providing unprecedented access to information. The access is unprecedented in the breadth of the total volume of information that is moving on-line and may be tapped for decision making.

It also is unprecedented when we consider the increasing percentage of the world's population that enjoys this access. As more and more information moves on-line and becomes available to more and more people, it is causing some fundamental changes in how we communicate, do business and think of the world we live in. Consequently, it is also causing fundamental changes in how criminals and miscreants commit crimes.

Throughout much of human history, the educated elites of every culture have jealously guarded their knowledge. Access to knowledge, whether in written or spoken form, was often the source of the elite's privileged position and often allowed them to dominate or control the great uninformed masses of uneducated humanity—information was and is still a means to power. "Outsiders" were never granted access to the store of wisdom unless they were inducted into the privileged elite. Now, however, the average I-Way traveler, wherever resident, with little more than a modem and a mediocre microcomputer, can access, analyze, and/or distribute information around the world on almost any topic.

Some pundits have concluded that we now live in an era where there are "no more secrets." By some estimates, early in the next century there will be more information published and available on-line than has ever been accessible in all the libraries on earth. How this torrent of information will be managed to ensure that the I-Way robbers do not wreak havoc and dominate the I-Way, nor have power over others, is now (or should be) the primary objective of every security and law enforcement professional whose business or government agency travels the I-Way.

ROADMAP FOR THE I-WAY

The I-Way can be compared in some ways to a roadmap for a superhighway. Some basic examples will help explain the I-Way in common terms.

When multiple computers (whether microcomputers or larger) are linked together by various communications protocols to allow digital information to be transmitted and shared among the connected systems, they become a network. The combination of tens of thousand of organizational networks interconnected with high-capacity "backbone" data communications and the public telephone networks now constitutes the global I-Way. However, there is a major difference in this environment that is important to consider for security and law enforcement professionals.

When the isolated "by-ways" of individual business or government agency networks become connected to the global I-Way, they become "off-ramps" potentially accessible to other I-Way travelers. The number and diversity of locations that provide I-Way "on-ramps" are vast and growing. Today, one can access the I-Way from public libraries, "cyber" cafes in many cities around the world, even kiosks in some airports. These and other locations provide I-Way on-ramps to anyone who has a legitimate account or an I-Way robber who can "hijack" one from an authorized user.

Typically, a business or government agency will use centrally controlled computers called *servers* to store the information and the sophisticated software applications used to manage and control their information flow. These systems could be equated to superhighway interchanges.

Business and government agency networks are considered private property and the information they contain as proprietary for the exclusive use of the organization. These business and government agency networks are connected to large networks operated by I-Way service providers (ISPs), such as UUNET, GTE, AOL, ATT, and others, who provide the equivalent of toll roads and turnpikes for the flow of information.

THE I-WAY: NO TRAFFIC CONTROLS

The I-Way challenges the security and law enforcement professional with an array of new and old responsibilities in a new environment. From the perspective of managing risks, this new access to information creates new kinds of dangers to businesses and government agencies. It also allows well-understood security issues to recur in new or unique ways. No longer can organizations assume they will obtain any security through obscurity, no matter where they are physically located. In other words, because there is an I-Way off-ramp they will be visible to I-Way robbers. Everything from a nation's most critical defense information to business information is vulnerable to easy destruction, modification, and compromise by unauthorized I-Way travelers.

Too often, careless managers fail to take adequate measures to safeguard sensitive information, which results in premature disclosure with attendant adverse impact. The major part of the controllable risk arises from inadvertent disclosure to the ever-vigilant eyes of the I-Way robbers and others, such as competitive intelligence analysts with I-Way access.

NO CENTRAL MANAGEMENT OR I-WAY POLICE

One of the most fascinating aspects in the I-Way growth saga is that it has developed largely through collaborative and unregulated efforts of the interested parties. Self-appointed leaders and task forces worked together to address the tricky technical details of the design and operation of this environment.

When the I-Way was limited to scientists, academic researchers, and government employees, such a collaborative framework was probably a very cost-effective means of controlling the virtual world. However, in the early 1990s, for the first time there were more commercial sites than educational and governmental sites using the I-Way. Since that time, matters have become increasingly complex. The informal array of social sanctions and technical forums for cooperation is no longer capable of ensuring a modicum of civilized behaviors.

SUMMARY

The advent of the motor car and highways presaged an increase in physical mobility and access to goods and services in remote areas. This mobility not only contributed to the economic growth of the nation, but also was exploited by the famous gangsters of the 1920s and 1930s to loot banks and elude the local police. Similarly, the creation of the I-Way will facilitate unparalleled access to information and the growth of the global economy, but we can also expect that criminals will grasp the new opportunities for crimes—probably well before many security and law enforcement professionals are comfortable operating on the Internet!

NOTES

1. The time of the agricultural period varies by progress of individual nations.
2. As with the Agricultural Age, dates vary for individual nations.
3. *Information Superhighway: An Overview of Technology Challenges*, GAO-AIMD 95-23, p. 12.
4. Ibid., p. 11.
5. Software that simplifies the search and display of World Wide Web supplied information.

2

What Has Been the Impact of the I-Way?

CHAPTER OBJECTIVE

This chapter will discuss the impact of the I-Way and provide some insights into its impacts on both individual capabilities and organizations—both public (governmental) and private sector (corporate/nonprofit). The focus will be on how I-Way technology has facilitated unprecedented access to information by ordinary people around the world.

IMPACTS ON BOTH INDIVIDUAL CAPABILITIES AND ORGANIZATIONS

It is apparent that the I-Way has rapidly become a significant element in modern society, figuring in advertising, films, television, even facilitating the rapid dissemination of investigative reports involving a U.S. president. The I-Way has provided many additional information services and they are all becoming easier to access. The two primary new avenues for increased volume of information access are via the Web browser and net-enabled e-mail. This increased access to information has been an advantage principally for law-abiding citizens and legitimate businesses, but it also offers both hardened and prospective I-Way robbers new high-speed venues for perpetrating their crimes and schemes.

Almost everyone working in America has been exposed to some form of computer technology. From the front line retail clerk at the local fast food franchise, to the Wall Street analyst, to the farmer planning his crop rotations, individual work performance has been substantially enabled by the widespread proliferation of microcomputer technologies. But the macro impacts on organizations are in some ways less remarkable than they have been for individuals. Go to any good computer store, or better yet, if you have I-Way access, browse the Web sites of major microcomputer manufacturers. You will discover a wide range of systems with memory, speed, and storage capabilities that would have been descriptive of large, mainframe computers in the early 1980s. For example, in the late 1980s a large regional bank in Southern California operated its electronic wire/funds transfer machine with only 48 MB of RAM and 120 MB of disk storage, and the system transferred billions of dollars nightly for the bank. Now the performance of an equivalent system is available to anyone with a few thousand dollars—and the nightly transactions run to the hundreds of billions of dollars, if not trillions.

In business, it has become in some ways a David versus Goliath world, where the advantages don't always accrue to the organization that can field the bigger battalions. Advanced information technology was once the province exclusively of governments, the military, universities, and large corporate entities. This is no longer true. Now anyone with a modest investment in hardware and software can acquire a powerful processor and attach it to the I-Way. It should be obvious that criminals and those with criminal intentions also have access to powerful information technology. The question remains as to how they will use it.

As we consider the potential for criminal actions directed against organizations, it is critically important to consider these factors. The same information technology we use to manage our organizations can and will be used by savvy I-Way robbers to the detriment of governments, businesses, and others.

When powerful microcomputers are networked, the communication capabilities inherent in these arrangements multiply their value. A single microcomputer standing alone is little more than a sophisticated typewriter or calculating machine. The real power comes when individual machines link together to create networks that will allow the flow of information from one person to the entire world. As a case in point, consider the story of Russia's transition from communism to democracy. When the military coup against Gorbachev occurred in the early 1990s, the military plotters seized control of all the classic means of communication: newspapers, telephones, and radio and TV stations. However, the anti-coup forces quickly drove their message onto the I-Way to get word to the outside world of the situation, and timely communications played a significant part in defeating an attempt by the most powerful military and police apparatus on earth to regain power over the Russian people.

The capabilities brought to the individual by the I-Way are considerable and growing almost daily. For example, anyone can now enjoy the ability to sign up for investment services from low-cost brokerages and stock market advisors and enjoy the kind of timely advice that for generations has been a perquisite of the rich and powerful classes. Grass roots political organizing and civic action are also enabled. Recently in California, a concerned parent scanned into a database and posted on a Web page the details of the state's list of sexual predators/ pedophiles, thus allowing average people to determine if there was a registered sex offender residing in their neighborhood.

From shopping for homes and automobiles (where on-line services promise to eliminate the brokers' monopoly of information) to traffic, weather forecasts, and directions prior to trips, the I-Way is providing more information to more people every day, and we are only at the beginning of that process! The major trend here is clear: there will be more information accessible to more people than has ever been possible in the past. How this information power will be used ultimately depends on the ethics and motives of the individual: I-Way robbers can use such power negatively.

INDISPENSABLE TECHNOLOGIES

Which of the many capabilities provided by the I-Way do average people really use? A very good source for this information is a recently published survey of 10,000 Internet and World Wide Web users.[1] In the survey, the percentages of respondents who considered email the most indispensable technology among those listed exceeded 93 percent. The World Wide Web itself was a close second, with a little over 90 percent of the respondents rating it as indispensable. All the other listed technologies rated substantially lower, with none over 30 percent in this survey.

In addition to showing how much the average person now values his or her e-mail, the survey also identifies other services and capabilities now available through the I-Way. One that is of particular significance to business organizations is the "chat" service (often referred to as "chat rooms"). In some sense, they are the virtual counterpart to neighborhood coffeehouses or lounges. They permit customers/participants to strike up conversations with old friends or new acquaintances via their keyboards in impromptu, real time, on-line discussions. The major difference is that often they allow one to use an assumed name, and participants may therefore completely misrepresent everything about themselves, particularly if they are in the room for some criminal purpose. Chat services have been implicated in everything from incidents of on-line pedophilia, to broken marriages, to solicitations for more violent crimes.

ORGANIZATIONAL IMPACTS

The major benefits to organizations of the I-Way and related technologies are significant and far ranging. In large part, the impacts may be characterized as dramatically lower costs for transmitting and sharing information. To appreciate how far we have come, before electronic mail became ubiquitous, it took as long as a week for first class postal mail, derisively called *snail mail* by I-Way aficionados, to travel from one coast of the United States to the other. Even the fax machine, which itself was a significant improvement over postal and overnight courier services, required dedicated fax equipment. Contrast these with the capabilities of I-Way e-mail. E-mail, which may transit the globe in seconds, allows recipients to retrieve their messages when it is convenient, and they need not be present at a predetermined location to receive them. Through the use of digital attachments, e-mail can carry more information in a convenient compression of transmission times.

Whereas the innocent e-mail user sees only increased speed and volume of communication, security and law enforcement professionals must understand how damaging even one message could be to a business or government agency. A single e-mail message could contain the whole strategic business plan of the organization or the source code to a breakthrough product, and be transmitted anywhere on earth in a nanosecond.

To show that this threat is much more than theoretical, consider the allegations involving two leading Silicon Valley software companies. Company A accused rival Company B of theft of trade secrets and proprietary source code. Company A's management alleged as one element in their complaint that a former Company A employee used his company-provided I-Way access to transfer source code of key products to his own personal account.

The employee then tendered his resignation. Upon arrival at his home-based office, the now-former Company A employee allegedly downloaded the stolen source code to his home computer system. Employed as a programmer consultant by rival start-up Company B, he reportedly used the purloined source code as the foundation for a remarkably similar product created at Company B.[2]

Another example is a former employee of Company X who was accused of transmitting the source code for a new digital device to rival Company Y. This scheme apparently was discovered only by accident when the highly confidential materials created such a long message that it caused the e-mail system to crash and allowed a system administrator to discover the purported scheme.

These two incidents are drawn from press reports in the media and it is likely that they are only the very tip of the iceberg. In fact, many organizations do not have the security systems and technologies to detect similar incidents. Due to the adverse publicity and the prospect of the lengthy criminal justice process, even those businesses and government agencies that have been victimized by I-Way robbers frequently do not report similar incidents to the proper authorities.

USING I-WAY ON- AND OFF-RAMPS TO SHARE INFORMATION

One of the truly remarkable developments in information technology has been the widespread use of the Web browser and related technology to deliver information to both internal employees and to the external customers of the organization. If e-mail could be described as a "virtual" duplication of the postal services into the global I-Way environment, then Web servers can be thought of as kiosks or bulletin boards. On these virtual bulletin boards, an organization can make accessible to target populations the information they need to make decisions and perform administrative, operational, or other functions. For example, one very common *intranet* (internal company I-Way) application is to provide a central "forms page" where employees find the most current version of forms to be downloaded and printed for everything from payroll deductions to medical reimbursements. Another use is to front-end a database in which is stored information that must be accessible to a widely dispersed population of users or broad cross section of I-Way travelers.

I-WAY BILLBOARDS, REST STOPS, AND CATALOGS

Currently, the most common and growing destination for the I-Way traveler is the business or government agency Web site. For the I-Way traveler, Web sites are a combination of the superhighway billboards, banks, shopping malls, rest stops, and even fast food delivery services. All of these services as well as hundreds of others can be located at the on- and off-ramps to the I-Way.

These Web sites are used by businesses for advertising, public relations, and marketing, as well as to sell or deliver products or services to I-Way travelers. Web sites may contain and dispense government information concerning everything from how to prepare and submit forms, to descriptions of the most wanted criminal fugitives, to recruiting advertisements for future employees. Even the most secretive United States government agencies, such as the Central Intelligence Agency, the National Security Agency, and others, have established Web sites which provide useful information to I-Way travelers.

The business and government agency Web sites are often the targets of miscreants, juvenile delinquents, and other I-Way robbers. Successful attacks against these Web sites can be disruptive and destructive to the reputation of the sponsoring organization. Therefore, the protection of the Web site must be an important part of the business or government agency plan for using this technology.

SUMMARY

The I-Way has provided a vast and constantly increasing source of information. In the Information Age, where information leads to power and competitive advantage, the I-Way has empowered individuals, business and government agencies, and even nations willing to exploit it. The advances in communications and systems technology has driven much valuable information to Web pages, and Web sites have been the foundation upon which is developing a global commerce replete with I-Way cities featuring virtual malls, banks, and other businesses and services. This aggregation of valuable products, services, and even money is bringing the I-Way robbers who can be expected to cause disruptions and other operational problems.

NOTES

1. Survey conducted by the Graphics, Visualization & Usability Group of Georgia Tech University in the first quarter of 1998.
2. Although based on actual cases, the names have not been used since the cases are still being adjudicated through the criminal justice process.

3

Dangerous Curves Ahead!

CHAPTER OBJECTIVE

This chapter explains the "I-Way" metaphor and the many similarities between the development of the National Defense Highway System (more commonly known as the United States interstate highway system) and the I-Way. These similarities can help us better anticipate some of the risks of I-Way technology. An overview of the risks will be presented through a discussion of how the technology has enabled crimes, as well as some of the statistics that presage a vast increase in I-Way crimes and also assess security and law enforcement professionals' current capability to respond to the anticipated surge in I-Way crimes.

COMPARING THE HIGHWAY AND THE I-WAY

The global Internet I-Way has often been compared to a global highway for information. United States Vice President Gore, in his December 1993 speech to the National Press Club, commented that ". . . today commerce rolls not just on asphalt highways but along information highways. . . . Think of the national information infrastructure as a network of highways, much like the interstates of the 1950s. These are highways carrying information rather than people or goods."[1]

Many other public officials and industry leaders have also used this convenient metaphor. Although there are many reasons why the comparison between the physical highways and the digital circuits for communication is not perfect, it nonetheless communicates an image that is useful. The highway metaphor can be especially helpful to security and law enforcement officers in better understanding the risks that are part of the I-Way environment. Using the information superhighway metaphor should encourage security and law enforcement professionals to understand that much past experience is, in fact, relevant in the Information Age. The I-Way is intended to communicate in the broadest terms the extended state of connectivity and some of the vast new capabilities arising from the global telecommunications infrastructure.

NEW CHALLENGES FOR SECURITY AND LAW ENFORCEMENT PROFESSIONALS

The I-Way has brought with it many new challenges to the security professional. Just learning the vocabulary and technical terms arising from the I-Way is a significant issue. Some also look at the challenges from the I-Way robbers, fraudsters, spies, and terrorists, as something completely new. However, if we look more closely we find that there is little that is truly new from the I-Way robbers. Few of the basic techniques or objectives of these criminals have changed. What is actually new is the *environment* in which they operate. It is now the Information Age and all business and government agencies that operate in the Information Age today inhabit a technology-driven environment. It is the microprocessor-based, network intensive environment alone that is new. Make no mistake, the "bad guys" and "girls" still have the same motives, opportunities, and rationalizations for committing their crimes.

Today's generation of criminals is committing crimes and frauds for precisely the same reasons that they and their predecessors have always committed crimes: it's how they choose to earn their livelihood. Criminals are attempting to do what they have always done: to steal, defraud, and subvert others for personal, corporate, national, and/or political gain. The methods they use for the most part are the same and only change when the I-Way environment requires them to change to achieve their objectives. However, to be successful in the Information Age, they must now commit crimes in the contemporary business environment. The rapid growth of the I-Way and I-Way commerce (also known as *electronic business* in some parts of the world) means that I-Way robbers must operate with knowledge of the I-Way!

If we really think about it, do we have any reason to believe that criminals are much different today than they were in the days of Jesse James? Even in a world featuring computers coupled with the digital, virtual I-Way, and the increased use of I-Way commerce (e.g., "cyber banking"), criminals still have the same objectives: take someone else's money and convert it to their personal benefit. However, the I-Way now allows them to have global mobility and escape in nanoseconds! They are no longer bounded by physical locations or very much by time.

A SHORT HISTORY OF CRIME

Let's look back at some examples of the "ages past." These examples are greatly simplified, but they support the idea that over the centuries the environment has changed, but criminals have remained the same, committing crimes for the same reasons that they have always committed crimes.

During the Agricultural Age (up to about 1745 in the United States, according to the Tofflers), robbers stole money from banks, stores, and people, and escaped on foot or on horses. Particularly in the "colonies," criminals were limited to areas they could walk or run to and/or away from. Using horses, they could make faster getaways! The only knowledge they required was how to ride a horse; where to go to get the money, goods, or other valuables they planned on stealing; and a plan for the crime. If they couldn't afford a horse, they could always steal one. So the horse was one of the tools for committing the crime and also perhaps the object of the theft. This, coupled with their other basic tools of a weapon and a plan, meant they were ready to commit their crimes.

With the advent of the Industrial Age (about 1745 to 1954 in the United States, according to the Tofflers) came the automobile, which greatly enhanced robbers' ability to steal. Robbers still robbed, but now they could steal from more banks, stores, and people. Furthermore, they were able to expand their crime areas because they could travel farther in less time because of the automobile. Also, they could get away faster and hide out farther from the crime scene. So, the automobile did for the robbers in this age what the horse did for them in the earlier age: expanded their crime areas; they also were able to get away farther and faster.

The advent of the superhighways exponentially increased the criminals' opportunities. No longer required to use dirt country roads and two-lane highways, the automobile coupled with the superhighway greatly expanded their crime area. As before, criminals used this new technology and enhanced environment to help commit the same crimes they had always committed and for the same reasons. In this case, as in days past, they purchased their method of transportation, this time the car, or they stole one. They still needed a weapon and a plan.

ADVENT OF THE SUPERHIGHWAYS

In most major westernized nations the central governments invested heavily in the middle of the 20th century to create modern high-speed physical highways. This was seen as a logical progression to allow the national economies of the country to fully benefit from the potential offered by the invention of the automobile at the end of the 19th century. As fascinating as the early automobiles were, their ability to impact national commerce was severely constrained by the lack of paved road networks that would allow them to pass quickly between cities and regions. As recently as the 1930s it could take weeks for an auto to traverse the continent from New York to California.

Germany led the way in the 1930s with the *autobahn*; the United States followed with the interstate superhighways; in England they are known as the *motorways* and in Italy are called the *autostrada*. All represented huge capital investments and took decades to complete. Why did national governments invest billions of dollars in taxes into such projects? Because these superhighways facilitated the flow of people, products, and in time of war, troops and war materials between and among the regions of the nation. One of the major consequences of these superhighway systems has been the beneficial spread of commerce to many cities. The advantages enjoyed by major metropolitan areas that were serviced by railroad lines, ocean or river ports, and major air terminals were now partially offset by the arterial superhighways of the nation. From mills, factories, fields, and warehouses, businesses created products and their contributions rolled away on trucks, cars, and scooters powered by the internal combustion engine and onto the superhighway system to distant locations. No longer did a business have to limit itself to the expense of locating in major transportation hubs.

In general, economists have argued that the superhighway systems contributed to the increased spread of industrial civilization and a generally higher standard of living for more people. Nation-states became a little more homogeneous as the physically mobile population relocated.

The Impact of Superhighways on Crime

One aspect of the automobile and superhighway system combination, one not anticipated by most citizens, was how quickly criminals exploited the new possibilities offered by this combination of technologies. Perhaps the most striking examples can be drawn from the legendary criminals and gangs of the 1930s in the United States. Bank robbers like Bonnie and Clyde, "Ma" Barker, and Al Capone exemplified the new breed of vicious criminals. Such criminals exploited submachine guns, combined with the mobility offered by the automobiles and highways to pillage and plunder hapless banks and businesses.

Frequently, criminals had better guns and cars than the police forces they confronted! Highly motivated by easy access to piles of money, they tended to strike quickly against the poorly protected banks in the smaller towns in the country, machine guns blazing if the hapless local police force made any effort to intervene. Striking quickly, exploiting the element of surprise, they were often successful and typically escaped by automobile and highway.

When local police authorities became sufficiently vigilant in one area, the criminals exercised geographic flexibility and traveled down the superhighway to the next unsuspecting small town. The fact that many of these vicious criminals ended up dead did not deter others from committing similar criminal acts in similar ways. They too were opportunistically exploiting the environment of their time to engage in their trade. They were the direct heirs of Jesse James and the train bandits who ravaged the Old West in the United States during the post-Civil War era.

Though legal sanctions continued to apply to improper acts even after the advent of the automobile and superhighway, a person who was willing to move on down the superhighway to the next town could perhaps do things that their geographically constrained cousin would never consider. The stereotypical American "cowboy drifter" was now a role nearly anyone in any advanced country could play. If one committed petty theft or a minor crime locally, one had the option to escape community sanctions via the superhighway to another state and start over again. As with the bank robbers, violent offenders of all kinds found that the easy escape by automobile offered continued opportunities to rape, murder, and steal.

The deeds of these criminals were often widely reported through newspapers and radio broadcasts. This broadcasting of their exploits sometimes made them into folk heroes, romantic Robin Hoods. Law enforcement was often portrayed as incompetent, lacking funding, knowledge, and jurisdiction to effectively pursue these criminals. Dishonor as a means of social control on behavior was weakened by the combination of increased mobility and the folk hero status ascribed to the criminals. Thus, the values, mores, and customs of the advanced nations were irrevocably changed by the combination of the automobile and the superhighway.

Throughout much of United States history, security and law enforcement responsibilities have primarily been a local affair. Training, scientific equipment, and technology such as radios or high-powered pursuit vehicles were nonexistent or in very short supply in the 1930s, and good detectives were as likely to break a case through physical or psychological coercion of suspects as through more professional police investigations. In such a world, the high-powered weapons, mobility, and use of the superhighway by criminal gangs were often a winning combination.

In the late 1800s, the Pinkerton Detective Agency was successful in obtaining contracts to safeguard railroads as a direct result of law enforcement's geographic limitations. In a similar fashion, the gang wars in Chicago and elsewhere in the 1930s resulted in a little-known United States federal government organization receiving a mandate to confront the crime problems of that time. The United States Federal Bureau of Investigations found itself tasked as the lead agency to confront the wave of violence that local security and law enforcement professionals were unable or unwilling to confront. With some degree of success, federal law enforcement was able to prevail over the machine gun–toting robbers of the 1930s.

SUPERHIGHWAY CRIME LEADS
TO I-WAY ROBBERIES

So why is all this history relevant to the security and law enforcement professional in dealing with the challenges raised by the I-Way? Let's compare the environment of the 1930s–40s in the United States with the I-Way world of the 1990s:

1930s–40s

Mobile criminals (automobiles + superhighways)

Select weakest targets for exploitation

Employ advanced technology (machine guns and commando tactics)

Sequential attacks against targets of opportunity

Local security and law enforcement poorly equipped for response

Geographic limitations hobble investigations and response

General decline in effectiveness of social controls due to mobility/technology (superhighways and automobiles)

U.S. federal government intervened via FBI (stop the bank robbers and bootleggers)

1990s

Mobile criminals (modems + I-Way)

Weakest targets subject to exploitation

Advanced technology (vulnerability scanners, information warfare tactics)

Sequential attacks against targets of opportunity

Local security and law enforcement poorly equipped for response

Geographic limitations (national borders) hobble investigations and response

General decline in effectiveness of social controls due to global mobility/technology (microcomputers and I-Way)

U.S. federal government intervened via FBI (stop the I-Way robbers and hackers)

When placed in perspective, one can see the I-Way robbers of the Information Age have much in common with the superhighway robbers of the Industrial Age. Based on the above, security and law enforcement professionals should understand that little has really changed over the years; therefore, the problems, issues, and approaches to dealing with them will be very similar. What must be emphasized is that what did not work before will not work now and what worked before may or may not work in the present. Law enforcement and security professionals should learn from history and use the methods and techniques appropriate.

One overwhelming distinction is obvious. Whereas in the earlier era the United States federal government could respond to citizens' concerns about rampant lawlessness by empowering the Federal Bureau of Investigation to enforce United States laws, times are now different. The I-Way is global in scope and growing most quickly in nations and continents that are not likely to take direction from the United States and where the United States has no jurisdiction. How will security and law enforcement professionals of any single nation influence the global response necessary to confront the more serious risks that the I-Way will create? In the absence of a global "I-Way Patrol" each individual nation's response is likely to fall short of effectively addressing the complete spectrum of criminal threats.

At a news conference after an all-day meeting at FBI headquarters of the Justice Ministers of the G-8 countries (the largest industrialized countries in the world) in December 1997, United States Attorney General Janet Reno said, "Criminals no longer are restricted by national boundaries. . . . If we are to keep up with cybercrime, we must work together as never before."[2] The news release from this important meeting went on to list the following areas where these major nations have agreed to collaborate:

Assign adequate numbers of properly trained and equipped law enforcement personnel to investigate high-tech crimes.

Improve ways to track attacks on computer networks.

When extradition is not possible, prosecute criminals in the country where they are found.

Preserve key evidence on computer networks.

Review the legal codes in each nation to ensure that appropriate crimes for computer wrongdoing are proscribed and that the language makes it easier to investigate the crimes.

Cooperate closely with the private sector to develop new ways to detect and prevent computer crimes.

Increase efforts to use new communications technologies, such as video teleconferencing, to obtain testimony from witnesses in other nations.

These are essential steps, even if they are general in nature. However, the past track record of nations cooperating in such efforts is not one of success, so one should not be overly optimistic about the future based only on these actions. The global reach of the I-Way and the difficulties of obtaining jurisdiction over perpetrators are the greatest challenges in dealing with I-Way robbers. To the extent that the collaboration of the G-8 nations ultimately extends to the other nations of the globe, perhaps under the broader auspices of the United Nations or other agencies, organizations can have increased confidence that even the most sophisticated I-Way robbers may ultimately face prosecution.

As law enforcement has adapted its methods and incorporated new technology to combat criminals, private organizations also have adopted various strategies to combat risks to their interests. It is likely that many organizations confronted with increasing risks from the I-Way will choose to respond as the railroad industry did in the 1880s in the United States, when they engaged the Pinkerton Detective Agency to help protect corporate interests against the James gang and similar highly mobile criminal gangs. It is possible, indeed likely, that many large organizations will choose to engage the resources of private sector specialists (cyber-sleuths or digital detectives) to help them resolve I-Way enabled crimes directed against them. This may occur because the limited resources in the public sector are directed to larger or more serious crimes, or simply because public agencies will generally take longer to complete an investigation due to the many competing priorities.

I-WAY ROBBERY STATISTICS: BELIEVE IT OR NOT

Before we present some of the available information concerning the prevalence of I-Way robbery, it's important to bear in mind some caveats. It has been said that there are three kinds of lies—"Lies, dammed lies, and statistics"— and that "Liars figure and figures lie!" With this in mind, this information is presented to attempt to show the extent of the I-Way robbery problem. Since much of the available data is derived from surveys, and since by their nature such surveys are confidential, the full accuracy of the results cannot be verified or validated. The information is presented to give security and law enforcement professionals some sense of the scope of the problem.

Recent press reports of the latest I-Way robberies are only the visible tip of the iceberg. According to the 1998 Price-WaterhouseCoopers and *Information Week* security survey of over 1600 MIS officials from over 40 countries, nearly 73 percent of organizations that responded had experienced break-ins involving network security.[3] Other documentary evidence is equally compelling. Fortune 1000 companies reported more financial losses due to computer security breaches and information theft in 1997 than ever before. Several corporations noted that they lost $10 million or more in a single break-in. System break-ins reported to the Computer Emergency Response Team (CERT) site are the highest ever.[4]

Why the dramatic increase in such reports and apparent losses? There are many factors that have contributed to this trend. In large part, these trends have developed because the I-Way makes every organization an on- and off-ramp, which puts computer systems at greater risk than ever before. With the rapid pace of growth in the I-Way, there are simply more computer systems that are now more accessible than ever to more people in more places on the planet. Because the I-Way–connected computers and networks contain more valuable information and other valuable assets (including digital forms of money), they are thus more important to businesses and government agencies than ever before.

The same applies to the I-Way for the I-Way robbers: the information which travels the I-Way and the ability to share methods, tools, and techniques are also their most important assets. Many of these tools and utilities are freely available to virtually anyone with a modem and I-Way access. There are perhaps thousands of public sites and an unknown number of private bulletin boards and chat areas in which the most clandestine and capable I-Way robbers in the underground share tools, techniques, and methods for defeating security measures. With a vast array of tools to draw from, is it at all surprising that I-Way attacks and robberies are becoming more common?

ROADBLOCKS TO THE I-WAY ROBBERS: ARE THEY WORKING?

Many information technology managers are quite concerned about the potential for I-Way robbers to harm their organization. Some managers may believe that if the United States government can't prevent intrusions, such as the high-profile defacing of the CIA and FBI Web sites, how are businesses and other government agencies, with significantly lower security budgets, going to stop I-Way robbers?

Stopping the I-Way robbers is more than just a theoretical issue. A recently published study conducted by War Room Research,[5] showed that most Fortune 1000 companies have experienced one or more incidents where an outsider successfully penetrated system defenses. More than 50 percent of the responding companies experienced more than 30 system penetrations in the past 12 months, and nearly 60 percent reported losing $200,000 or more from each intrusion.

In a separate study published jointly in 1998 by the Computer Security Institute and the FBI, 520 United States companies reported total losses of $136 million from computer crime and systems security breaches in 1997. This represented a 36 percent increase from 1996. Nearly 54 percent of respondents cited the I-Way as a frequent point of attack, about the same percentage of those who identified internal systems breaches as a frequent point of attack.[6]

With the vast increase in the numbers of people accessing and using the I-Way, it seems likely that more attacks will be attempted from outside of organizations. Prior to the I-Way ramps, most security staff considered the threat to be 80 percent internal and 20 percent external, but with the advent of the on- and off-ramps, the threat now seems to be about 50 percent internal and 50 percent external. It is not known how many intrusions are simply never detected. What is known is that many of those that are detected are not reported to law enforcement for investigation.

According to the same CSI-FBI study quoted earlier,[7] of the companies that knew they experienced a computer crime or detected system break-ins, only about 13 percent actually reported the crimes to law enforcement. The most common reason cited in the survey for not reporting known computer crimes to law enforcement is the fear that the organization will suffer adverse reactions from customers and prospective business partners due to negative publicity.

THERE IS NO I-WAY PATROL TO STOP I-WAY ROBBERS

It will come as no great surprise to security and law enforcement professionals that criminals are willing to make the effort to transition their trade to the I-Way. Recall the classic comment by convicted bank robber Willy Sutton, who when asked why he robbed banks told a reporter, "Because that's where the money is!" Following that comment, *where* is the money in today's global economy? It is, as almost every high school student now knows, in computers, wire transfer networks, and the global I-Way itself! It would be totally unrealistic to expect Willy's heirs to change their chosen profession merely because computers and networks are supplanting highways and automobiles and cybercash on the I-Way and off-ramps is supplanting cash in bank safes.

Although computer crime has existed for decades, some experts believe that computer technology today is roughly where automotive technology was in 1905 and that we have not yet seen the full extent of computer-related crime. Jonathan Winer, Deputy Assistant Secretary of State in the international narcotics and law enforcement arm of the United States State Department has said, "We have created an information superhighway without speed limits and without traffic controls."[8] Many public and private sector representatives have expressed significant concern over the ability of criminals to use the I-Way to launder money and commit other crimes.[9]

CAPABILITIES AND LIMITATIONS OF LAW ENFORCEMENT

If tidal waves of criminal enterprise are about to overwhelm the I-Way and impact this new commercial medium, what can we expect from the "I-Way patrol"? Unless things change drastically, it would seem not much! First, every security and law enforcement professional must understand that, at present, there is not any single, central organization with responsibility and capability to patrol and protect the global I-Way: there is not (at least yet) a global "I-Way patrol." The reasons are readily apparent considering the current state of the planetary political organization.[10]

The nation-state remains the primary organizing unit for most of the earth's population, and it is unlikely that any country would tolerate an international I-Way patrol with jurisdiction to seize and prosecute suspects or even proven perpetrators (their citizens) of activity which is criminal in another country. The uproar in Mexico when United States government agents seized and prosecuted a drug cartel–affiliated physician for his involvement with a United States Drug Enforcement agent's murder provides a real world example of the consequences of unilateral trans-border law enforcement. However, to put these matters in a little different perspective, imagine the uproar in the United States if a non-United States police force had authority to arrest United States citizens because they posted comments that were considered sacrilegious to another country's religious/spiritual leadership!

Rather than creating a global I-Way patrol, it's more reasonable to expect updating of existing extradition treaties to address this very real problem as probably the best short-term answer to the problems of obtaining jurisdiction over I-Way robbers. For example, note that Argentina initially declined to extradite to the United States a young man who admitted he hacked into a number of United States government systems via the I-Way, including NASA's systems. Although this was a criminal act under relevant United States statutes, he had not violated any laws of his homeland. Although he ultimately gave himself up to authorities and pled guilty to the charges, his surrender was voluntary. The inconsistencies in legal language, statutes, and codes from country to country are just one of the major problems associated with policing the global I-Way. In the absence of well-developed international agreements and treaties, and lacking any sort of I-Way patrol or even common policing standards, it is likely that organizations will be subject to criminal activities originating in another country; yet there may be no local authority capable of or willing to pursue a criminal investigation against the I-Way robbers.

GLOBAL CONNECTIVITY VIA THE I-WAY EQUALS GLOBAL EXPOSURE!

This simple truth is the key factor that helps explain why risks have increased due to I-Way connectivity. It is vital that security and law enforcement professionals know how radically different this new environment is. As recently as the late 1980s, the most common form of nonemployee computer crime probably involved a teenager in the local telephone dialing area using a *war dialer*[11] to try to emulate the movie "War Games." In that era, a company could protect itself against a wide range of risks with relatively inexpensive security technology. However, in today's era of global connectivity and access one should not assume that what was sufficient for simpler times will suffice for the present. Those organizations that choose to ignore their increasing vulnerability and trust haphazard security measures may well suffer serious losses. Potential I-Way robbers are not likely to ignore forever poorly protected on-ramps that have valuable assets.

An I-Way robber is no more likely to ignore an easy network firewall penetration than was his distant relative in the 1930s to pass by an unlocked bank vault! This means that just as banks and businesses in the past had to harden their facilities, hire trustworthy guards, install video surveillance cameras and alarms to safeguard their cash vaults, today's "digital data vaults" require enhanced protection. When organizations fail to invest adequately in protection, they run the risk of damage or loss of their key assets.

SUMMARY

Careful study of the above information and other publicly available data concerning I-Way crimes reveals several common themes. First, it appears that I-Way and computer/network enabled crimes are a rapidly growing component of global crime statistics. Second, no one in business, government, or academe really knows the full extent or the complete nature of I-Way crimes that have already been committed or are being committed at this moment. Last, we can conclude that although the I-Way and information access–enabling technologies like the Web browser-server combinations are creating more complex environments, we should not expect that complexity alone will protect valuable resources against losses. Criminals over the ages have proven themselves highly adaptable, and they already appear to be capable of and willing to exploit the new I-Way environment for their benefit.

To fight criminals in their various environments over time, new laws have been written and new enforcement methods have been devised. With the advent of "horseless carriages," horse theft laws evolved to include laws relating to the theft of the new vehicles. Similarly, the epitome of effective law enforcement changed from the town sheriff leading a posse of deputies on horseback to roadblocks staffed by state police and highway patrol officers. Radios were installed in police cars to increase mobility and improve response time; these were supplemented with personal communications units and later mobile data terminals. As with the criminals, law enforcement officers have also been challenged to adapt, learning in earlier ages to ride horses, drive automobiles, and now to exploit computers and networks to combat the latest generation of "digital desperados."

NOTES

1. Remarks by the Vice President, National Press Club, Washington, DC, December 21, 1993.
2. "Nations Band Together Against Cybercrime," Reuters, 10 Dec. 1997.
3. *Information Week*, August 29, 1998.
4. Tim Wilson, "Profits Embolden Hackers," *InternetWeek*, March 23, 1998.
5. War Room Research Report summarized in *Computerworld*, August, 1998.
6. See CSI-FBI 1997 report at http://www.gocsi.com.
7. Ibid.
8. "Reuters NewsBits," Tuesday, September 15, 1998, 9:47 AM.
9. Ibid.
10. War dialer is a software program that dials telephone numbers "looking" for the tone of a computer modem. Once found, it records that number to be subsequently dialed-up by the hacker who would then attempt to gain unauthorized access to the computer.

4

I-Way Bandits, Laws, Politics, and Other Issues

CHAPTER OBJECTIVE

The objective of this chapter is to provide an introduction and overview of the crimes, laws, and related issues surrounding the use of the I-Way. The material is presented in the form of "snapshots" of the topics to provide the security professional and law enforcement professionals with a quick overview of the I-Way environment.

UNDERSTANDING THE GLOBAL PICTURE

Now that you have been introduced to the I-Way and you hopefully are beginning to understand its ramifications on society, governments, businesses, and the security and law enforcement professions, you must understand that "you're not in Kansas anymore!" Just as our superhighways brought together towns, villages, and cities of the individual, industrialized nations, the I-Way has brought together the people, businesses, and governments of the world as never before. It is also an environment where I-Way robbers are travelling to places they never could have reached before—with lawmakers, law enforcement, and security officers in hot pursuit. This requires security and law enforcement professionals to think, plan, and act from a global perspective. Due to technology and the I-Way, we have moved from looking at "our" world as shown in Figure 4–1 to looking at the world as shown in Figure 4–2.

Figure 4–1

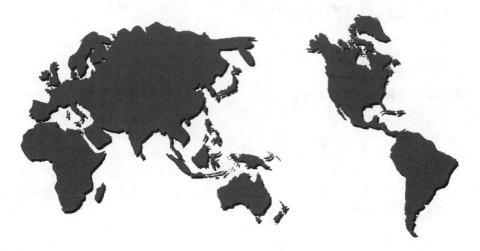

Figure 4–2

In reality, our I-Way world is even more complicated, crowded, and compressed, and looks more like Figure 4–3.

One of the biggest challenges facing today's modern security and law enforcement professional is learning how to think and operate in this new, dynamic, technology-driven, global environment. This point cannot be over-stated: you must learn to think and act with a global perspective.

The following example is provided to assist in understanding exactly what that means. Security professionals were advised from various sources that person(s) unknown were attempting to gain access to outside telephone lines at various businesses and government agencies within the United States. They were using social engineering[1] tactics. Their obvious purpose was to be able to make free long-distance calls (to exchange either verbal or

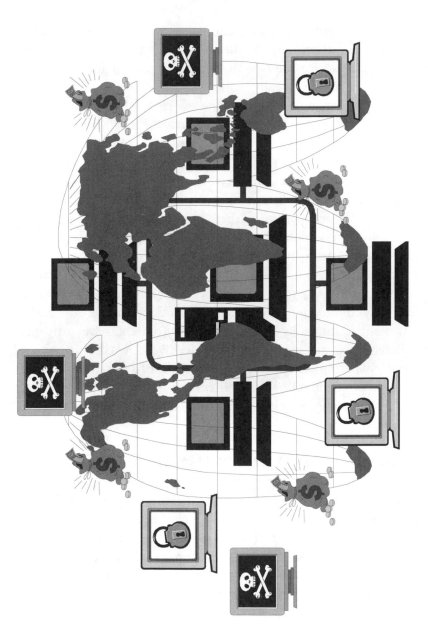

Figure 4–3

computerized information) and have the business or government agency pay the bill. They were asking the person they called to enter certain numbers, special characters through the touch tone phone. This "code" enabled the long-distance line connection.

One of the security individuals notified of this latest telecommunications fraud scam asked if this just applied to telephones in the United States. What is wrong with such a question? It seems logical enough doesn't it? No, it does not when thinking globally.

In our global environment, telephone switches, which today are computers that do the telephone operations and carry the information along the I-Way, are sold by international corporations to businesses and government agencies around the world. Don't forget that these telephone switches can also act as on-ramps to the I-Way, and are globally connected. Businesses and government agencies today use the same or compatible hardware and software, regardless of the physical location of their offices. Remember, to work globally, technology must be globally compatible. Thus, the threats, vulnerabilities, and risks associated with those switches are a global problem and must be dealt with by security and law enforcement professionals around the world.

There are very few exceptions to this I-Way truth: No I-Way crime problem is truly country dependent. It is hardware and software dependent.

Lieutenant Commander Robert Garigue of Canada's Department of National Defense was quoted as saying, "No one drives down the highway with no probability of having an accident. But you have to be a smart driver and you have to have in place the seatbelt and other built-in protections like airbags. It is a multi-leveled approach but ultimately the driver has to know the risks."

SAME JOB, DIFFERENT ENVIRONMENT

It is important for the security and law enforcement professional to keep the use of the I-Way, use of technology by I-Way robbers, and the related laws in perspective. For when we boil it all down, with very few exceptions the security and law enforcement professionals have the very same problems they've always had, vis-à-vis their responsibility for protecting the assets of the company or government agency by deterring and preventing the misuse, theft, and/or destruction of assets; if a criminal act occurred on, or because of, their business's or government agency's "on-ramp" leading to the I-Way, their job is still to assist in identifying the criminals and supporting any investigation, disciplinary action, and/or prosecution related to the criminals.

If you are a security or law enforcement professional, and within your company or government agency you or another department of security professionals do not have that responsibility, then that responsibility is either not assigned to a security professional or not assigned at all. In either case, it is a cause for concern, for only trained security professionals can adequately carry out the responsibilities as noted above. "Trained security professional" may mean either a business/corporate security or information systems security professional—ideally one in the same.

One cannot leave such matters to the information technology group or the auditors. Neither of them is trained to perform the job. Information technology personnel are more concerned with system performance and meeting the systems needs of their customers, and rightly so. Once past the user ID and password access control processes, their interest usually stops. Auditors look for compliance to laws, policies, and procedures. That is their emphasis. Furthermore, for them to be involved in protecting the I-Way often presents a conflict of interest—they would have to audit themselves. That is not a very objective approach.

However, in making these statements, it is assumed that the security professional is up to the challenges, both in experience and technical training. If not, one must question whether or not they are truly professionals or just "in a security job." Today's and tomorrow's security and law enforcement professional must understand the I-Way, computers, and networks. *Understanding* is defined as having a working knowledge of such systems and being able to ask the correct questions when you don't—and also understand the answers!

So, as a security and law enforcement professional, don't get sidetracked or look at I-Way crimes as something that are totally different. Yes, in some respects they are different, just as it was different when criminals started using automobiles instead of horses. However, the basic security and law enforcement crime prevention and investigative principles still apply!

WHAT IS THE DEFINITION OF I-WAY CRIME?

Although lawmakers of the world are each beginning to pass various laws for dealing with crimes specific to the I-Way, two other types of laws are also being used to charge and prosecute offenders. They are:

- ◆ General criminal laws
- ◆ Computer crime laws

Most I-Way crimes are prosecuted under other well-known, non–I-Way, non–computer crime laws such as wire fraud, mail fraud, and transportation of stolen property. Today, at least in the United States and most developed countries of the world, those in or partially in the Information Age have enacted at least one or more laws related to computer crime.

In order for some act on the I-Way to be considered a crime, it must obviously have violated some law. There may be photographs, graphics, cartoons, or jokes we do not like, but that does not make them criminal. Freedom and privacy, such as they are on the I-Way, are very precious. So, in order to maintain some semblance of that at least, we must "take the bad with the good" in order to help assure our freedom of speech and expression.

Before discussing the specific international, United States, and state laws related to I-Way crimes, some discussion as to what constitutes an I-Way and computer crime is in order.

What Is an I-Way Robbery—A Form of Computer Crime?

Computers are used as tools to commit crimes, just as in the past criminals used explosives and blowtorches to break into safes. And just like explosives and blowtorches, computers can be used for good or evil. It all depends on the person using them. Computers are also the target of criminals, just as safes are targets. As stated earlier, years ago, an American bank robber was asked why he robbed banks. He replied, "Because that's where the money is!" In this modern era, little has changed. Why do criminals use the I-Way to break into computer systems? Because that's where they can manipulate information to defraud the company or the government agency. That's where the money is, and the I-Way is the "yellow brick road"!

Since the I-Way obviously is a global network of computers, computer crime laws can and are being used to prosecute I-Way robbers.

Computer Fraud versus Computer Crime[2]

The Association of Certified Fraud Examiners (ACFE)[3] has published a *Fraud Examiner's Manual* which provides some excellent definitions and discussions on the topics related to defining computer crime and computer fraud. They are quoted below:

Computer Fraud

A general definition of *computer fraud* is: Any defalcation or embezzlement accomplished by tampering with computer programs, data files, operations, equipment, or media, and resulting in losses sustained by the organization whose computer system was manipulated. The distinguishing characteristic of computer fraud is that access occurs with the intent to execute a fraudulent scheme. The Delaware statute illustrates this point.

> Whoever knowingly . . . without proper authorization, accesses . . . any computer . . . for purpose of: (1) devising or executing any scheme to defraud [another], or (2) obtaining money, property, or services . . . by means of false or fraudulent pretenses, representations or promises shall be guilty of computer fraud."

Computer fraud statutes have established two very important principles. First, the statutes contain definitions of computer-related terms. These statutes allow the prosecutor to sidestep having to explain to the jury technical "computer speak" and its cumbersome fit with common law terminology. Second, the statutes create an offense based on proof of access with a particular intent. Success in carrying away property (money) does not have to be proven. Tracing the flow of proceeds is likely to be difficult without paper records and access may be the only provable event.

Computer Crime Laws Affecting the I-Way

Because of the serious problems I-Way crimes cause businesses, governments, and individuals, federal and state legislators have enacted new laws to fit these types of crimes, also known as "I-Way robbery," "cybercrimes," or "techno-crimes." Some of these new laws have been tested in court while others have not. What is interesting to note is that many of the non–computer crime laws can and are being used to prosecute computer criminals. The reason for this is primarily due to the fact that the old laws have been tested and validated over the years while some of the new computer laws have not. Additionally, older laws are easier for prosecutors, judges, and juries to understand. When it comes to I-Way crimes and other forms of computer crime, the KISS (Keep It Simple Stupid) principle still applies.

Computer crime is generally defined (to paraphrase the U.S. Department of Justice) as a crime committed where use or knowledge of computers is required. *Computer-assisted crime* is defined as a crime in which the computer is used to assist in perpetrating the crime.

Some Classes of I-Way Crimes

I-Way crimes and other computer crimes and frauds can be classified by various methods; however, the simplest method would appear to be to classify them as defined in the various Unites States federal and state statutes. Examples of these are:

♦ Accessing systems without authority
♦ Accessing systems or information in excess of authority
♦ Violating the privacy and other rights of users
♦ Violating systems rules
♦ Interrupting or stealing services, e.g., computer time
♦ Tampering with Web sites, software programs
♦ Misusing information by using it for other than its intended use, e.g., selling it
♦ Using the I-Way for pornographic purposes
♦ Using the I-Way to commit a fraudulent act or other criminal act

THE INFORMATION AGE AND THE I-WAY LAWS

In the previous chapters, there was some discussion on the difference between the Agricultural Age, the Industrial Age, and the Information Age. Many nations, like the United States, are in the Information Age where information and the systems that process, store, and transmit information are the basis for the majority of a nation's economic power and where the majority of workers are employed in white-collar jobs. However, when it comes to the lawmakers of the country, their processes and jurisdiction, we find some interesting problems that the security professional should keep in mind when dealing with I-Way crimes, laws, law enforcement, and the criminal justice system. It is (aside from normal politics) also something to keep in mind when reading about and trying to understand the I-Way environment.

The primary problem is this: nations' lawmakers are using processes developed over the years when their nation was in the Agricultural and Industrial Ages. Many, if not most, of these lawmakers have yet to understand how to think globally when it comes to understanding the I-Way and change their processes accordingly. Others may understand but are reluctant to try to change things because of the potential loss of power and authority that would occur. For example, imagine that one day every citizen has a secure computer and each votes, under majority rule, for whatever laws we wanted passed. That, the purest form of democracy, would make the Congress obsolete. All we would need is people to write proposals for new laws which would be voted for or against by the citizens. You don't need a legislator to do that, just their staff who generally write the drafts anyway. It would be a totally revolutionary use of the I-Way and would drastically change so much of our political processes, for example, dealing with lobbyists.

This Information Age is very different from the two ages that preceded it. At the expense of being somewhat redundant, let's take a moment to revisit that issue again. During these first two periods, life was slower, information traveled slower, and there were physical limitations such as those on natural resources. In the United States we had the two great oceans on either side of us which made it more difficult for any hostile nation to attack us, and our criminal element was also bounded by physical and political boundaries.

The lawmakers of the United States, both federal and state, could pass laws and pretty much be assured that some government enforcement agency would be given the responsibility and authority to investigate allegations of violations of those laws. Unlike dealing with today's I-Way issues, the lawmakers usually had authority and jurisdiction over the person who committed the crime and the place where the crime was committed. The lawmaking process from the Agricultural Age and Industrial Age have been carried over into the Information Age. However, as we have seen in the discussion thus far, we are in a different environment where criminals only need a computer and an I-Way on-ramp. Then, at literally the speed of light, they can commit a crime in a nanosecond from the other side of the globe, and disappear just as quickly.

I-Way Privacy

Think of what has been said thus far. Then consider, as an example, how Congress can pass a law outlawing gambling on the I-Way. A person operates an I-Way Web site for casino gambling. That operator resides in Monte Carlo. That person takes all bets from anyone in the world. The gambler lives somewhere in the United States and, using the credit card or whatever system the Web site casino accepts as appropriate, places a bet. It may be against the laws of the United States, but the casino is not in the United States. The gambler uses an Internet Service Provider (ISP) to access the I-Way and send in the bet.

Who will know that the gambler broke a United States law? In today's society, not even the gambler may know that it was against the law, so that is an issue. Since it may be difficult to prove intent, then another problem arises: how will police know this person violated I-Way law(s)? Will the ISP read all our e-mail for indications of such violations? How many of us would want that? Not even the ISPs want to do that. It's almost like having the person that built the public road be required to enforce the speed laws. Besides, with literally millions, if not billions, of daily e-mail messages circulating along the I-Way, who is capable of reading and screening the content of each of these?

Should government agents be allowed total access to ISPs in the United States and then with a "keyword search program" scan all e-mail messages of the ISP's customers searching for the word *bet,* and when they find a violation of law, initiate an investigation? This may sound unrealistic, but indications are that it is already being done in some countries and being proposed in others. (See http://www.fe.msk.ru/libertarium/ehomepage.html)[4] to see what the Russian security people are proposing vis-à-vis this precise issue. SORM (system of efficient research measures), according to the same site, would, among other things, ". . . provide for reading of all information (both incoming and outgoing) belonging to specific subscribers of the network(s) in question."

The United States, the European Community, and other nations have stated that they are concerned about protecting the rights and privacy of I-Way users. As time goes on, this issue will become more serious and will be more relevant to those responsible for I-Way security and "policing" their on-ramps to the I-Way. For example, as telemedicine becomes more closely integrated into how medical practices are performed, the issue of patient records being transmitted over the I-Way from one doctor or hospital to another will undoubtedly be compromised, based on today's I-Way security. Thus, the potential modification or public disclosure of records will occur, undoubtedly followed by lawsuits.

If such problems and "invasions of privacy" have occurred in the past on non–I-Way–connected computers, the chances of it happening on I-Way–connected systems are pretty much 100 percent! For example, according to *InformationWeek* magazine as far back as the May 17, 1993, issue, the Resolution Trust Corporation saw nothing wrong with copying the files of a whistleblower. This was done, according to the report, with the permission of the Justice Department and the corporation's legal counsel.[5]

A newspaper[6] printed an article discussing a Federal Trade Commission (FTC) survey that determined that "hundreds of companies are collecting personal information about consumers, and without telling them, selling the data. . . . The Federal Trade Commission also recommends that Congress put into law restrictions from and about children who use the Internet. . . . People who don't use the Internet frequently cite privacy concerns as their reason for staying offline." In other words, there are people who are afraid to get on the I-Way because of privacy issues, thereby missing the many benefits of such I-Way access, probably to their own detriment in many instances.

The FTC survey looked at 1400 Web sites selected at random and found 85 percent collected some personal information; 14 percent offered notice of that collection; and less than 2 percent had a "comprehensive privacy policy."

Are additional privacy laws necessary? Another newspaper article[7] states that "A group that says it represents small Internet business has threatened to make public the e-mail addresses of 5 million America Online (AOL) members if AOL continues to bar their businesses from pitching products to its (AOL) subscribers." AOL said, "We would avail ourselves of any legal remedies we need to protect our members . . . from this threat. . . . We see this threat as some sort of cyber-terrorism. . . . AOL members have made it clear 'they do not want junk e-mail' . . ."

Based on the above, a case therefore can be made for some type of legislation so that ISPs such as AOL can protect their customers' privacy. The United States Federal Trade Commission has developed a model for I-Way privacy legislation which includes the following four elements[8]:

1. Web sites would be required to advise those that access their site how they collect information and what information they collect.
2. The Web site owners would offer their visitors choices as to how the information gathered about them can be used.
3. The Web sites would allow access to the private information collected from their visitors and the opportunity for the visitors to correct inaccurate information.
4. The Web site would be required to provide "reasonable" security to protect the integrity and security of the visitors' information.

If Congress were to pass additional I-Way privacy legislation, the issue, then, as with all other I-Way related laws, is who will enforce the laws, who will monitor the I-Way to ensure the law is obeyed? In addition, how will the laws be enforced when the corporation collecting the personal information resides outside of the borders of the United States? Will the United States implement trade sanctions against the country where that corporation resides? Bar the corporations of the United States from any business relations with that corporation? All things in life are possible, but some are not likely. This is one of them that falls into the "not likely" category.

In the United States, the federal Electronic Communications Privacy Act (ECPA) prohibits unauthorized eavesdropping and unauthorized access to messages and information stored or transmitted by computers. The law was primarily enacted to stop alleged abuses after the time of Watergate, but has since been updated to include the newer issues of computers and the I-Way, especially as they relate to privacy. However, privacy issues may be getting some support outside of the United States. According to *Wired* magazine's May 1998 issue, page 135[9]: "Beginning October 25, 1998, a group of Brussels bureaucrats . . . will oversee implementation of a new privacy policy throughout Europe. Under this regime, known as the European Data Protection Directive, any country that trades personal information with the U.K., France, Germany, Spain, Italy, or to any of the other 10 EU states will be required to embrace Europe's strict standards for privacy. No privacy, no trade. It's that simple. . . The new rules will oblige every country within the European Union to a common set of standards that bind governments and corporations to a rigorous system of privacy protection."

This is a very interesting issue, not only because of its requirements, but also as an indication of something very far-reaching that is caused by the I-Way. Because of the privacy concerns, coupled with today's electronic commerce on the I-Way, a nation or group of foreign nations can pass a law or issue a formal directive that basically dictates how another nation and/or international business will deal with an issue, such as implementing some mandatory I-Way security measures. So if, for example, you are a security person working for a United States international corporation with clients and business relationships with the European Community and you use the I-Way to conduct business, you may want to get a copy of this new directive because you may be required to provide the required protection based on the European security requirements.

But wait! Not so fast! According to *USA Today* (3/27/97), the Organization for Economic Cooperation and Development, meeting in Paris, France, approved a plan to allow law enforcement agencies to "eavesdrop on the Internet." This organization is made up of 29 countries. Of course, the United States endorsed the measure. However, according to the report, the guidelines included: "The fundamental rights of individuals to privacy, including secrecy of communications and protection of personal data, should be respected in national cryptography (coding) policies." How is the security professional to interpret such guidelines? If you are required as part of your responsibilities to ensure the privacy of the employees' personal information, don't take the matter lightly, as many a lawsuit for millions of dollars can be the result. It is a difficult but interesting dilemma.

It has also been reported that only three of the 15 European Union countries have enacted the privacy plan into law. The report also stated that the "White House has been scrambling to ensure that U.S. Web sites aren't hindered by a strict European Union electronic privacy directive set to hit this October." Is that an indication of how much the United States currently supports privacy?

In addition, Director of the FBI Louis Freeh told a meeting of the International Association of Chiefs of Police that "software vendors should be required by law to offer a security feature allowing law enforcement to decrypt encrypted communications."[10]

I-Way privacy concerns are very real. If you want to prove it to yourself, search the I-Way for *cookies*—not the chocolate chip variety, but the computer variety that transmit information to the Web site to which you have just linked. I-Way browsers can be set up in such a manner as to require your specific permission to "set a cookie," but there have been some sites that will not even let you access their site unless you allow them to set a cookie—usually these sites set multiple cookies. If you are interested in further information on this topic, there are many Web sites that deal with the subject. Use your I-Way search engines and just type "privacy." The authors found over 390 separate links relative to this topic.

I-WAY AND COPYRIGHTS

The I-Way has increased the violations of copyright laws. As we shall see when we discuss hackers in another chapter, it is a widely held belief that hackers and others who cruise along the I-Way believe that all information belongs to everyone. It should be free to all—no secrets, no controls over who uses the information. This is their ideal world. So, it was just a matter of time before the issue of copyright violations over the I-Way became a serious problem, and it has over the last several years due to the explosion of I-Way travelers. According to an unnamed federal investigator: "On December 16, 1997, President Clinton signed the No Electronic Theft Act, a controversial law that will help software companies in their battle against high-tech "Robin

Hoods." Under the new law, a person who willfully infringes on copyright-ed material worth at least $1000 is subject to criminal prosecution even if no profit is gained from the infringement. . . . The new law closes the 'LaMac-chia loophole' named for a 1994 incident in which David LaMacchia, then a student at the Massachusetts Institute of Technology, was charged with vio-lating copyright laws after he offered copyrighted software for free on his electronic bulletin board. A federal court acquitted him of criminal charges because copyright laws, at that time, stipulated that violators must receive financial gains for stolen intellectual property. . . . According to one major software group, software companies lose about $11 billion in annual world-wide revenue because of piracy, $2.6 billion of it in the United States."

There are several interesting points to be made here. It is interesting that dollar amounts relating to I-Way crime losses, computer-related loses, are always quoted in very large numbers. In this case, it would be of interest to determine exactly how these numbers were derived. When trying to iden-tify, locate, and pin down the individual(s) who came up with such numbers (an almost hopeless task in many cases), one finds that the numbers are gen-erally not based on any scientific methods, but a SWAG (and we all know what those are!).

The other interesting point is that most of the violations are occurring overseas. Some of the biggest violators are in Asia. Although the major vio-lating nations have signed agreements to enforce copyright laws, such enforcement appears to occur only when the software corporations put polit-ical pressure on the United States, who in turn does the same to the violat-ing nations.

It is easy to see why copyright violations are rampant in Asia and else-where. In these nations fighting their way into the Information Age, it is a logical choice. Of course there are those in every nation who are rich and prosperous, but the majority of people and local businesses in these coun-tries are not rich. These are nations of "haves and have-nots" and a very small or nonexistent middle class. Yet, a strong majority middle class is vital to a nation becoming an economic power and a strong Information Age nation. These governments, small businesses, students, and universities cannot afford to pay the prices charged for software products in the quantities need-ed, but they must have the technology to develop their information infra-structure, rapidly educating their citizens in technology in order to pull themselves up the economic ladder and compete internationally. Their pri-ority is to build an Information Age nation as quickly and cheaply as possi-ble, so the choice is simple; the illegal copying of software, books, and other forms of information is one way of helping. The problem is compounded by the recent downturn in the Asian economies, which may exponentially increase the number of violations.

In the United States, the problem is still financially based but more of it is done by individuals. A family with both parents working, trying to raise their children, while paying the mortgage is trying to also ensure that their children are computer literate and prepared for working in the new century. If they have a choice between a free copy of a suite of software application programs selling retail for $695, or going to the local computer store and buying the software, which will they choose, especially after hearing the amount of money some software corporation executives earn in a year?

According to Robert Kruger, Business Software Alliance (BSA) vice president,[11] "Internet use is growing 700 percent a year. . . . Internet piracy could even eclipse traditional forms of piracy and make what's in the market now appear quaint." BSA is an industry-funded watchdog representing software vendors in the United States. Kruger wants to see more legislation, education, and enforcement to help eliminate piracy. He further mentioned that of the 30 complaints received concerning Singapore, no one had as yet been prosecuted. This is not unusual for reasons described above.

GOOD I-WAY ENCRYPTION VERSUS THE UNITED STATES GOVERNMENT

Increases in economic espionage (according to the FBI) and the theft of trade secrets and sensitive information make the need for security to protect the United States' economic lead and competitive advantage critically important. With the ever-increasing reliance on global commerce through the I-Way, the need for encryption of information residing on storage systems and I-Way transmissions is a necessity.

However, in the United States a very basic disagreement has been taking place. For several years now, businesses have been lobbying for unlimited use of the best encryption available to protect their I-Way transmissions, but the United States Department of Justice, the United States Attorney General, and the FBI especially, have been roadblocks; they believe that they, under current legal guidelines, should be able to read all encrypted transmissions in order to help build a prosecutable case against individuals under investigation. They call for a system called *key escrow* (where a third party holds the key or portion thereof to decrypt an encrypted transmission and/or file.If the FBI wanted the key in order to read the file, they would use a process that included justifying a search warrant, etc.)

The export issue boils down to the number of bits to be used in any software product that encrypts international transmissions. The standard has been 56 bits; however, that encryption has been broken, with reportedly less than $225,000 in hardware and software. Imagine what a large corporation or government agency could do with the millions of dollars at their disposal. There are exceptions grudgingly granted by the government; for example, Netscape reportedly has been granted approval to use 128-bit encryption to communicate with its customers worldwide. One wonders if there is some caveat to the permission that neither side will talk about. One also wonders if the limited security offered by 56-bit encryption products is chosen deliberately to allow easy breaking of the code by United States government agencies.

Most private firms and those outside the influence of government agencies (those not using government funds for research contracts and grants) desire and require the best encryption that our vendors can provide. It would seem that the protection benefits of excellent encryption far outweigh the benefits to law enforcement of poor encryption, since the law still requires more evidence than the results of a "decrypted wire tap"—especially since the number of cases where federal wiretaps would be used relative to today's I-Way crimes is rather small.

The government's desire for access may be paranoia by some or just a concern that the United States and other nations help maintain, protect, and support personal liberties and privacy at a time when, because of the I-Way, they are threatened with each related technological advancement. One only has to read about the Russian's SORM (previously mentioned) to wonder how close we are to being placed in a similar position.

During a hearing held by a Senate Judiciary subcommittee, FBI Director Louis Freeh allegedly stated that "network service providers should be required to have some immediate decryption ability available permitting agents to readily descramble encrypted message that pass through their system."[12] The hearing reportedly was a "stacked deck" created by Senator Jon Kyl (R-Arizona), Chair of the Judiciary subcommittee on technology, terrorism, and government information. It was reported that "Out of seven witnesses, five were current or former law enforcement agents. No privacy or civil liberties advocates testified. Some companies including FedEx apparently dropped out when they'd have to pay lip service to key escrow if they wanted to speak."

In Brussels, "The European Commission urged governments, including the United States, to take a hands off approach to regulating the technology needed to ensure that Internet transactions are confidential."[13] If the United States government continues to have its way on controls and also gets "back doors" placed in encryption products, then can someone find that back door and read the "secrets"?

Another issue is the very good encryption product being developed and sold commercially in other countries. United States laws don't apply to them so they can keep their sensitive information better protected. In order for the government's system to work, all other forms of encryption must eventually be outlawed for use within the United States. How many international, foreign corporations want to use encryption software that has the "back door" with their United States subsidiaries?

One last comment about the encryption issue: if someone posts an encryption software program (that would violate federal export rules if sent outside the United States) on a Web site in the United States, with a caveat that said "for downloading and use only within the United States," and it was downloaded by someone outside the United States, would any government official know? Would the one who posted be prosecuted? Who would know the foreigner downloaded it? How can this practice be stopped?

As always, more information on the topic can be found by using your I-Way search engine and searching for "encryption," "key escrow," or similar phrases.

GAMBLING AND PORNOGRAPHY: TO FILTER OR NOT TO FILTER—THAT IS THE QUESTION

United States legislators, federal and state, not understanding this new environment, suggest placing site "filters" to screen out certain I-Way sites. Out of a hundred million sites, which do you filter? Of course, some are obvious by the site name, for example, "Gambling.com." However, not all are so obvious. Besides that problem, how do you identify what is illegal? If you filter out sites that have the word "gambling" in their name, then you may also filter out "gamblers anonymous" sites whose purpose it is to help people rid themselves of their gambling habit.

Another example is filtering for "not for children's eyes" sexual content. If you filter out for words such as "breasts," then women interested in breast cancer information can't get to that information. As you can see, the situation is not as simple as it may seem to some lawmakers who do not understand this new environment.

If the ISP does not provide the filtering for their customers, then who will? Should some federal or state investigative or police agency do it? None of us wants 1984 to come in 1999, thank you very much! Besides, what I-Way users want some ISP or government agency censoring our e-mail and Web site access? Furthermore, the public has said quite clearly in most law enforcement jurisdictions in the United States that the limited budget priorities are to get rid of the illegal drugs, stop violent crime, and stop gangs. Nowhere is the public saying that their priority is to stop I-Way crimes, except for child pornography.

One may argue that child pornography is gaining public and lawmaker attention and that the public wants something done about it. Yes, maybe. But again, the issue is not an easy one to solve or resolve. An interesting case is the one where a couple in California had a "pornography" site for adults, legal by California laws. An investigator purposely brought up the site on his system in Tennessee where such material was indeed considered pornographic by Tennessee standards. The couple was convicted of violating the Tennessee law, even though the site and couple were physically located in California and the investigator in Tennessee, an adult, viewed the site.

The example illustrates several points: (1) You can be convicted of a state's I-Way–related law even if you have never physically been in that state or own property in that state, and (2) on the I-Way, you must apparently comply with all laws in all states to stay out of trouble. It is believed that their conviction is being appealed.

So, who will know? Who will investigate? Who in the United States will shut down the Monte Carlo casino because it violates a federal United States law? It is somewhat similar to the United States drug problem. We have found after spending billions of dollars that we cannot control with any hope of success the activities within the boundary of another country. We just have to look at Mexico and Colombia to see very clearly our folly. Then again, the United States keeps trying. Will I-Way robberies be just another sad example of spending billions of dollars in a non-cost-effective manner?

According to one FBI source, I-Way gambling "is believed to be a $200-million-a-year industry." The Florida Attorney General has reportedly reached an agreement with Western Union to stop wiring money for offshore companies, which have been using Western Union to receive or send money related to gambling activities. In New York, the FBI office filed complaints against 14 managers and owners of six I-Way sports betting companies operated off-shore.

An article posted on http://www.info-sec.com entitled "Controversial Gambling in the Internet Becomes a Billion-Dollar Business," by Miriam Steffenses, states that the senator from Nevada wants to outlaw I-Way gambling. Any guesses why in a state where gambling is legal? "Internet gambling is also accessible for children, it is irresponsible," he allegedly told the Washington Post.

On the other hand, according to the same article, a "Cyber-Casino-Chief" said in reply to Senator Kyl's remark that whoever bets "had to reckon six months in prison and a fine of $2,500": "In order to apply that, one would need the KGB." The casino owner also allegedly said, "That is pure hypocrisy. These people do so as if they take care of game-addiction, but not a single one of them wants to give up billions of dollars of lottery-revenues in his (Kyl's) state."

In July 1998, Senator Kyl's "Internet Gambling Prohibition Act" was added to a major spending bill. This was done, according to an FBI source, even though a report by the Department of Justice "criticized the gambling bill for being inconsistent and overly broad." This is strong criticism coming from the same people who have to try and enforce this law, assuming it is passed into law and is not thrown out of court as has been the case with at least one other significant law, the "Communications Decency Act." Congress is considering a law that would tie school funding with the requirement that school computers install filters to filter out what some call "cyber trash." Again, who will define what that is? Do we want politicians to do that for us? Consider their "decency track record" beginning with the United States Chief Law Enforcement Officer—the President.

IT AIN'T SPAM—IT'S MARKETING

The I-Way is being inundated by unsolicited e-mails and Web site messages, which are used by various businesses to try to sell products. This unsolicited junk mail is a great business marketing tool because it is extremely cheap and can be sent to literally millions of people with the click of a mouse. *Spam*—electronic junk mail—includes any possible topic one could think of, such as pyramid schemes, selling products (some fraudulent, like the cure for cancer), get-rich schemes, hate mail, and real estate ads.

The problem is no different than any other unsolicited mail we receive in our "snail mail" boxes. We don't ask for it but we get it. One reason is that the United States Post Office makes a great deal of money from junk mail.

This holds true for the spammers also. Spam is no different from a telemarketing call, or the flyers stuck on your car windshield in the parking lot. From the looks of parking lots when one of these "industrial age spammers" has been there, most people just throw the flyers on the ground. Somebody has to clean up the parking lot. On systems somebody has to clean up after them also, either the ISP or the user.

Congress has "heard the call of the people," and has begun the process of enacting legislation to stop spamming. According to an article[14] by Janet Kornblum, staff writer, some spammers have begun to add disclaimers to their mass mailings which state that their mailings comply with the Consumer Antispamming Act. What is interesting to note is that the Act has not been passed by Congress, nor made into law. It appears that the bill will be eventually passed by Congress and signed by the President. It is interesting to note that some *anti*spammers are against the proposed law because they believe that it states that spamming is illegal in only certain cases. Thus the conclusion reached is that if it is not expressly prohibited, it is not illegal. So, Congress may have the opposite effect than its intended purpose, unless the bill is changed prior to passing both houses of Congress.

At least one group, "Coalition Against Unsolicited Commercial E-Mail (CAUCE)," has a Web site, http://www.cauce.org, and is reportedly an "all volunteer organization, created by Netizens to advocate for a legislature solution to the problem of UCS (a/k/a/ "spam")." Again, by using a search engine and typing the word "spam," one can find more than enough information on the topic.

The more serious issue of spamming is the fact that it can deny use of the system due to the shear volume of spam received through corporate and government agency systems, one to each user ID. A CNN on-line news article, February 23, 1998, "NETCOM Slugs it out with Usenet Users Over Spam," stated that a "Usenet Death Penalty or UDP, was announced a week ago in response, supporters say, to Netcom's inactivity against spam messages posted by its users." According to a Cabal Network Security (reportedly an on-line group which also fights spam) spokesman, Netcom U.S. has not acted to stop spamming and has ignored the "growing public outcry against this problem."

Another example of the seriousness of the spam problem was when Ameritech.net delayed e-mail messages that were sent from America Online (AOL) to prevent the junk e-mail from overloading the Ameritech.net.[15] This was done because spam had targeted AOL's users, and listed Ameritech.net as a return address. It was reported that AOL rejected millions of the messages and returned them to the alleged sender—Ameritech.net. "Alleged" because someone could have spoofed the system to mask the true sender.

The designated "Spam King," Sanford Wallace of Cyber Promotions, Inc., has recently stated that he will seek permission from ISPs before sending bulk e-mail to their customers. He has been the subject of numerous lawsuits. In the latest, he reached a $2 million dollar settlement with Earthlink Network Inc.[16]

I-WAY PORNOGRAPHY—ADULTS, CHILDREN, AND VIRTUAL CHILDREN

All types of people use the I-Way; therefore, it also has its "red light districts." The difference is that on the I-Way there are no zoning laws, so these sites may be found anywhere along the I-Way. Those who are intent on viewing "pornography"[17] and who have been receiving their magazines in plain brown paper envelopes, can now receive them electronically, and share their information on the I-Way.

No one knows whether or not this has become a growing problem or the I-Way just made it more visible. In either case, it is a great concern to governments, parents, and most people. Law enforcement officials have pretended to be children on I-Way chat sites and have "lured" these criminals in sting operations. Many of the photographs and such are stored on I-Way Web sites and bulletin boards overseas and beyond the reach of law enforcement, except of course, for the law enforcement in that country.

If an effort to stop pornography within its borders, the United States passed the "Communications Decency Act" in 1996.[18] The act makes it illegal for anyone to "display in any manner available to a person 18 years of age, any comment, request, suggestion, proposal, image, or other communication, that, in context, depicts or describes in terms patently offensive as measured by contemporary community standards sexual or excretory activities or organs regardless of whether the user of such service placed the call or initiated the communication."

This law was subject to a court challenge by groups such as the ACLU. The United States District Court, Eastern Pennsylvania, District of Pennsylvania, found the law to be a violation of the United States Constitution. District Judge Dazell was quoted as saying, "As the most participatory form of mass speech yet developed, the Internet deserves the highest protection from government intrusion . . . just as the strength of the Internet is chaos, so the strength of our liberty depends upon chaos and cacophony of the unfettered speech the First Amendment protects." The United States Supreme Court decision supported the lower court decision. They said in part: "The Internet is an international network of interconnected computers . . . [which] now enables tens of millions of people to communicate with one another and to access vast amounts of information from around the world. The Internet is a unique and wholly new medium of worldwide human communication. . . . Taken together, these tools constitute a unique medium known to its users as cyberspace—located in no particular geographical location but available to anyone anywhere in the world. With access to the Internet . . . tens of thousands of users are engaging in conversations on a huge range of subjects. It is no exaggeration to conclude that the content of the Internet is as diverse as human thought." The United States Supreme Court found that "The record demonstrates that the growth of the Internet has been and continues to be phenomenal. As a matter of constitutional tradition, in absence of evidence to the contrary, we presume that government regulation of the content of speech is more likely to interfere with the free exchange of ideas than to encourage it. The interest in encouraging freedom of expression in a democratic society outweighs any theoretical but unproven benefit of censorship."

However, in 1998, New Mexico passed a law that made it illegal to give minors access to "indecent" material online.[19] It is widely assumed that the law will be challenged and sent the way of the CDA. In New York, in a similar case, a federal judge ruled that the legislative body of the state could not impose enforceable laws relative to I-Way content restrictions that affected companies outside of New York. United States District Court Judge Loretta Preska stated, "The Internet is one of those areas of commerce that must be marked off as a national preserve to protect users from inconsistent legislation that, taken to its most extreme, could paralyze development of the Internet altogether."

Congress continues to write and pass legislation concerning the issue of pedophiles. The latest attempt relates to the prosecution of adults who knowingly contact minors (children under the age of 18) through the Internet for the purpose of engaging in sexual activity or sending obscene material.[20]

One of the federal agencies that has been involved in investigating child pornography has been the United States Customs Service. According to an article published in www.govtech.net, they have had some success in gaining some international cooperation. Prior to 1977, they had success in using obscenity statutes—subsequently, Congress enacted specific child pornography statutes and the Child Protection Act of 1984.

In 1997, New York Attorney General Dennis Vasco said that their 18-month "cybersting" operation, "Operation Rip Cord," identified more than 1500 suspected child pornographers and had made 120 arrests in the United Kingdom, Germany, and the United States.

There are two methods that the child pornographers are using to circumvent or evade the law. The first is by using software and morphing or designing virtual children. They expect that since it is not a real child, only looks like one, no law is broken. They have found out that "resembles a child" has been part of some anti–child pornography laws; thus they can and have been prosecuted for such offenses, at least in California.

The second method is through the use of encryption techniques to mask their transmission of system storage files. Also, it is rumored that pedophiles and others have used *steganography*, which is another word for hiding something "in plain sight." This technique has been around for many years beginning as far back as in the time of Sparta. Examples are microdots, invisible ink, and null ciphers. A possible example is sending a person a graphics file containing a picture of a tree. If the receiver knows where to look, he can continue to enlarge a leaf on that tree and eventually see a child pornography picture. The use of steganography by I-Way criminals offers a serious challenge to security and law enforcement professionals.

The issue of child pornography is one that is getting the greatest amount of attention and support from all those involved in I-Way legislation and law enforcement, and rightly so. It also has had some successful international operations in coordination with other countries' law enforcement agencies. This cooperation, building on its success and lessons learned from its failure may offer the best opportunity and precedent for building an international I-Way law enforcement bridge.

INTERNET HOAXES

Another major irritant for I-Way users, besides spam, is the numerous hoaxes that have been sent by e-mail, posted on Web sites, and passed on by word of mouth. They have gotten so numerous that there are now even Web sites which lists hoaxes (Is that a hoax?). One of the sites is the Web site of the Computer Incident Advisory Capability (CIAC) of the United States Department of Energy. They caveat their information by saying that "CIAC does not have the resources to investigate and/or confirm every hoax currently circulating." They make a good point in saying that "You can help eliminate 'junk mail' by educating the public on how to identify a new hoax warning, how to identify a valid warning, and what to do if you think a message is a hoax." They have identified approximately 20 hoaxes to date. Their site includes a discussion on the history of hoaxes, how to identify them, and more. As a security and law enforcement professional, when you hear of some new virus threat or e-mail threat, it is highly recommended that you check this and other anti-hoax Web sites before "perpetuating" the hoax. It will save time, trouble, and embarrassment.

Since hoaxes fall more in the line of practical jokes, there are no laws that specifically address this subject; however, if the hoax led to defamation of character or violation of other laws, then obviously prosecution may be possible.

OTHER I-WAY CRIMES, MISDEMEANORS, AND IRRITANTS

As was discussed earlier, the I-Way is used by all kinds of people. Therefore, one would expect the same kinds of weirdos, strangers, juvenile delinquents, racists, stalkers, and rapists that one would find on the streets of any city. These people use the I-Way as they have used the telephone, print, and any other means of communication to meet their objectives.

Some of the unfortunate trends, possibly because of cheaper computers, easier access to the I-Way, and the growing numbers of users, include more use of *flaming* (sending nasty, hostile notes in place of walking up to people and telling them what you really think of them); more racists' Web sites, more examples of bigotry; and all the other hateful things that we humans do to each other.

It is unfortunate that this great communications system and massive knowledge database has begun to change from a great opportunity for people around the world to share, learn from each other, better understand each other, and help each other, into more of a "virtual big city." A recent example was one individual who violated a law that makes race-based threats a crime. This individual allegedly sent the following message to approximately 60 Asian students at the University of California, Irvine: "I will personally make it my life's career to hunt you down and kill you."

As a security officer or law enforcement professional for your company or government agency, you are going to be required to protect the employees against such acts and/or investigate them. It is important to understand that these I-Way robbers take from all of us on the I-Way when they do things in violation of federal laws, state laws, company policy, procedures, and if nothing else, things in bad taste. As human beings, as security officers and law enforcement professionals, we appear to be starting to win the war against violent crimes. However, the I-Way robbers are growing in number and in crimes. We must do more to stop them. We can begin by understanding the I-Way, the crimes, and the criminals, and developing security skills to defend against them.

INTERNATIONAL, UNITED STATES FEDERAL AND STATE LAWS, STATUTES, AND REGULATIONS

The purpose of this section of the chapter is to provide an overview and framework for the discussion of Internet crimes. In order to do so, some discussion of the related laws is necessary. However, it is not our intent to go beyond the basic, laymen's view. To do so is beyond the scope of the intent of this basic, introductory overview of the issue of Internet-related crimes.

As nations enter the Information Age, they develop their national information infrastructures (NII), and connect to the global information infrastructure (GII). As was the case with the superhighways, businesses and governments find that the NII and GII are used not only by honest people, but also by the I-Way robbers. When these businesses and governments have identified these criminals, and in some cases even had them arrested, they have found that there may not be any laws that apply, there are no international laws that can be used, or that they lack jurisdiction over the criminals.

The I-Way becomes complicated due to the matter of jurisdiction. In the cases of I-Way crimes, is the jurisdiction based on the location of the criminal and the criminal's computer system; the computers in between the criminal's computer and the victim's computer (the unwilling accomplices); or the victim's computer? For example, if I sit at my computer in my home in Paris, go through a New York City computer, and break into a computer in Tokyo, who has jurisdiction? Who will prosecute me, and under what laws of what country?

Once that is decided, and assuming you knew the identification of the criminal and had sufficient evidence for prosecution, is there sufficient support for extradition? Each country, including the United States, generally does not like to extradite its citizens to a foreign country for prosecution. If the citizen's country's legal system does not have a similar law relative to the criminal offense for which the citizen is to be extradited, then the chances of extradition have been almost zero.

The I-Way is borderless, unbounded by physical roadblocks. This also brings out an interesting question. If a security officer or investigator accesses Web sites and dial-up systems in other countries, identifies and obtains evidence relative to criminal activity of someone in that other country when the criminal activity took place in the investigator's country, has that security person or investigator overstepped his or her authority? In other words, does he or she lack the jurisdiction for doing what he or she just did? Maybe not, but don't be surprised if a defense lawyer brings it up if for no other reason than to muddy the prosecution waters.

Looking again at the comparison of the superhighway and the I-Way, we see that there are many similarities. You may recall that it was not that long ago when criminals in their automobiles out-ran "the law" by escaping to another jurisdiction. In some cases, the conditions of "hot pursuit" applied, where a law enforcement officer was able to pursue outside the officer's jurisdiction. However, in those cases the pursuit was usually within the same state—sometimes outside the state, but not across international boundaries. If we look at the "hot pursuit" on the I-Way, we find that this is not the case. In today's environment, the criminal justice system components (e.g., law enforcement officers) must coordinate with their counterparts (e.g., the judges) for search and wiretap approval, and then attempt to track down the I-Way robber. Cliff Stoll's book, *The Cuckoo's Egg*, explains the difficulties of accomplishing this task.

However, that is the easy part. When they find that the I-Way bandit is in another country, then the matter is elevated "through channels" to the Department of Justice and the State Department. The State Department coordinates with its counterpart in the country or countries that are the conduit for the I-Way crime or where the I-Way robber resides. Then each nation goes through its internal procedures and then back again to the United States and down to the investigative office. Of course, there is also the involvement of Interpol to either help in coordination, or get in the way as another bureaucratic hoop to jump through. Some processes have been improved but it still is not easy.

When crimes are being conducted in nanoseconds, these requests for assistance may be of little use since they take weeks to months to carry out. One of the other countries may not even have a law that applies, so no action at all will be taken by the government agencies or other countries. Even if they have an applicable law, there may be political reasons why they will not provide investigative assistance.

Such issues are still being discussed at national and international levels. As this new environment matures, so will its applicable criminal laws. However, nations have yet to agree on many international criminal issues that arose before the I-Way, so there should not be any expectations of quick fixes as they relate to common, applicable laws related to I-Way–related international crimes.

United Nations

Many nations are quickly entering the Information Age and are just as quickly becoming the victims of the I-Way robbers. More and more of these nations are passing computer crime laws that also apply to that portion of the I-Way under their jurisdiction. It is beyond the scope of this book to provide copies of each nation's computer crime laws. However, it was felt that the United Nations' viewpoint would provide the readers with a global perspective of the problem, concerns, and recommendations of this international body.

The United Nations' document "International Review of Criminal Policy—United Nations Manual on the Prevention and Control of Computer-related Crime," provides an excellent overview of the entire issue of international computer crimes and laws. It is very applicable to the I-Way as it relates to substantive criminal laws concerning privacy, the holders of information and data, procedural law, and international cooperation. A portion of it relating to the issue of computer crime which is relevant to I-Way crime is quoted below:

A. Definition of computer crime
20. It is difficult to determine when the first crime involving a computer actually occurred. The computer has been around in some form since the abacus, which is known to have existed in 3500 B.C. in Japan, China, and India. In 1801 profit motives encouraged Joseph Jacquard, a textile manufacturer in France, to design the forerunner of the computer card. This device allowed the repetition of a series of steps in the weaving of special fabrics. So concerned were Jacquard's employees with the threat to their traditional employment and livelihood that acts of sabotage were committed to discourage Mr. Jacquard from further use of the new technology. A computer crime had been committed.
21. There has been a great deal of debate among experts on just what constitutes a computer crime or a computer-related crime. Even after several years, there is no internationally recognized definition of those terms. Indeed, throughout this Manual the terms computer crime and computer-related crime will be used interchangeably. There is no doubt among

the authors and experts who have attempted to arrive at definitions of computer crime that the phenomenon exists. However, the definitions that have been produced tend to relate to the study for which they were written. The intent of authors to be precise about the scope and use of particular definitions means, however, that using these definitions out of their intended context often creates inaccuracies. A global definition of computer crime has not been achieved; rather, functional definitions have been the norm.

22. Computer crime can involve criminal activities that are traditional in nature, such as theft, fraud, forgery and mischief, all of which are generally subject everywhere to criminal sanctions. The computer has also created a host of potentially new misuses or abuses that may, or should, be criminal as well.

23. In 1989, expanding on work that had been undertaken by OECD, the European Committee on Crime Problems of the Council of Europe produced a set of guidelines for national legislators that enumerated activities that should be subject to criminal sanction. By discussing the functional characteristics of target activities, the Committee did not attempt a formal definition of computer crime but left individual countries to adapt the functional classification to their particular legal systems and historical traditions.

24. The terms "computer misuse" and "computer abuse" are also used frequently, but they have significantly different implications. Criminal law recognizes the concepts of unlawful or fraudulent intent and of claim of right; thus, any criminal laws that relate to computer crime would need to distinguish between accidental misuse of a computer system, negligent misuse of a computer system and intended, unauthorized access to or misuse of a computer system, amounting to computer abuse. Annoying behavior must be distinguished from criminal behavior in law.

25. In relation to the issue of intent, the principle of claim of right also informs the determination of criminal behavior. For example, an employee who has received a password from an employer, without direction as to whether a particular database can be accessed, is unlikely to be considered guilty of a crime if he or she accesses that database. However, the principle of claim of right would not apply to the same employee who steals a password from a colleague to access that same database, knowing his or her access is unauthorized; this employee would be behaving in a criminal manner.

26. A distinction must be made between what is unethical and what is illegal; the legal response to the problem must be proportional to the activity that is alleged. It is only when the behavior is determined to be truly criminal that criminal prohibition and prosecution should be sought. The criminal law, therefore, should be employed and implemented with restraint.

United States Federal and State Legislation

The definition of computer crime varies somewhat from state to state. In some states, using a computer to defraud or commit other crimes may make it a special type of violation. There are certain computer crimes that are specified by federal legislation, such as attacks upon or misuse of government-owned systems.

There are many varied statutes (various federal and at least 49[21] different state statutes) relative to computer crime. Each of these statutes has its own and often different elements of proof. Generally the elements of proof include: knowingly accessing or otherwise using a computer, without authorization or exceeding authorization, with intent to commit a fraudulent act. As in most cases, proving intent, the willful doing of the illegal act, is usually the most difficult element to prove. On the I-Way, the complications are increased by the vastness of the playing field and the number of players.

United States I-Way Related Laws

In dealing with I-Way robbery, the security and law enforcement professional will find that the computer crime and computer fraud laws at both the federal and state levels can be used, assuming that the criminal justice system will eventually become involved and that the business or government agency is interested in prosecuting offenders under one or more of these statutes.[22]

Federal Laws

There are many laws already in existence that can be used to prosecute I-Way crimes and frauds, although they were not enacted with such crimes in mind. Among the United States federal laws that can be used are: (1) wire fraud, (2) mail fraud, (3) interstate transportation of stolen property, and (4) racketeer-influenced and corrupt organizations.

There have been some federal laws enacted which are specific to computer crime, fraud, and protection. These include: (1) Electronic Funds Transfer Act, (2) Computer and Fraud Abuse Act, and (3) Computer Security Act.

The violation of older federal laws is cited in many cases as the reason why a computer is to be searched. The use of such laws offers a simpler case to present to judges and juries. Many times, it avoids the complications associated with computer terminology and use. Some of the more relevant federal laws are as follows:

◆ 15 U.S.C., Section 1693n, Electronic Funds Transfer Act
◆ 18 U.S.C., Section 1343, Wire Fraud

◆ 18 U.S.C., Section 1341, Mail Fraud

◆ 18 U.S.C., Section 2314, Interstate Transportation of Stolen Property

◆ 18 U.S.C., Section 1961, Racketeer Influenced and Corrupt Organizations (RICO)

◆ 18 U.S.C., Section 3109, No-knock Statute

◆ 18 U.S.C., Section 2701, Stored Communications Access

◆ 18 U.S.C., Section 2510, Wiretap

◆ 18 U.S.C., Section 1029, Electronic Communications Privacy Act

◆ 18 U.S.C., Section 1030, Fraud in Connection with Federal Interest Computers (Computer Fraud and Abuse Act)

◆ 42 U.S.C., Section 2000aa, Privacy Protection Act

State Laws

States are also affected by computer crimes. Some states enacted new legislation specific to computer crimes while others amended their current statutes. At last check, 49 states had either amended their current statutes or enacted new legislation (Vermont had not). According to the U.S. Department of Justice, 25 states have enacted specific computer crime statutes and 24 states have amended their criminal statutes. Some states use separate codes and some states use categories such as "crimes against property." The first state to respond to computer crime was Florida, whose legislation went into effect on August 1, 1978.

The following specific state laws should be reviewed when conducting a computer crime or fraud investigation[23]:

Computer Crime Act—Specific State Statutes

Alabama (1985): Ala. Code 13A-8-101

Arkansas (1987): Ark. Stat. sec. 5-41-102, 5-41-106

Colorado (1979): Colo. Rev. Stat. Ann. sec. 18-5.5-101

Connecticut (1984): Conn. Gen. Stat. Ann. sec. 53a-250

Delaware (1984): Del. Code tit. 11, sec. 931 to 939

Florida (1978): Fla. Stat. Ann. sec. 815.01

Georgia (1981): Ga. Code Ann. sec. 16-9-90

Hawaii (1984): Haw. Rev. Stat. 708-890

Idaho (1984): Session Laws of Idaho 1984, ch. 68, p. 129, adding Idaho Code sec. 18-2201

Illinois (1979): Ill. Stat. Ann. ch. 38, sec. 16D-1, 16D-7

Iowa (1984): Iowa Code Ann. sec. 716A

Louisiana (1984): La. Rev. Stat. 14:73.1 through 5

Michigan (1979): Mich. Comp. Laws Ann. sec. 752.791

Mississippi (1985): Miss. Code Ann. sec. 97-45-1

New Jersey (1984): N.J. Rev. Stat. sec. 2A:38A-1 & 2C:20-23

New York (1986): N.Y. Penal Law Art. 156

North Carolina (1979): N.C. Gen. Sat. 14-453

Oklahoma (1984): Okla. Stat. Ann. tit. 21, sec. 1952-1956

Rhode Island (1979): R.I. Gen. Laws sec. 11-52-1

South Carolina (1984): S.C. Code sec. 16-16-10

Tennessee (1983): Tenn. Code Ann. sec. 39-3-1401

Texas (1985): Tex. Penal Code sec. 33.01-33.05

Utah (1979): Utah Code Ann. sec. 76-6-701

Virginia (1984): Va. Code Ann. sec. 18.2-152.1

Wyoming (1982): Wyo. Stat. sec. 6-3-501 through 504

Amended States' Criminal Statutes

Alaska (1984): Ala. Stat. sec. 11.46.740 & 11.81.900(b)(44); Alas. Stat. sec. 11.46.200(a)

Arizona (1978): Ariz. Rev. Stat. sec. 13-2301E, 13-2316

California (1979): Cal. Penal Code sec. 502

Indiana (1986): IC 35-43-1-4, IC 35-43-2-3

Kansas (1985): Kans. Stat. sec. 21-3755

Kentucky (1984): Ch. 210, Acts of 1984, adding Ky. Rev. Stat. sec. 434.840

Maine (1975): Me. Rev. Stat. Ann. tit. 17-A sec. 357(1964)

Maryland (1984): Md. Ann. Code Art. 27, sec. 14.6

Massachusetts (1983): Mass. Gen. Laws Ann. ch. 266, sec. 30(2)

Minnesota (1982): Minn. Stat. Ann. sec. 609.87

Missouri (1982): Mo. Ann. Stat. sec. 569.093

Montana (1981): Mont. Code Ann. 45-6-310

Nebraska (1985): Neb. Rev. Stat. sec. 28-1343

Nevada (1983): Nev. Rev. Stat. sec. 205-473

New Hampshire (1985): N.H. Rev. Stat. sec. 638:16

New Mexico (1979): Computer Crimes Act of 1979, N.M. Stat. Ann. sec. 30-16A-1

North Dakota (1983): N.D. Cent. Code sec. 12.1-06.1-08

Ohio (1986): Ohio Rev. Code Ann. sec. 2901.01 and 2913.01

Oregon (1985): Or. Rev. Stat. 164.377

Pennsylvania (1983): Pa. Stat. Ann. tit. 18, sec. 3933

South Dakota (1982): S.D. Codified Laws Ann. sec. 43-43B-1

Washington (1984): Wash. Rev. Code Ann. sec. 943.70

Wisconsin (1981): Wisc. Stat. sec. 943.70

Identification and summaries of the state laws are available for review as Appendix B.[24]

SUMMARY

The gambling issue, Decency Act issue, spamming issue, and hoaxes are all typical examples of events caused by the reliance on and use of the I-Way. People began to use it as a totally government-free environment—no speed limits, no stop signs—for the absolute uninhibited flow of information and communication. However, politicians and lawmakers have been gaining momentum in pushing their Agricultural and Industrial Age processes onto this Information Age environment as the numbers of I-Way travelers and our dependency on the I-Way have increased. As of this writing, legislatures at both the state and federal levels are continuing to write and enact laws dealing with controls over actions on the I-Way. It is assumed that this "battle" will continue as we enter the 21st century.

There are action, reaction, controversy, and political overtones—sometime not too subtle. Either in the middle or as part of the problems and solutions are the security and law enforcement professionals.

The Clinton Administration is said to be crafting an "Electronic Bill of Rights." The editorial from the Orange County newspaper, August 9, 1998, states: "Congress lurches into cyberspace. . . . Lots of poorly crafted legislation to control the Internet is moving through legislature." Columnist Harry Hammitt, writing in the August 1998 issue of www.govtech.net, said "Committing to Privacy? The Clinton administration's interest in privacy may be motivated more by politics than an interest in the public's privacy rights."

Right or wrong. That is the current environment on the I-Way, full of new warning signs, speed zone signs, stop signs, radar traps, and potholes; and the United States Congress and state legislators continue to try to find their way along the I-Way without a roadmap.

NOTES

1. *Social engineering* is a combination of those techniques used by criminals, con artists, or the like, who want something from someone and try to talk the victim into doing something. They may use coercion, implied threats, lies, or whatever verbal tactics will work to help them get what they want from their victim.
2. The definitions used in this section were taken from various sources, including the Association of Certified Fraud Examiners, Department of Justice documents published by that agency, the Federal Bureau of Investigation, and the National Institute of Justice. It is recommended that the reader search these agencies' Web sites for more extensive discussions and information on this topic.
3. Further information on ACFE can be found at http://www.acfe.org.
4. All I-Way addresses are subject to change. If the address is not available, keyword searches will usually find the information.
5. It is not the intent of the authors to say whether such examples are legal, ethical, or such. It is our intent, as it is with other examples throughout this book, to provide the reader with the information so that the

ramifications of the I-Way can be better understood, thus, adding to the security professionals' knowledge, which would help them better secure their portion of the I-Way and investigate wrongdoing.

6. "Web-site privacy lacking, FTC finds," *Orange County Register*, Business Section, June 4, 1998.

7. "Group says it'll post AOL members," *Orange County Register*, Nation/World Section, January 1, 1998.

8. *InternetWeek*, July 27, 1998.

9. http://www.infowar.com/class_1/Class1_051498b_j.html-ssi

10. *Information Security*, December 1997.

11. http://www.news.com/News/Item/Textonly/0,25,21367,00.html?pfv

12. Reported in http://www.info-sec.com/crypto/crypto_09049/a.html-ssi.

13. See http://www.infoseek.com/Content/.

14. http://www.news.com/News/Item/0,4,24871,00.html?dd.ne.t.wr, CNET News.com, August 3, 1998, "Spammers jump gun on legislation."

15. "Ameritech delayed AOL E-mail to duck storm of spam," *Orange County Register*, July 29, 1998.

16. "'Spam King' now will pay for privilege of E-mailing you," *Computerworld*, April 6, 1998.

17. For the purposes of discussion and understanding of the definition of pornography, which varies from state to state, we will define it as "naked people shown in whatever manner that violates the law where it is viewed."

18. Shelley M. Liberto, "Supreme Court Strikes Down Decency Act in Defense of Internet 'Chaos,'" *WWWIZ* magazine, September 1997, Legal Issue.

19. *Net Insider* article by John Borland, March 9, 1998.

20. Reported in http://www.news.com/News/Item/Textonly/0,25,23108,00. html?st.ne.nipfv, June 12, 1998.

21. As of our last research, only Vermont did not have a computer crime law.

22. All laws noted were the most current available at the time of this writing. Obviously, security officers should verify the most current laws available if they intend to use them for any type of criminal justice action.

23. Much of this information was made available by the National Institute of Justice. It is recommended that their Web site be visited for additional information.

24. Our thanks to the International Computer Security Association for providing the authors with a digital version of these laws from their Web site: http://www.icsa.net.

I-Way Robbers and Other Miscreants

CHAPTER OBJECTIVE

The objective of this chapter is to profile the various miscreants one may encounter while using the I-Way for private or government agency business. By understanding them, one can gain an understanding of how to begin to protect the assets that these miscreants have targeted for theft, manipulation, or destruction, as well as support any associated investigative processes.

HISTORY OF I-WAY ROBBERS

The juvenile delinquents, spies, fraudsters, sexual deviants, and other miscreants who travel the I-Way generally represent a cross-section of those that have been around for probably as long as humans have been around. As soon as one human had something considered of value, some other human probably tried to find a way to get it or destroy it. It seems to be part of the evolution of human beings, for the problem is not confined to the I-Way, nor is it confined to the United States. It is a global problem. Crime has never been the sole possession of any one race, religion, society, community, or nation.

As was stated earlier, the environment is really the only major difference between these I-Way robbers and the other miscreants found in every society today. The change in environment does not change the type of people involved or their motives. They are still the same scoundrels who want something someone else owns, or out of jealousy or just plain meanness want

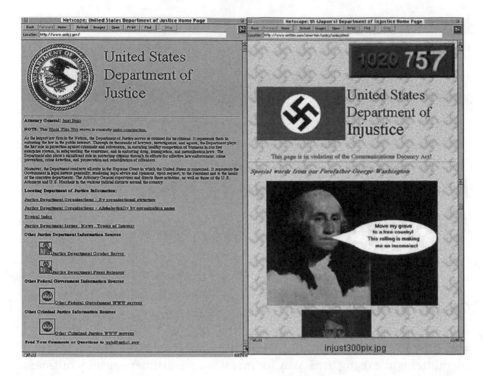

Figures 5–1A and 5–1B U.S. Department of Justice

to deprive the owner of that thing of value. Others soon will want, and will try, to kill someone through the I-Way, perhaps through tele-medicine; so, soon we can probably add murderers to our list of spies, terrorists, pornographers, and other criminals traveling along the I-Way.

Many of those who run rampant on the I-Way today already have a long history (longer in terms of today's rapidly growing and evolving I-Way) of criminality and juvenile delinquency. For example, where once they used the signs along the superhighway to spray paint their messages and gang identifications, these new I-Way juvenile delinquents and hacker gangs now break into Web sites to spray their graffiti (see Figures 5–1 through 5–3). These miscreants have attacked hundreds of Web sites over the years and have changed them, deleted them, or denied their use by legitimate I-Way travelers.

As more and more customers and businesses are on the I-Way, it is imperative that they as well as the security and law enforcement professionals all understand the dangers and consequences of not protecting their Web sites. Loss of business and public embarrassment, at a minimum, will be the results of this lack of protection.

Figure 5–2A   Republic of Indonesia

Figure 5–2B   Republic of Indonesia

Known generally as *threat agents*, all of these miscreants pose threats to the businesses, government agencies, and honest citizens on the I-Way. A short review of techno-crime history will assist in understanding these I-Way robbers, for, as historians say, if you don't know where you've been, you won't know where you are going.

In the 1970s, techno-crimes such as computer fraud were rare, and those that did occur were rarely reported because the companies or government

Figure 5–3A United Kingdom

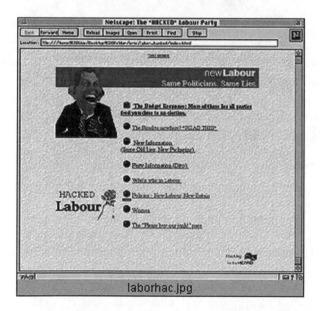

Figure 5–3B United Kingdom

agencies did not want the public to lose confidence in them and in their newly installed computers. After all, they were touting the dawn of the computer age, at a cost of millions of dollars. Perpetrators generally were computer specialists: programmers, computer operators, data entry personnel, systems analysts, and computer managers—insiders. After all, they were the only ones who knew how to operate and use the technology, and the only ones who were able to gain physical access to them. Thus, the threats were always internal because there were no physical connections from these systems to the outside world. Theft was generally not an issue since these systems, though worth millions of dollars, were extremely heavy and difficult to move. Since the vast majority of these systems were not externally networked, almost 100% of the threats were from insiders.

In the 1980s, the type and frequency of techno-crimes changed due to the personal computer, telecommunications advancements, and networking. The internal types of perpetrators were expanded to include workers who were suffering from financial or personal problems, the disgruntled, the bored, and those tempted by curiosity and/or the challenge. This was also the time of the external hacker. The advancement in the I-Way, telecommunications systems, cheaper, more powerful computers, modems, dial-up systems, and computer bulletin boards gave more potential I-Way robbers more opportunity because of both the availability of the tools and access to the systems increased. During this period, the external threats began to grow. Most information systems security professionals during that period and into the early 1990s placed the threats at approximately 80 percent internal and 20 percent external.

In the 1990s and into the 21st century, international crime and frauds developed and will continue to develop, due to increased international networking—the Global Information Infrastructure (GII), which is based on the I-Way. Also, the new technologies of the private branch exchange (PBX) and cellular phones, both of which are computer based (microprocessors) brought with them the telecommunications criminals who have increased in number as the technology became cheaper, more powerful, and more widely used. They too now drive up the ramps that lead to the I-Way. Perpetrators generally are the same as in the past but now include more international criminals, hackers, and phreakers because of the ease of international access. With the integration of telecommunications and computers into the I-Way, as well as the integration of government agencies and businesses into the I-Way, the threats appear to be approaching an equal split between internal and external threat agents: 50 percent internal and 50 percent external.

WHO ARE THESE I-WAY ROBBERS?

I-Way robbers are the miscreants who use computers and telecommunications systems as their tools and targets for unlawful, immoral, and/or unethical purposes. They can be anyone from "normal" employees, organized crime members, white-collar workers, drug dealers, people in debt, people wanting revenge, greedy people—anyone, under the right circumstances. They can be anyone who has the motive, opportunity, and rationalization for perpetrating their criminal act.

Internal versus External Miscreants

One method of categorizing these people is by their location relative to their target (victim)—internal and external. This method can also assist the security professional in developing a protection plan based on threats, vulnerabilities, and risks to mitigate the opportunities of these criminals. Outside risks often require additional and/or different protection schemes than do inside risks.

Although these internally based and externally based miscreants share some things in common, such as techniques and motives, they will be discussed separately because it provides for a clearer understanding of these threats, which is important if one is to develop a program to safeguard assets from these miscreants. If for no other reason than that external threats are receiving all the publicity, they will be discussed first.

OUTSIDER THREATS

Classes of Outsider Threats

Outsiders have increasingly become a threat to the I-Way and the computer systems on it, due primarily to national and international networking of systems. Some classes of outsiders are as follows:

- Hackers
- Phreakers
- Vendors/suppliers
- Ex-employees
- Employees of associated businesses
- Competitors
- Foreign government agents (spies)

♦ Customers
♦ Subcontractors
♦ Terrorists
♦ Contractors, for example, maintenance personnel
♦ Outside auditors
♦ Consultants
♦ Political activists

There are a number of business and technological developments that will increase the outsider threats. These include:

♦ The number of computers internationally continues to increase past 100,000,000
♦ The number of computers in the United States continues to increase past 25,000,000
♦ Computer literacy, worldwide, is on the rise
♦ Telecommunications and networked computers continue to increase worldwide
♦ More people will be telecommuting
♦ Increases in outsourcing continue
♦ Increased use of technologies such as EDI, EFTS, POS systems
♦ Strategic, advanced systems increasingly become the targets as economic competition grows
♦ Terrorism is growing and it is only a matter of time before they begin targeting computers as a target of opportunity
♦ Former Soviet Union countries' agents are selling their computer expertise to the highest bidders
♦ Information warfare is growing as one of the 21st century's methods of waging war

Outsider Motivations

Many external threat agents share the same motivations as the insiders. In addition, some other motivations of outsiders include:

♦ Revenge of a former employee
♦ Competitors wanting inside information
♦ Former employees' curiosity to see if their previous user IDs and passwords still work

◆ Political agenda
◆ Nationalistic economic pressures
◆ Patriotism
◆ Religious fervor

The Hackers

One of the biggest challenges facing security and law enforcement professionals today is the hacker. This is not only because of some of their increasingly sophisticated methods, but also because of their sheer numbers.

Initially, hackers were just considered intelligent kids who experimented with computers (Levy, 1984), but times changed and when the news reporters played up their stories, the term *hacker* began to be used as a label, not for the computer enthusiasts who loved learning new things and programming computers, but for those who illegally accessed the computers for their personal pleasure, for vandalism, and later for criminal purposes.

This general term for those who break into computer systems (gain unauthorized access), now predominantly via the I-Way, may be incorrect, but it is now part of the I-Way culture. Some have tried, unsuccessfully, to differentiate between hackers and the miscreants on the I-Way, but to no avail. The term has stuck; therefore, it will also be used here.

Hacker Profile

It is generally agreed among those dealing with hackers that the average United States hacker profile back in the 1980s and early 1990s was as follows:

◆ Caucasian
◆ Male
◆ Young (14 to mid-20s)
◆ Very intelligent
◆ Avid computer enthusiast
◆ Introverted
◆ Insecure
◆ From middle to upper middle income family

This is logical when one thinks that at the time the majority of United States citizens were caucasian, only families with sufficient income could afford computers, and these were primarily two-income families with both parents working. So, to help "junior" to prepare for college and the future, computers were bought. Some parents probably believed that it was a good way for junior to stay out of trouble, and it was the modern-day equivalent to the babysitter. Furthermore, those that were more extroverted generally had friends, more activities and social events to concern themselves with. Thus the insecure, introverted boy took refuge with his computer—his friend.

It is beyond the scope of this book to try to explain why it is that hackers are predominantly male. It may stem from the fact that the computer field seems to be of interest more to males than to females. It may be that males prefer violence—possibly stemming from the caveman days of hunting and protecting their turf. Many a hacker began with computer games and computer games have grown more graphically violent over the years. For whatever reason, hacking is generally a male-dominated sport!

Motivations of the Hacker

The opinions of security professionals and the hackers themselves tend to agree that computer hackers are mostly motivated by their desire to:

♦ Learn about computers as a hobby
♦ Defy authority
♦ Respond to a challenge
♦ Beat the system
♦ Cause disruption
♦ Show contempt for others
♦ Show how smart they are

Types of Hackers

There are three basic types of hackers (Levy, 1984; Kovacich, 1993). They are:

1. The Curious, who break into computers to learn more about them.
2. The Meddlers, who break into computers because they are interested in the challenge of breaking in, and looking for weaknesses in the system.
3. The Criminals, who break into computers to commit a crime, to act for personal gain.

The Curious Hacker   It is generally agreed that the first true hackers came from the Massachusetts Institute of Technology (MIT) in the fifties and sixties. Many of that initial group belonged to MIT's Technical Model Railroad Club (TMRC). These hackers had an insatiable curiosity, the kind that caused them to wonder what made things work and how to make them operate better. So they took things apart to see how they worked and then found ways to make them work better. They naturally gravitated to the computer. These early hackers enjoyed learning about computers and how to expand the computer's capabilities, as opposed to those who wanted to learn just enough to get by for their classes. They began to develop their own terminology: a piece of equipment that didn't work was called *losing;* a ruined piece of equipment was *munged* (Mash Until No Good); someone who insisted on studying for a course was called a *tool;* and garbage was *cruft* (Levy, 1984).

The term *hack* had previously been used to describe MIT college pranks. However, members of the TMRC used it in a more serious vein to refer to computer programming exploits which were clever, innovative, and had style. The "Hacker Ethic" was: "Access to computers—and anything which might teach you something about the way the world works—should be unlimited and total. Always yield to the Hand-On-Imperative!" (Steele et al., 1983).

Their philosophy was one of sharing, openness, decentralization, and getting their hands on machines at any cost—to improve them and improve the world. They believed that computers could do much to improve the world. Rules that prevented them from taking matters into their own hands were not worth discussing—not to mention obeying. They believed that information should be free; they mistrusted authority. They believed they should be judged on their skills and not by their degrees, age, race, or position. They believed that art and beauty could be created on a computer and that computers could change lives for the better. They were young, intelligent, free spirits who lived for the computers they learned from and modified, and for the software they wrote and made more and more efficient (Levy, 1984).

As computers began playing a more and more important role in our daily lives, our dependency on them continued to increase. We could not take chances that unauthorized users would gain access to them. In order to safeguard these computers and their information, additional security controls were put in place. These passwords, software licenses, copyright notices, protected programs, and other controls were totally contrary to the hackers of old. Thus began the adversarial relationship between the hackers and the people responsible for safeguarding the computers and the information stored, transmitted, and processed therein. Although this relationship started in earlier years, a line was now drawn in the sand. This didn't deter the hackers; in fact, it probably increased their eagerness to break into the computers. This was an increased challenge to their egos and their talents—like a bullfighter waving a red cape in front of the bull. How could these young bulls resist?

The Meddler—The Juvenile Delinquent The next generation of hackers had the spirit of the older hacker generation but was more active in computer penetrations. Some called this type of hacker the *meddler* (Steele et al., 1983). The meddler is a hacker who is inquisitive and also an irritant to the staff of the computer system he or she tries to penetrate. This person normally tries to uncover information about a system, such as the type of system, the passwords for it, how it works, what type of software it uses, and a telephone number to dial-in to it. After discovering the information, the hacker will then try to access the system without authority. This inquisitive person, in the days of dial-ups and before the I-Way expanded into what it is today, used a "war dialer" (hacking software that continuously dials telephone numbers looking for the computer modem tone) as their primary tool. Then the hacker used various types of software or just guesses to identify a user's identification and passwords to gain access.

Today, these miscreants use search tools such as Yahoo, Lycos, and Excite to search the I-Way for hacking tools, download the hacker software programs (or security programs that have been turned into hacking tools), identify a target, and then just execute the programs. This will be discussed in more detail in the following chapters. Although this is a very simple process it continues to work.

The meddler is interested in the challenge of trying to break into systems and discover their uses, how they operate, and generally to learn as much as possible about them. This type of hacker has even been known to identify vulnerabilities and correct them, or recommend corrections to the computer operations staff—not so much out of kindness but out of ego by "kicking sand in their faces." Many of these hackers, like those before them, are the types who take apart a clock, radio, or other electronic equipment just to see how it operates; the people who built a crystal radio set and later a computer. They too were not only curious but usually had no intention of destroying the system's software, files, or information stored on the computer. The primary difference between these hackers and the earlier hackers was that they accessed computers without any approval or authority. If they were challenged, they became the juvenile delinquents of the I-Way.

The True Criminal Element As the meddler generation of hackers began to gain unauthorized access to computer systems in violation of the new computer crime laws, which were rapidly becoming active at both the state and federal levels, some of them began to destroy information, steal information, and damage system files. Additionally, their use of the systems cost the owners money. Computer costs were generally charged back to customers directly or indirectly through budget allocations, based on time on the systems. The use of the computer literally meant that time was money!

As they began to penetrate computers, they bragged about their exploits to fellow hackers, through hacker computer bulletin boards. These hacker computers linked through telephone lines enabled them to talk to one another. It is interesting to note that many of the hacker bulletin boards had better security than the billion-dollar corporations' systems they had penetrated! Now these hackers, along with the true hackers and meddlers, often operate their own Web sites on the I-Way.

These penetrations and subsequent unauthorized entry and manipulation of computer files, such as credit records, caused more and more harm and increased publicity. Because of public outrage and legislation, hackers began to face confiscation of their equipment by federal and local law enforcement officials, many times to the surprise of the parents who saw their son's computer being carted away as evidence!

Although there are still those computer and telephone hackers who fit the profile of the hackers of the fifties, sixties, and seventies, the late eighties saw two new types of hackers. The first were the international hackers who began penetrating computers in the United States from as far away as Europe. The case gaining the most publicity was one in which a hacker was traced from Lawrence Berkeley Lab to Hannover, Germany (Stoll, 1989). It was subsequently determined that the hacker was being paid by the KGB to break into U.S. computers; hacking had become an international profession! The second type of hacker began penetrating the telephone switching systems for the sole purpose of selling toll-free international telephone calls to anyone with $15 or $20. They became known as the *phreakers*.

The new challenge is to stop these hackers and phreakers who are causing annual losses in the billions of dollars. According to Jerry Swick, Senior Investigator, MCI: "According to law enforcement and private sector experts, business losses from telecommunications fraud are estimated at more than $4 billion per year. The average loss per incident to users exceeds $50,000. Tele-crooks, hackers, and 'phone phreaks' are invading corporate telephone and voice messaging systems at an unprecedented rate." This type of activity disrupts an organization's valuable communications network and causes losses of revenue. Telecommunications fraud creates an expensive problem that affects consumers and your businesses. As the telephone becomes more integrated into the I-Way, it will open up an entirely new source of threats, vulnerabilities, and risks.

International Hackers International hackers are a growing concern and many have targeted systems in the United States, especially those of the Department of Defense. These juvenile delinquents and foreign governments' information warriors have become more sophisticated, better equipped, and more vicious than their predecessors. It was rumored that a group of Dutch hackers offered their support to Iraq during the Persian Gulf War. They have denied making any such offer. The financial systems of the United States have come under increased attacks, and some of the most serious are from Russia's criminal elements.

The Phreakers While the hackers were busy breaking into computer systems, another type of hacker was busy breaking into telephone switching systems and making telephone calls around the world without paying for them. One of the first to gain notoriety was called "Captain Crunch." He allegedly found that a free whistle enclosed in each box of cereal, when held to the telephone handset, made the same sound as the telephone switching equipment. It provided him the ability to make free long-distance telephone calls. Another was known as "The Cracker." This person began at the age of fourteen to explore the telephone switching systems (Landreth, 1985).

Phreakers specialize in telecommunications hacking. They prefer private branch exchanges and telephone switches. In writing to one another and others, they change the letter *f* to *ph*, some say for "phone," which is why they are now known as phreakers. Today, these juvenile delinquents and criminals pose some of the most serious challenges to security and law enforcement professionals. Some of them have skills that rival those of engineers at the telecommunications corporations.

These hackers and phreakers formed hacker gangs and often were at war with each other. Some shared information and others were rivals. The rival gangs often attacked each other as do the street gangs of today. Gangs such as the Masters of Deception, Legion of Doom, and numerous others were generally loosely formed groups of young hackers who enjoyed the camaraderie of sharing information and attacking systems together.

Profile of the I-Way Fraudster

Technology fraudsters, like other techno-criminals previously discussed, can be anyone from organized crime members, white-collar workers, drug dealers, people in debt, people wanting revenge, to greedy people—anyone, under the right circumstances. Fraud offenders differ little from the average person. According to the Association of Certified Fraud Examiners, most offenders commit fraud for the same reasons most criminals commit crimes:

- ◆ Motive
- ◆ Opportunity
- ◆ Rationalization

These studies also indicate that most computer crimes have been committed for personal financial gain, for the intellectual challenge, to help the organization, or due to peer pressure.

I-Way Terrorists

For the technology-driven terrorists—the I-Way terrorists—the I-Way may soon become the vehicle of choice of tomorrow as car bombs are today. *Terrorism* is basically the use of terror and violence for political purposes, as in a government trying to intimidate the population or an insurgent group opposing the government in power. The FBI defines terrorism as ". . . the unlawful use of force or violence against persons or property to intimidate or coerce a government, the civilian population, or any segment thereof, in furtherance of political or social objectives." The U.S. CIA defines international terrorism as ". . . terrorism conducted with the support of foreign governments or organizations and/or directed against foreign nations, institutions, or governments." The U.S. Departments of State and Defense define terrorism as ". . . premeditated, politically motivated violence perpetrated against a non-combatant target by sub-national groups or clandestine state agents, usually intended to influence an audience. International terrorism is terrorism involving the citizens or territory of more than one country."

A terrorist, then, is one who causes intense fear; one who controls, dominates, or coerces through the use of terror. With more and more businesses, government agencies, and users becoming more and more dependent on the I-Way, it is just a matter of time before the I-Way terrorists begin committing their acts. However, instead of car bombs and germ warfare, they will be using logic bombs and computer viruses.

Why Use Terrorist Methods?   Terrorists generally use terrorism when those in power do not listen, there is no redress of grievances, and/or when individuals or groups oppose current policy. They believe that there is no other recourse available. A government may want to use terrorism to expand its territory or influence another country's government.

What Is a Terrorist Act?   Generally speaking, terrorism is what the government in power says it is. Some of the questions that come up when discussing terrorism are:

♦ What is the difference between a terrorist and a freedom fighter?
♦ Does "moral rightness" excuse violent acts?
♦ Does the cause justify the means?

Results of Terrorist Actions   Terrorist acts tend to cause an increase in security. They may cause the government to decrease the freedoms of its citizens in order to protect them. This in turn may cause more citizens to turn against the government, thus supporting the terrorists! It also causes the citizens to become aware of the terrorists and their demands. Terrorists cause death, damage, and destruction as a means to an end. Sometimes, they get a government to listen, and sometimes they succeed in creating social and political changes.

We can see the beginning of this trend in the United States. We are willing to give up some of our freedom and privacy in order to have more security and personal protection, as in increased airport security searches and questioning of passengers.

Current terrorist targets have included transportation systems, citizens, buildings, government officials, military barracks, and embassies.

Terrorist Technology Threat Environment   Today's terrorists are not only using technology to communicate (e.g., e-mail) and technology crimes to fund their activities (e.g., credit card fraud, illegal bank money transfers); they are beginning to look at the potential for using technology in the form of information warfare against their enemies. Because today's technology-oriented countries rely on vulnerable computers and telecommunications systems to support their commercial and government operations, this sort of terrorism is becoming a concern to businesses and government agencies throughout the world. It is estimated that this will increase in the future.

The advantage to the terrorist of attacking these systems is that I-Way terrorism can be accomplished with little expense by very few people and cause a great deal of damage to the economy of a country. They can conduct such activities with little risk to themselves since these systems can be attacked and destroyed from the base of a country friendly to them. In addition, they can do so with no loss of life, thus avoiding the extreme backlash against them that would arise if they had destroyed buildings and killed many people.

Economic and Industrial Espionage—I-Way Spies

When we look at rapid, technology-oriented growth, we find nations of "haves" and "have-nots." We also see corporations that conduct business internationally and those that want to do so. The international economic competition and trade wars are increasing. Corporations are finding increased competition and looking for a competitive edge, every competitive advantage.

One way to gain an advantage is through industrial and economic espionage. It is true that both forms of espionage—political and industrial—have been around as long as there has been competition. However, in this Information Age, competitiveness is more time-dependent, more crucial to success, and has increased dramatically, largely due to technology. Thus, we see the increased use of technology to steal that competitive advantage and, ironically, these same technology tools are what are being stolen. In addition, we now have more sensitive information consolidated in large databases on I-Way networked systems with security that is often questionable.

Industrial and Economic Espionage Defined   To clarify what we are talking about here, definitions of industrial espionage and economic espionage are in order. *Industrial espionage* is defined as an individual or private business entity sponsorship or coordination of intelligence activity conducted for the purpose of enhancing a competitor's advantage in the marketplace. According to the FBI, *economic espionage* is defined as "Government-directed, sponsored, or coordinated intelligence activity, which may or may not constitute violations of law, conducted for the purpose of enhancing that country's or another country's economic competitiveness."

Economics, World Trade, and Technologies   What allowed this proliferation of technologies to occur? Much of it was due to international business relationships among nations and companies. Some of it was due to industrial and economic espionage.

The Information Age has brought with it more international businesses, more international competitors, and more international businesses working on joint projects against international competitors. This has resulted in more opportunities to steal from partners. Also, one may be a business partner on one contract while competing on another, thus providing the opportunity to steal vital economic information. Furthermore, since we are now a world of international business competitors, the global power of a country is today largely determined by its economic power. Thus, in all reality, we are in the midst of worldwide business competition, called by many an *economic war*, and the I-Way is developing into the main battleground.

Even the Russians view economics as a major factor in information warfare. Dr. D. S. Chereshkin, Vice President of the Russian Academy of Science, Institute of Systems Analysis, Moscow, Russia, in a brief thesis entitled, "Realities of information warfare," stated:

> The new information technologies, being realized as modern information infrastructure, determine the effectiveness of a country's economy. At the same time, all this [sic] technologies makes the life fundamentals—power stations and transport systems—very sensitive to any destructive influence which can be given to information infrastructure. . . . But what types of information weapons are known today? . . . Means for destruction, distortion or plunder of information files. This warfare gives the opportunities to put out of action all highly technological infrastructures.

This world competition, coupled with the I-Way and other international networks and telecommunications links, has provided more opportunities for more people, such as hackers, phreakers, and crackers, to steal information through these networks. The end of the Cold War has also made many exspies available to continue to practice their trade, but in a capitalistic environment. After all, the United States encouraged these Cold War spies to become capitalists to build a democracy, a middle class, and private businesses. So, what do these people know? They know how to spy. Now instead of doing it for patriotism, they do it for money. After all, they are now capitalists!

These ex-KGB,[1] ex-CSR, and ex-GRU (as well as active) agents are professionals, but the most dangerous are the Ph.D. computer scientists who were trained by the KGB, GRU, and others. They have many decades of experience and have reverse engineered IBM mainframes in the "good ol' days." These are the ones to fear most, the ones who without sheer luck and/or a lot of money spent on security will not be caught.

Proprietary Economic Information   This new world environment makes a corporation's proprietary information more valuable than ever. When we talk about proprietary economic information, we are talking about, according to the FBI, ". . . all forms and types of financial, scientific, technical, economic, or engineering information including but not limited to data, plans, tools, mechanisms, compounds, formulas, designs, prototypes, processes, procedures, programs, codes, or commercial strategies, whether tangible, or intangible . . . and whether stored, compiled, or memorialized physically, electronically, graphically, photographically, or in writing." This assumes that the owner takes reasonable measures to protect it and it is not available to the general public. These types of information are key targets for the industrial and economic espionage agents and much of this information is available via the I-Way.

Economic Espionage Vulnerabilities   The increase in economic espionage via the I-Way is also largely due to corporate vulnerabilities to such threats. Corporations do not adequately identify and protect their information, nor do they adequately protect their computer and tele-communications systems with their on- and off-ramps to the I-Way. They do not have adequate security policies and procedures; employees are not aware of their responsibilities to protect their corporation's proprietary information, for example, what information should not be posted on a Web site or sent via e-mail. Many of the employees and also the management of these corporations do not believe they have any information worth stealing or believe that "it can't happen here."
  Therefore, the combination of

  ♦ A nation's or corporations' information which is valuable to other nations and businesses
  ♦ The amount of money which some are willing to pay for that information
  ♦ The increase in miscreants willing to try to steal that information
  ♦ The increase in I-Way ramps to businesses and government agencies
  ♦ The vulnerabilities of systems on the I-Way off-ramps
  ♦ The lack of security as a high priority for businesses and government agencies
  ♦ The ability to steal that information on a global scale

all add up to some very dangerous times for those with information worth protecting and major challenges to the security and law enforcement professionals with the responsibility for that protection and investigating incidents.

Economic Espionage Risks   When corporations fail to adequately protect their information, they are taking risks that will, in all probability, cause them to lose market share, profits, business, and also help in weakening the economic power of their country.

Info-Warriors and Cyber-Warriors

Information warfare (IW) is the term being used to define the concept of 21st century warfare, which will be electronic and information systems driven. Since it is still evolving, its definition and budgets are muddy and dynamic. The federal government agencies and even departments within the Department of Defense (U.S. Air Force, U.S. Navy, Office of the Secretary of Defense, National Security Agency, U.S. Army) all seem to have somewhat different definitions of IW. As you would expect, these agencies define IW in terms of strictly military actions; however, that does not mean that the targets are strictly military targets.

Information warfare, as defined by the U.S. Defense Information Systems Agency (DISA), is "actions taken to achieve information superiority in support of national military strategy by affecting adversary information and information systems while leveraging and protecting our information and information systems." This definition seems to be a good summary definition of all the federal government agencies' definitions as noted above.

The federal government's definition of IW can be divided into three general categories: offensive, defensive, and exploitation. For example: to deny, corrupt, destroy, or exploit an adversary's information, or influence the adversary's perception is offensive; to safeguard ourselves and allies from similar actions is defensive (also known as *IW hardening*); and to exploit available information in a timely fashion, in order to enhance our decision/action cycle and disrupt the adversary's cycle, is exploitative.

In addition, the military views IW as including electronic warfare (e.g., jamming communications links); surveillance systems; precision strikes (e.g., if you bomb a telecommunications switching system, it is IW); and advanced battlefield management (e.g., using information and information systems to provide information on which to base military decisions when prosecuting a war).

One may wonder how civilians can be involved in a country's information warfare activities—after all, isn't that between governments and their military forces? Remember that during World War II, the allies bombed cities and private factories of the Axis forces. Today's and tomorrow's cities and private factories are on the I-Way, a nation's information infrastructure, and its Web sites. The Chinese of the People's Republic of China have the view, as do most other countries, that information warfare will include the civilian community:

> The rapid development of networks has turned each automated system into a potential target of invasion. The fact that information technology is increasingly relevant to people's lives determines that those who take part in information war are not all soldiers and that anybody who understands computers may become a "fighter" on the network. Think tanks composed of non-governmental experts may take part in decision making; rapid mobilization will not just be directed to young people; information-related industries and domains will be the first to be mobilized and enter the war. (The British Broadcasting Corporation Summary of World Broadcasts, August 20, 1996, translated from the *Jiefangjun Bao* newspaper, Beijing, China, June 25, 1996, page 6.)

Based on a combination of the definitions noted above, one can look at information warfare as being a factor in information, systems, and telecommunications protection. The info-warriors, cyber-warriors, techno-spies, I-Way terrorists, or whatever one wants to call them present additional increased challenges to all those on, attached to, or concerned with making the I-Way a safe place to travel, visit, and maintain as a free space for sharing information and learning.

Remember that these armies of info-warriors are looking at the targets presented along the I-Way, and the first of these are commercial, nonmilitary. The weapons that they will use can be categorized as attack, protect, exploit, and support weapons systems. They have the funding and identification of targets and are developing plans and sophisticated application programs to attack a nation's information infrastructure, which includes sites on the I-Way.

Insider Threats

Who Is an Insider?   An *insider* is a company employee or person on contract to the company. It may also be defined as anyone who has authorized access to the systems leading to the I-Way and to travel on the I-Way itself, from physically inside a government agency or business or company-approved location.

Position of the Insider   The position of the insiders who pose risks on the I-Way is basically anyone who has access to the computer systems, input documents, or output documents. These include, but are not limited to:

    Auditors
◆ Security personnel
    Marketing personnel
    Accountants
    Financial analysts
    Management
    Inventory personnel

Insider Motivations   Earlier, the triad of motive, rationalization, and opportunity was discussed. These apply to insiders also. Some of the possible motives could be:

◆ Financial gain
    Revenge
    Challenge
    Curiosity

Some of the possible rationalizations could be:

◆ Underpaid
    Didn't get but deserved promotion
    Work goes unrecognized

Some of the opportunities could include:

    Lack of audit trails
    No access controls to systems or files
    Lack of separation of duties
    A high degree of trust in employees' honesty

Threat Recognition There are various indicators that could point to an employee who has perpetrated or who may be considering perpetrating an I-Way robbery. Some characteristics or profiles of an insider who presents a threat include:

♦ Bankruptcy
♦ Divorce pending
♦ Substance abuse
♦ Unexplained wealth
♦ Big spender
♦ Constantly complaining
♦ Hostile
♦ Emotional instability
♦ Signs of extreme stress
♦ Profound personality changes
♦ Expressed feelings of being victimized by peers, employers, or organization

Opportunists and Miscellaneous Miscreants

As had been stressed throughout this book, the I-Way is only a vehicle, just as the automobile and the horse were—it's a way to get around! Therefore, one should not be surprised to see those who are interested in adult or child pornography, racism, or bigotry perpetrating frauds and scams or other unacceptable behavior while cruising the I-Way.

They are not unique to the I-Way. The security and law enforcement professional who has come across these types of people on our streets prior to the construction of the I-Way for public travel will find these same types of people on the I-Way for the very same reasons as before. They are the same people, thus not unique to the I-Way. One should not be surprised to find them on the I-Way, in the neighborhood, and knocking on the door of the system nodes along the I-Way of businesses and government agencies.

The security and law enforcement professional should know that there are those employees who, for reasons of sexual gratification, get-rich schemes, or out of curiosity, are willing to open the businesses' or government agencies' doors leading to the I-Way and let these people in. There are also those who use tactics, tools, and techniques to break the door down. How they break that door down is important for the security and law enforcement professionals to understand if they are to protect the assets of their employer or investigate I-Way robberies.

Some take advantage of novices on the I-Way, new drivers with "learner's permits" on the I-Way. For example, one trend is choosing Web site names that are similar to other more well-known sites. During the NASA Mars mission, many people wanted to get more information about the mission, but were more accustomed to going to a ".com" site than a ".gov" site. Those who pointed their browsers to http://www.nasa.com instead of http://www.nasa.gov were in for a shock when an advertisement and photos of naked women popped up on the screen. The same can be said for http://www.whitehouse.com instead of http://www.whitehouse.gov or http://www.sharware.com instead of http://www.shareware.com. There are many other examples.

Was this done deliberately or was it coincidence? Was it good marketing strategy? Is it illegal? Unethical? What about the firm that diverted an alleged competitor's on-line viewers to their own site? These are some of the questions and incidents that appear to be occurring more frequently as more and more people travel the I-Way while others see the users as potential customers—or victims.

Of course, then there are the pranksters who have gone from throwing rolls of toilet paper all over someone's house, car, and yard (usually in the middle of the night) to listing one's home address on the I-Way as a place for a good time, or anything in between.

One person wrote a computing help column in the *San Francisco Chronicle* newspaper (computers@sfgate.com) asking for help in getting his or her address off a Web site. It seems that someone had listed the address as a place to get a massage. Over 50 young men had shown up at the front door at all hours of the day and night. This may seem funny, but not if it is your address.[2]

The following scenario is offered as a possible use of I-Way robberies for gaining more security budget:

> Discretionary spending, the amount Congress budgets every year for such programs as roads, fighter planes and education programs, has declined steadily to the point it is 12 percent below the 1990 level, according to a congressional study. . . . In inflation-adjusted 1998 dollars, discretionary outlays dropped from $630 billion in 1990 to $553 billion this year, the Joint Economic Committee study said. Discretionary spending, those programs in the federal budget that Congress must vote on each year, now comprises only one-third of all federal spending. The other two-thirds goes to fixed entitlement and mandatory programs.[3]

So, less discretionary budget means more agencies fighting over their share of the third that is left. The latest Department of Justice—and specifically the FBI—public relations efforts before congressional committees relative to economic espionage, hackers, and techno-terrorist threats have presented many briefings and hacker cases to obtain more budget. The FBI's new "I-Way crime center," with an alleged start-up budget of $30–40 million to basically catch hackers, is one part of that budget battle.

SUMMARY

Security and law enforcement professionals in their careers meet all kinds of miscreants. The I-Way is no exception. These threats to the assets of the business or government agency can come from the inside or from the outside. Before security officers can be successful in protecting their business's or government agency's assets, or law enforcement officers can be successful in investigating I-Way robberies, they should have a basic understanding as to who these people are, their motives, and profiles.

Those from within the business or government agency—insiders—and those that are not directly employed by the business or government agency—anyone who is under financial pressures, is greedy, vindictive, jealous, or hostile—can be a threat. They are sometimes called *threat agents*. A threat agent can be anyone under the right circumstances with the motive, opportunity, and a rationalization for his or her illegal acts. They are crackers, phreakers, embezzlers, con artists, sexual deviants, spies, and terrorists.

By gaining an understanding of these threat agents, the security and law enforcement professionals will be in a better position to help mitigate their threats. By taking away one or more of their opportunities, motives, and/or rationalizations that have led them to come after the assets the security officers are charged with protecting, these miscreants' efforts can be thwarted, or at least mitigated or more successfully investigated.

The hacker problems have escalated and so has their impact. This problem is compounded by the increase in attacks by foreign hackers. New technology has brought new types of crimes, the requirement for new types of investigative techniques, and a new language—"techno-talk." The risks to the I-Way are growing and so are the challenges to law enforcement, security officials, and the criminal justice system. I-Way robberies are becoming more sophisticated and no longer being perpetrated by "just kids."

Criminals are perpetrating them with the same goal as other, less-sophisticated criminals—fraud driven by greed.

The majority of criminal justice system members lack computer and telecommunications expertise to adequately investigate and prosecute the I-Way robbers. However, they can expect to become more involved in technology-related crimes. There is also a general lack of knowledge throughout the entire industrial security profession as to how best to address this problem. This makes it very difficult for members of the criminal justice system to adequately do their jobs as they relate to these types of crimes. Additionally, the public demands that priority be given to the investigation and prosecution of violent crimes such as murder, rape, drug selling, and gang-related crimes. "Victimless crimes," technology-related crimes, and white-collar crimes committed via the I-Way continue to receive a lower priority.

NOTES

1. Central Intelligence Service—*Centralnaya Sluzhbza Razvedkyin* (CSR); remaining elements of the Committee for State Security, the *Komitet Gosudarstvennoy Bezopasnosti* (KGB); and the chief intelligence directorate, the *Glavnoye Razvedyvatelnoye Upravleniye* (GRU).
2. *Orange County Register Connect*, August 16, 1998.
3. *Orange County Register,* April 7, 1998.

6

I-Way Targets

CHAPTER OBJECTIVE

This chapter discusses the assets typically targeted by I-Way robbers. It also provides a brief overview of the increased importance of "intangible" information assets to the knowledge-based businesses and government agencies of the Information Age and some of the ways that the global adoption of I-Way technology brings increased risk to these assets.

I-WAY ROBBERS AT THE WALL?

When businesses and government agencies connect to the Internet, management very frequently believes they have nothing of value to an I-Way robber. They may even believe the new I-Way business environments are safer than an equivalent operation in physical space. After all, no one will be sticking a gun in anyone's face demanding money. However, some of this attitude is attributable to ignorance of all the possible reasons that could inspire an I-Way robber to seek unauthorized access or use of businesses' and government agencies' networks and systems. The potential motivations and possible targets range from the obvious to those that may be less apparent to managers accustomed to thinking in terms of only physical/tangible assets. It is important for security and law enforcement professionals to understand this and communicate with management so that management understands the problems.

WHAT SHOULD BE PROTECTED AGAINST I-WAY ROBBERS?

The most important step in determining what assets to protect in businesses and government agencies is to first understand what may be valuable and important, then to learn to think like the opponent, the I-Way robbers themselves. Although the I-Way robber "in training" may gain skills and experience in breaking into systems along the I-Way for intellectual sport, at some point some "cross the line" and begin to actively seek financial gain from exploiting their knowledge. They represent a real threat to businesses and government agencies that fail to prepare adequately to withstand or respond to their activities. There are documented cases too sensitive to discuss here of hackers or those with hacker skills being hired, threatened, or blackmailed into conducting I-Way robberies for organized crime groups or others. They even go so far as to threaten or kidnap members of families.

Since the global I-Way allows the I-Way robber free rein to I-Way–connected systems anywhere on the planet, you should not assume that you will be dealing only with citizens of your own nation or even from the same continent. This further complicates the already formidable challenge of protecting the businesses' and government agencies' assets since now you must consider what could be of interest to anyone from anywhere!

Business Information

The raw material of the Information Age is information, and the refined ore is knowledge, the "how best to do what needs to be done" components of information. When assessing the assets of a business or government agency, first consider who, in both the personal and professional context, could have need of or benefit from access to information and knowledge resident in the enterprise. The list of potential threat actors includes all those outlined in the previous chapters. Also, consider the possible abuse of sophisticated automated search tools such as bots, web-crawlers, and intelligent agents, which may be employed by opponents against the businesses' and government agencies' information, networks, databases, and files accessible via the I-Way ramps.

As the person responsible for safeguarding some portion of the I-Way, ask the following series of questions. They are not intended to be exhaustive, but to inspire thought and help elicit whether there may be any highly motivated opponents who could be inclined to exploit the I-Way to the detriment of the businesses and government agencies.

1. Has the business/government agency or its officers insulted or offended officers or executives of competitors, collaborators, or others in a recent business situation?
2. Has the public relations group perhaps snubbed a powerful stock market analyst, a popular journalist, or a major foreign correspondent?
3. Has a foreign government had its request for establishing a facility in its nation declined by the business/government agency, or has a foreign competitor been denied a license to key technology from the business/government agency?
4. Is the business/government agency the target of any publicly known probes, inquiries, or investigations by local, state, federal, or international governmental entities for any reason?
5. Are there any rumors circulating on the I-Way, whether true or not, about questionable activities of the business/government agency, its executives, or staff?
6. Is it known that the business/government agency is involved in controversial activities like animal experimentation?
7. Is it known that the business/government agency provides services, products, or advice to "pariah" nations such as Myanmar (Burma) or Libya?
8. Has the business/government agency put itself between parties in conflict, such as the insurgents in a Third World nation and the current government?

If the answer to any of these questions is yes, the business/government agency is probably at an increased risk for some unfortunate attention from these sources or from I-Way robbers working on their behalf to provide redress. Whether the motive is to find the "smoking gun" of a business's or government agency's complicity or duplicity, or to obtain highly valuable technology or digital products, an I-Way intrusion is a potential avenue of approach that creates little risk to the perpetrator.

However difficult and dynamic is the process for understanding the wide range of potential threat actors and their motivations, it is an essential element that helps adjust an I-Way protection program to address changes arising from the mix of motivations. These motivated opponents often create significant spikes in the risk profile facing businesses and government agencies.

In the days before the I-Way, the capability of even highly motivated opponents to act adversely to the business or government agency was limited to those with convenient geographic access to facilities, people, or other tangible assets of their targets. The I-Way now provides a high-speed avenue to reach a target from anywhere on the planet, which makes it much easier for motivated I-Way robbers to act. Couple the reduced barriers of time and space with the limited ability of most law enforcement agencies to investigate and the often poor security of even major businesses and leading government agencies, and we have a situation that provides many opportunities for the I-Way robbers to practice their trade. This means the person responsible for I-Way security has a very serious challenge, and that the opponent has many advantages.

Only after you have a solid appreciation of everyone who might have a reason to target the enterprise should you move to the next step. Assessing what may exist in the business/government agency that could be of interest to competitors, opponents, or other opportunistic I-Way robbers is then a much more feasible task.

Each of the following categories should be considered. The I-Way security officer, in cooperation with the broader business/government agency security groups (physical security and information systems security) should conduct a formal inventory as part of the risk assessment. The objective of this inventory is to identify, in cooperation with legal counsel and executive management, which of the business's or government agency's assets have the greatest value to the business/government agency and which, if improperly obtained by motivated opponents, could cause the greatest damage to the business/government agency's interests. The inventory of potential targets will also provide the framework that will help prioritize protective measures.

As difficult as it is for security and law enforcement professionals, they need to think like the "bad guys." This is especially important in dealing with I-Way robbers, since what they seek may often not be the asset that is of greatest financial value to the business or government agency, nor the asset with the highest "street value." If their motivation is to harm the business/government agency—for example, by short-selling the company's stock—then they may not steal information to sell at a profit, but may merely release the most embarrassing information found in computers and networks, so the target's reputation will suffer. If their desire is to humiliate the business or government agency, they may achieve that with a simple defacing of the Web site with crude language or offensive graphics.

Power and Reputation

I-Way robbers gain status and prestige in the underground community based on whose I-Way network and system security they crack. Intruding into the local community college to change a few grades for classmates is not considered the same level of achievement as penetrating the security of a famous multinational corporation. Therefore, if the business or government agency has a high profile, they may be targeted for a "drive-by attack" by I-Way robbers merely because of their name or status.

It is another well-known phenomenon that more skillful hackers have a proclivity to "mentor" and train those more junior. In a recent high-profile case, code named "Solar Sunrise" by the FBI, the young Israeli hacker who used the name "Analyzer" allegedly instructed two junior accomplices in northern California in the subtle nuances of breaking and entering systems. Many businesses' and government agencies' I-Way connections were violated as the trio practiced their techniques. Thus businesses and government agencies could find themselves hacked either as proof of an accomplished I-Way robber's abilities or as a training assignment for the junior or trainee hacker under the tutelage of the "journeyman."

Access to Other I-Way Ramps, Networks, and Systems

Perhaps one of the least obvious and potentially most significant reasons to target a specific business or government agency is the particular locus it occupies on the I-Way. To managers accustomed to thinking of their business or government agency as a merely physical entity in the stream of commerce, it may be difficult to accept that the web of electronic connections that constitutes the I-Way may bring undesired attention from a wide range of threat agents.

Even if the business or agency itself has nothing of special value, the I-Way conduits it may utilize to provide goods, services, or other benefits to some other businesses and government agencies may be the cause for undesirable attention from I-Way robbers and other miscreants. The many issues explored below describe a wide range of potential reasons to penetrate an otherwise innocent or undesirable victim and abuse their systems.

Safe Harbor and Staging Base

In some circumstances the poor security at a location will make it a convenient staging area for operations against the ultimate target located at another business or government agency. Such situations are more likely if the intervening businesses and government agencies have extensive I-Way relationships with large or high-profile businesses and government agencies with valuable digital assets. This is one of the downsides to major businesses or high-profile government agencies extending their networks to vendors in what are described as *extranets*. Unless security standards are enforced for all participants in the extranet, they may create an unmarked back door that can allow the I-Way robbers direct access to the business/government agency's "crown jewels" with no need to first circumvent a tough firewall security system.

Back Door or Special Relationship

The existing relationship between a vendor and its customers may provide a convenient route into a primary target. Especially when management does nothing to ensure that minimum security controls protect key vendor I-Way connections, they run the risk that outsiders and other customers of the vendor may gain unauthorized access to the business or government agency. Another possibility is that they may use the I-Way connections to access sensitive information concerning the targeted business or agency stored at the vendor's location. The I-Way robbers may also gain initial entry to the vendor's networks by invading other customers connected to the vendor's network. This "transitive property" and possibly trusted I-Way ramps may create vulnerabilities that can dramatically extend the risk to information far beyond the visible relationships of traditional business operations.

Dead Drop

If businesses' and government agencies' systems are poorly protected, they may find that although they are not the direct target of an I-Way robber, their servers may be used as a convenient place where the fruits of a crime are stored.[1] For example, the servers may be used to temporarily store *warez*[2] (pirated software that has had the copy protection and licensing information stripped out) or other stolen software. The warez operators may then grant other pirates access to the files and let them download the illegal software.

Alternatively, systems may be used to store gigabytes of pornography. In one high-profile case at a national laboratory in the United States, staff members abused their control over systems to operate a sideline business providing I-Way access to pornography. In this case, the systems administrators were acting without approval and apparently for personal gain by charging outsiders for access to the materials. They simply allowed anyone who paid for the privilege to access the lab's computers via the I-Way to view and download the graphic files.

Special Tools or Unique Networked Resources

Although a business or government agency may have information of only limited commercial value, if it has a unique, powerful, or valuable resource

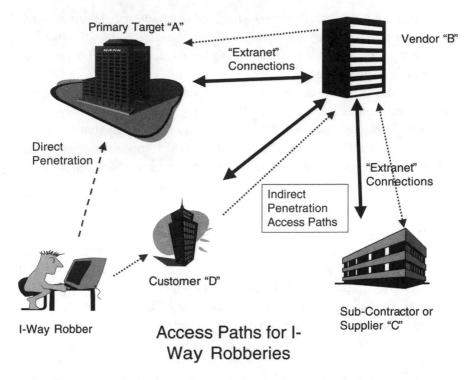

Primary Target "A"

"Extranet" Connections

Vendor "B"

Direct Penetration

"Extranet" Connections

Indirect Penetration Access Paths

Customer "D"

Sub-Contractor or Supplier "C"

I-Way Robber

Access Paths for I-Way Robberies

Figure 6–1   Access Paths for I-Way Robberies

which could be of use to a criminal scheme of an I-Way robber, the resource may become a target (see Figure 6–1). For example, the business or agency may own or lease a powerful supercomputer and the I-Way robbers need such a system to attack encrypted files or to run very large dictionary systems for cracking passwords on accounts. As other sophisticated technologies become connected to the I-Way, expect the resourceful criminals to find ways to use them to their benefit.

Proprietary Technology

Obvious targets of I-Way robbers include valuable digital technology (application software or source code) developed by the business or government agency for its own use or as a potential new product or service. There have been a few publicly revealed cases where software companies have lost the next generation of their source code to an I-Way robber who invaded the company network and then posted the source code to the I-Way. In another example, it is alleged that consultants working at the request of a subsidiary of a giant company may have invaded the network of their arch rival in an attempt to obtain proprietary computer source code. Obtaining the code was apparently the key element in a plan to create a "killer" application designed to cripple the rival.

In the first case, no one was ever identified or prosecuted for the alleged theft. In the second, the matter is still in court, so final conclusions cannot be drawn. However, there are very likely many other cases that have never been made public. More incidents are likely in the future as more businesses and government agencies derive their competitive advantage from the I-Way.

Intangible Assets

Of special importance and concern to many businesses and government agencies is ensuring adequate protection of intellectual property (IP)[3] and trade secrets in the era of high-speed I-Way connectivity. This high priority on safeguarding intellectual property is not misplaced. In today's high-technology businesses and government agencies, 50 percent or more of the value of the businesses and government agencies may reside in intangible assets, including the trade secrets and other valuable forms of intellectual property. It is believed that 80 percent or more of the IP assets of a high-technology company are contained in one or more computer and network systems environments, whether databases, computer-aided design systems, or document management systems. Although most managers agree that businesses and government agencies have increased staff productivity through widespread adoption of the I-Way, the technology also creates an entire series of new challenges. The most serious of these challenges lies in ensuring that the digital versions of the businesses' and government agencies' trade secrets and IP are adequately protected against unauthorized access, modification, disclosure, misappropriation, and infringement. When it takes only a tiny fraction of a second to transmit the results of decades worth of research in digital form to another country, it becomes clear that businesses and government agencies must do more in the Information Age to protect this valuable yet portable asset.

One major challenge in protecting digital versions of IP is in determining exactly what is valuable IP, then determining where, both physically and logically, the business/government agency has placed trade secrets and other forms of intellectual property. Too often the business or government agency legal department is focused only on the need to prepare nondisclosure documents and file legal briefs in support of patent applications or infringement litigation. Although these are important tasks, they must also provide detailed advice and assistance to help the technology managers establish adequate protection for the digital forms of IP which populate the business I-Way and which could leak out onto the external I-Way if not properly secured. If they do not, there is a high probability that valuable IP will be unnecessarily at risk. This will happen because, in the absence of effective direction from corporate lawyers, the information technology (IT) staff will be hard pressed to tailor protective measures for the trade secrets and IP of the enterprise. The IT department will run the risk of over-protecting non-trade secret information if they are too rigorous, and of possibly under-protecting the crown jewels of digital proprietary information and trade secrets if they are too lax.

The next challenge is being able to know and prove who has had access to the business's or government agency's digital trade secret information as it flows through the I-Way. Often the internal I-Way contains Web-based applications designed primarily to provide easy sharing of information. Typically, access controls, where they exist, are based on shared or easily guessed or "sniffed"[4] fixed passwords. Often this vulnerability is combined with inadequate audit trails that do not show exactly who accessed what information and when they had the access. In the absence of these measures, the business/government agency may not have an adequate program in place to safeguard the digital versions of intellectual property. The business/government agency may not be able to show who had legitimate access to the IP materials and distinguish these accesses from unauthorized activity.

Courts, at least in the United States, are very reluctant to make judgments against an allegedly infringing business or government agency when the owning/originating business/government agency has failed to take "reasonable" precautions to safeguard its trade secrets and other intellectual property against theft or misappropriation. As more and more intellectual property is generated, stored, and processed in digital form, management must ensure that it is exercising reasonable efforts to protect its intellectual property or risk losing ownership rights over these assets. Since there is no single, authoritative source of what may be considered "reasonable" protection for digital IP and trade secrets, businesses and government agencies should err on the side of doing more than the minimum to provide some safety margin.

A firewall system on the business/government agency's I-Way off-ramp gate may ensure that external I-Way robbers cannot gain easy access to internal systems containing trade secrets and critical information. However, it will do nothing to prevent those inside, or those who gain access to company networks and systems through other means, from using the I-Way to send trade secret information to customers or confederates outside the business or government agency, through e-mail and postings to Web chat rooms and other public forums. For this reason, I-Way protection measures for digital IP and trade secrets must address both insider and outsider threats, especially where access to the I-Way is possible.

Business Plans and Strategies

It is important to understand the overall direction of the business or government agency. Typically the information available in business plans and strategic documents will answer questions such as: What is the business/government agency planning to do? Where will it invest? Who will lead the effort? What is the expected amount of the investment? What is the expected (or required) return on investment? Who will benefit? Are there documents (including spreadsheets, presentations, and databases) on any server or I-Way–connected system that outline in detail: the business/government agency's plans; labor relations plans; contract negotiation strategies, litigation strategies, and so on? These materials could significantly help the opposing parties prevail over the business/government agency in public contests. Is there a Web server or other system used to conduct internal debates concerning the efficacy or other issues concerning management, diversification or outsourcing plans, or other issues of a long-term and strategic nature? If these materials are network accessible to a large number of staff, they could well be targeted and accessed. The intruders may be seeking to block efforts of your business/government agency, design a counter-strategy, or provide the relevant documentation to the representatives of your competitor or opponent who engaged them to obtain the information.

Research and Development Plans and Activities

Once past any roadblocks on the I-Way off-ramp, an I-Way robber may well make a direct line for any servers or systems that could help him or her obtain information concerning the business's or government agency's new products and services. Learning the status of new and alternative products; investment priorities; plans to enhance current or future products; capabilities, features, or functions of new products; acquisition plans; or critical items or materials could all immediately be useful to a wide range of prospects from stock analysts to foreign competitors to organized labor seeking an upper hand during contract negotiations.

Employee Files and Other Human Resources Data

Web-based systems operated by the human resources department may provide access to a wide range of potentially valuable information including: salary, bonus plans, or other compensation; stock option allocations; performance counseling or disciplinary files; and employees' home addresses, home telephone numbers, social security numbers, and other key identifiers (driver's license, vehicle license, access card information). Often such systems allow individual staff members to access and update their personal information using a default user ID and password. Since users rarely ever change passwords unless forced to do so, there is a good chance that an I-Way robber will be able find his or her way into this information. This information may be desired by private investigators working on behalf of former spouses or competitors looking for the most vulnerable, underpaid candidate for a recruiting pitch. In the realm of deranged I-Way robbers, access to residential information may facilitate physical stalking or worse.

Facility Floor Plans and Blueprints

Any information that could assist competitors in duplicating the efficiency and effectiveness advantages of your business or government agency may be sought. If knowledge of floor plans or the blueprints to a particular device would allow competitors to deduce unique business process or engineering advantages not common in the industry, they should be considered key targets. Any servers containing such information that are accessible via the internal I-Way should be appropriately secured. Plans, documents, or reports that indicate the presence, operation, or limitations of physical security measures (alarms, sensors, CCTV/monitoring systems, card access systems), especially when associated with high-value components, raw materials, or finished products, are another likely target. This information may be used to facilitate more traditional crimes like burglary, theft, and armed robbery.

Customer Accounts and Product Information

One of the most successful early applications of the I-Way has been to provide an electronic catalog via a Web server where I-Way travelers may shop. If these I-Way shopping malls are not well planned and carefully protected, the contents may be vulnerable to an I-Way robber who may steal customer credit card account numbers and other customer information. Alternatively, they could change the delivery addresses of purchases. Information concerning the quantity of products sold, perhaps the pricing, any special terms, and other information, may be useful to competitors or prospective suppliers.

New Product Plans and Timing

Marketing plans and supporting materials may provide timing, key investments, target accounts, or other milestones that could be used by competitors to thwart introductions, delay acceptance, or otherwise diminish market success or acceptance of new or improved products. When placed on the business's or government agency's internal Web servers, they are an obvious target—a fact that is not frequently appreciated. Some managers display the attitude that marketing is little more than common sense, and that plans and documents provide no additional benefit to competitors beyond what they could deduce by thoughtful consideration of the opponent's position. However, if the plans and documents are sufficiently detailed, they may be more akin to battle plans, the loss of which could jeopardize the survival or success of the products or services.

Inventions and Technical Data

Lists, databases, or compilations of invention disclosure documents that identify the inventors or provide key technical insights could allow competitors to anticipate direction, capability, or intentions of the business/government agency, develop alternative products, or emphasize shortcomings or limitations of the improved products or services. If these materials are displayed in a simple-to-access Web server environment, they could be easily compromised by an I-Way robber working internally to the business or one who successfully evaded the firewall, with serious consequences.

Financial Conditions

Current or forecasted financial activities, status, or conditions or the business/government agency's investments could provide potential acquirers or opponents insight as to strengths or weaknesses of the business/government agency. Quarterly performance estimates of publicly traded businesses and government agencies obtained in advance of the public announcement of the results could allow investors to trade more successfully in the company's stock. The plans or activities of government agencies can have significant impact on the economy, which means that budgets and priorities may be sought from among the I-Way. This information may be sought by I-Way robbers either through direct attacks against the major servers or individual desktop computers of specific analysts.

Product Development and Production

Sometimes systems and servers containing this information are outside the control of the IT departments. The engineers or technical staff operating such systems may not fully appreciate the value and importance of the contents, or may believe that no one could benefit from the stolen contents without a formal engineering or scientific background. The fact is, an I-Way robber does not need to know how to use the stolen materials, only how to take all essential elements for reselling it to an outsider. Engineering and design factors that impact development and manufacturing of current and future products, the volume of production by product type, known or suspected defects or quality issues with current or future products, actual cost of manufacture of current and future products, and other manufacturing or production issues may be determined if an intruder gains access to the servers or systems containing this information.

SUMMARY

I-Way robbers will target businesses and government agencies for many different reasons. Therefore, the targets they may seek will differ widely depending on their specific motivation. It may not be possible to protect all I-Way–accessible assets perfectly, but every business and government agency must conduct a risk assessment to determine what may be valuable as well as what may be vulnerable, then make appropriate security decisions.

NOTES

1. For example, Mitnick's alleged use of accounts on the Well to store the source code taken from Shimomura's systems.
2. Pronounced as *wares*.
3. For government agencies, *sensitive information* may be inserted for *IP*. This, of course, is nation dependent.
4. "Sniffed" means to read user access information transmitted on the network.

7

I-Way Robbers: How Do They Do It?

CHAPTER OBJECTIVE

The objective of this chapter is to discuss the tactics, tools, and techniques used by the I-Way robbers to obtain information or other valuable property via the I-Way.

WHY ARE I-WAY PROTECTION PROBLEMS INCREASING AND WHY ARE THE ATTACKS SUCCESSFUL?

Before discussing the way that I-Way robbers attack systems, a summary of the reasons why these attacks are gaining in number and are successful is presented in order to better explain the methods that are being used and why they are being used. I-Way security problems have increased and the I-Way robbers are successful for several reasons, including:

- ◆ A more distributed computing environment
- ◆ More networking both nationally and internationally
- ◆ Convergence between computers and telecommunications systems
- ◆ Capability for more remote systems maintenance
- ◆ Cheaper hardware and software
- ◆ Poor information systems security because it is a low priority

♦ More individuals growing up with computers have turned into computer vandals—why break a business's store windows and spray-paint walls when they can break through I-Way ramp barriers and spray-paint Web sites?

♦ Less morality and social pressure to conform to society's standards

♦ Opportunity for criminal gain with little international recourse by law enforcement agencies

♦ General standardization on specific hardware and software (e.g., TCP/IP, UNIX, browsers, and Windows 95, 98, and NT environments) allows known vulnerabilities to be found and exploited before vendor patches are developed and implemented

♦ Systems are generally easier to use

♦ More hackers, although most are much less technically competent than in the past

♦ A few smart, very sophisticated hackers with a great deal of technical competency

I-WAY ROBBERS' BASIC APPROACH

I-Way robbers who attack the systems networked on the I-Way generally use a common attack approach. (See Figure 7–1.) Their sequence of attacks usually follows the scenario below:

♦ Research target organization—identify the target, then research it by doing a search using one or more of the search engines that can be found on the I-Way; collect information; gather documentation and system identification.

♦ Identify target's vulnerabilities—another source of information is the CERTs (Computer Emergency Response Teams) announcements notifying all those on their Internet subscribers list as to new-found systems vulnerabilities and how to eliminate or at least mitigate the vulnerabilities. Normally, attackers keep up with these vulnerabilities from the CERTs and use them to attack systems faster than the targeted businesses or government agencies can correct the vulnerabilities.

♦ Use the basic software tools, such as the ones identified below, and begin the attack. Once inside, the attackers steal, modify, or destroy information.

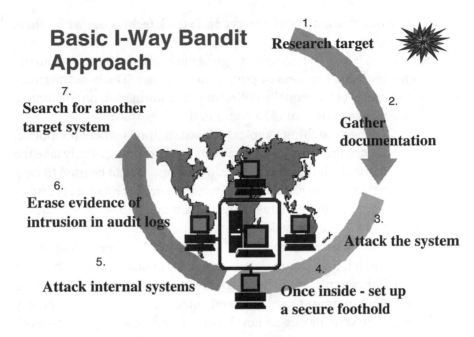

Figure 7–1   Basic I-Way Bandit Approach

Depending on the attacker objectives, the attacker may:

1. Install a covert back door that circumvents protection systems in order to get back in later
2. Search for other systems that are networked to the system just penetrated, and attack them in a similar manner
3. Log-off the system. The attacker may or may not erase the audit trail records identifying what he or she has done and then log-off the network.

BASIC I-WAY ROBBERY TECHNIQUES

Theft and Social Engineering

Based on the above general, systematic approach, the attacker must gather information about the target from many sources. The I-Way itself provides an excellent vehicle for the attackers to share information and collect information on a global scale. They can use the I-Way to search out their targets and to share information about a target and attack techniques with others around the world.

Sometimes it may be necessary to gather information directly from the target, whether it is a business or government agency. The basic methods for doing so are by (1) personally collecting the information on the target's site, (2) social engineering, or (3) a combination of both.

You may recall watching a typical television drama where the police, trying to catch a criminal involved in fraud or drug dealing, covertly take the person's garbage and sift through it for information that can be used to help their investigation. I-Way robbers often use the same technique. They frequently rummage through the trash bins of their target looking for clues to assist them in successfully attacking that target.

So, what are these "trash collectors" looking for? They are seeking information that will tell them more details about the computing environment of the target. For example, there may be boxes in the trash that had been used to transport new computer hardware and software. One of the boxes may have been used to ship the target's new I-Way firewall product, new network server, routers, switches, or the new version of the operating system.

In addition, they will look for memos, telephone books, anything with names, positions, and telephone numbers that may give a hint as to the user IDs and passwords people may be using—possibly passwords themselves. Even expired passwords provide good information because they may indicate a pattern that would lead allow easy guessing of the new password. For example, if I am required to change my password every month, I may choose a word with a sequential set of numbers. So when I have to change my password, I use "password2" in February. Then in March, when I am again required to change my password, I use "password3." This meets the security requirements to change passwords on a monthly basis as well as the security requirement to use alphanumeric characters for my passwords, but it also means that anyone who finds my old password could easily predict my current and future passwords.

The information also may be gathered by posing as an employee, vendor, prospective employee, or even as a janitor on a night shift (when there are probably fewer people around). All it takes to obtain almost unrestricted access to a target site is either getting hired by the janitorial service or finding out what work clothes the janitors use, and stealing or buying a similar set. Photo ID badges used by the organization pose little deterrent to a determined I-Way robber. With just a little bluffing, they may tell the security guard that they are new employees and they have an appointment to get an

ID badge in the morning. In the interim, the janitorial company has told them to sign in as a visitor. More likely than not, the guard will allow the access for the single evening, which may be all that is required.

This is only one way of "social engineering" your way into the targeted facility. The objective is to convince someone to allow you access to the target facility. Once inside, you have many hours to find information that will assist you in breaking in to the computer system. If you are lucky, maybe someone even left a computer operating and connected to the organization network at the end of the work day. Such a lucky break will allow the fortunate intruder to act as an authorized user with access to the system.

Social engineering is used quite often for gathering information necessary to successfully attack a system on the I-Way. *Social engineering* is nothing more than the ability to trick information out of someone and/or make him or her do what you want.

For example, taking an organization's phone book out of a dumpster may give the I-Way robber the names of key people who have the information required to break in to a major network or application containing the most critical information of the organization. Then the approach would be to call the target during nonbusiness hours—the later at night the better—because all the higher level managers, if not all managers, will most likely have gone home. You call the systems operations group, who typically will be working 24 hours a day, and tell them you need access to their maintenance port to do some on-line maintenance. You give them as the name of your company, their primary computer vendor; since you know what systems they have from documentation obtained in previous searches or by calling up someone in the target and asking them what computers they are using. Again, social engineering techniques apply. You can claim to be a high school student and looking for a company with a certain type of computer for a high school science class to tour. Normally, you will be referred to the public relations or marketing people. In either case, these individuals have been known to give out a great deal of information. You can also pose as a computer salesperson, or other people who can get information because of who they claim to be.

The most essential skill for social engineering is the ability to make other people believe what you tell them. If the operations person is hesitant in providing information, some nice talking may work: "Look, I understand your concern and I appreciate your position, but we both have our jobs to do. Mine is to do some system maintenance for you. Your company called in the first place so it's not like I want to be here this late at night either. Look, is Bob Johnson there?" (You found Bob Johnson's name in some documentation and found that he was the director of operations.) "His name is listed on the work order with telephone number 234-2345." Normally, it's the specific and detailed nature of the information provided to the contact that leads him or her to believe the request is legitimate. After all, how could anyone know that much information unless it was legitimate?

If that approach does not work, then some intimidation may work: "Look. If you don't give me the information I need to perform the maintenance, I really don't care. I can go home early, no problem! Let me have your name and position please so that when my boss asks or this Johnson guy asks why the work was not done, I can tell them to talk to you. I don't care!" That technique works quite often, and once you are in, you are in!

If none of those techniques works, maybe it is time to try an easier target. Unless the I-Way robber has specifically targeted a business or government agency, he or she will generally move on to an easier target. After all, they need to spend time on-line cracking systems and cruising down the I-Way for other systems to attack. Most I-Way robbers don't want to be delayed spending time talking to people and researching new ways to get the information they need to mount a successful attack.

Social engineering works because people basically think other people are honest and unless they had some guidance and awareness briefing on what to say and *what not to say*, they are normally very helpful and provide the requested information.

Other Techniques Used by Both Insiders and Outsiders

The following are some methods that may be used by attackers:

- ◆ Data Diddling: Changing data before or during entry into the computer system; for example, forging or counterfeiting documents used for data entry, or exchanging valid disks and tapes with modified replacements
- ◆ Scavenging: Obtaining information left around a computer system or in the computer room trash cans
- ◆ Computer Manipulation—Data Leakage: Removing information by smuggling it out as part of a printed document; encoding the information to look like something different and removing it from the facility
- ◆ Computer Manipulation—Piggybacking/Impersonation: Physical access is one method used; for example, following someone in through a door with a badge reader, electronically using another's user ID and

password to gain computer access, or tapping into the terminal link of a user to cause the computer to believe that both terminals are the same person

♦ Computer Manipulation—Simulation and Modeling: Using the computer as a tool or instrument to plan or control a criminal act

♦ Wire Tapping: Tapping into a computer's communications links to be able to read the information being transmitted between systems and networks

System Manipulation

Many software applications have been written and techniques used by the I-Way robbers. The terms for these types of application programs have become standardized over the years. Most I-Way robbers use a variation of hacker tools, but they generally can be classified as follows:

♦ Trojan Horse: Covert placement of instructions in a program that cause the computer to perform unauthorized functions but usually still allow the program to perform its intended purpose. This is the most common method used in computer-based frauds and sabotage.

♦ Trap Doors: When developing large programs, programmers tend to insert debugging aids that provide breaks in the instructions for insertion of additional code and intermediate output capabilities. The design of computer operating systems attempts to prevent this from happening. Therefore, programmers insert instructions that allow them to circumvent these controls. I-Way robbers take advantage of these trap doors, or create their own.

♦ Salami Techniques: Involves the theft of small amounts of assets from a large number of sources without noticeably reducing the whole. In a banking system, the amount of interest to be credited to an account is rounded off. Instead of rounding off the number, that fraction may be credited to a special account owned by the perpetrator.

♦ Logic Bombs: A computer program executed at a specific time or when a specific event occurs. For example, a programmer could write a program to instruct the computer to delete all personnel and payroll files if his/her name were ever removed from the file.

♦ Computer Virus: Malicious code that causes damage to system information or denies access to the information it spreads through self-replication.

Using the I-Way to Search for Tools

When an I-Way robber needs tools to attack I-Way targets, they usually come from three sources:

1. Friends
2. Their own developments
3. The I-Way

The first two speak for themselves, so only the I-Way will be addressed. Very little equipment or skill is needed these days to attack systems on the I-Way:

◆ The attacker obviously must have access to the I-Way, which is usually through an account with an Internet Service Provider (ISP).

◆ Once on the I-Way, the attacker points the mouse to the "SEARCH" icon and then types in "hacker," "hacker software," or specific tools that the I-Way robber had heard about, for example, "SATAN."

◆ Then, the I-Way robber must be able to download the tool. This is also generally an easy task, as often the attacker only has to click on the "download" icon.

◆ The I-Way robber then identifies the target or randomly attacks various targets by executing the attack tools programs. It really is just that simple!

I-WAY ROBBER TOOLS

Most of the I-Way robbers use common and readily available programs found on the I-Way. Many of these programs were intended for the use of systems administrators to assist them in identifying the vulnerabilities of their systems so they could subsequently patch the holes. Following are some of the most common programs used by attackers.

◆ SATAN (Security Administrator Tool for Analyzing Networks): A testing and reporting tool that collects a variety of information about networked hosts. SATAN was developed for security administrators to assist them in identifying vulnerabilities in their systems that would require patching. This tool is also commonly used by hackers to identify and then attack the vulnerabilities of networked systems. This public domain tool can be found and downloaded from numerous sites on the Internet.

♦ As an example of how easy it is to find these software tools, the authors, searching on the I-Way using the terms "SATAN AND software," found numerous sites where SATAN was available (after sifting out the sites with religious connotations). The following site was one of several sites found.

♦ This site identified numerous addresses where SATAN could be found in North America alone:

URL-http://www.ensta.fr/internet/unix/sys_admin/satan.html

North America:

ftp://ftp.mcs.anl.gov/pub/security/

ftp://coast.cs.purdue.edu/pub/tools/unix/satan/

ftp://vixen.cso.uiuc.edu/security/

ftp://ftp.acsu.buffalo.edu/pub/security/

ftp://ftp.net.ohio-state.edu/pub/security/satan/

ftp://ftp.cerf.net/pub/software/unix/security/

ftp://ftp.tisl.ukans.edu/pub/security/

ftp://ftp.tcst.com/pub/security/

ftp://ftp.orst.edu/pub/packages/satan/

ftp://ciac.llnl.gov/pub/ciac/sectools/unix/satan/

♦ COPS (Computer Oracle and Password System): COPS is a publicly available collection of programs that attempt to identify security problems in a UNIX system. COPS does not attempt to correct any discrepancies found; it simply produces a report of its findings.

♦ ISS (Internet Security Scanner): A software program that checks a range from beginning to end of a set of IP logical addresses on a network to determine what systems, by address, are on the network.

♦ Crack: Crack is a software program that attempts to guess passwords based on dictionary entries, user ID, and user name. It requires a password file (/etc/passwd). The new version can be used across an entire network.

♦ FBRUTE: Similar to Crack, this software program can decrypt encrypted password software using a dictionary.

♦ RootKit: According to BellCore this tool was first noticed about 1993. It is targeted to specific systems (originally SunOS 4.1.X); a new version targets LINUX. RootKit is a combination of attack programs used as a "patched" login that allows any ID to access the systems through a backdoor password.

♦ Tripwire: A software program that checks files and directory integrity, it is a utility that compares a designated set of files and directories to information stored in a previously generated database. Any differences are flagged and logged, including added or deleted entries. When run against files on a regular basis, Tripwire enables you to spot changes in critical system files and to immediately take appropriate damage control measures. Tripwire is also available on the Internet.

♦ Finger: This is a UNIX protocol that can be used to obtain information about users logged on to a system. It provides information that can be used by attackers, such as when the account was last used and from what location the user last connected.

SOME COMMON ATTACK METHODS

Some of the more common I-Way attack methods can cause millions of dollars in lost revenue due to denying use of Web sites, and modifications of Web sites cause embarrassment to their owners. Spoofing, session stealing, and other attack methods have been plaguing the I-Way. There are patches and remedies to avoid being the victim of most of these common attacks; however, many businesses and government agencies have not installed the fixes—including many United States Department of Defense systems. There is no excuse for such lack of security. Ironically, the Defense Department is supposed to defend this nation but often can't seem to defend its own systems![1]

Denial of Service[2]

Denial of service means to block use of the I-Way or related system. There are various methods to deny service or access to a system on the I-Way. One example is to send a big ping packet. For example, on some systems, the attacker can send a packet (ICMP Echo Request) bigger than 65,507 bytes (ping -1 65510 target system). The reassembled fragments overflow the

TCP/IP stack. This attack works on various hardware; however, the vendors and others have been developing patches to prevent such a denial of service.

Web Server Modifications

Attacking Web servers has been the latest fad among many of the miscreants on the I-Way, generally the juvenile delinquents. It's equivalent to juvenile delinquents spray-painting a wall, building, or sign with graffiti. However, in the hands of someone more devious, it can be used for making political statements, diverting others through links to a competitor's site, and many other devious schemes which are only limited by the I-Way robber's imagination.

The problem is that the common gateway interface (CGI) scripts (phf, AnyForm, FormMail, convert.bas, .bat files, custom scripts) allow for the creation of Web pages, but these CGI scripts are vulnerable. Again, patches, and other techniques, can be used to minimize this risk.

IP Fragmentation

This attack method is accomplished by making a fragment so the TCP header is split between two fragments (Fragment 1: Part of the TCP Header, Fragment 2: Rest of TCP Header with port number). For example, in Fragment 1: Put in "phony" port (e.g., port 80); Fragment 2: Use TCP header with port 23. When the fragments are reconnected, the port number is overwritten.

Password Sniffing

One technique to successfully attack a system on a busy subnet is to change the system configuration to make it a network sniffer. Thus, the attacker can collect user IDs and passwords flowing through the network. (See Figure 7–2.)

ISP Attack

In this attack, the attacker sends a false message, usually to numerous servers that offer newsgroups, and "convinces" them to send back information such as server passwords.

Spoofing

This method of attack requires the prediction of future sequencing numbers. The attacker spoofs the trusted system into believing that the attacker's systems is another, authorized trusted system, while simultaneously blocking that other trusted system. (See Figure 7–3.)

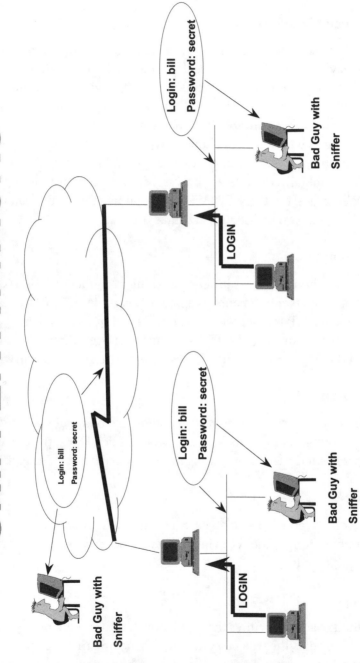

Figure 7–2 Sniffer Attacks

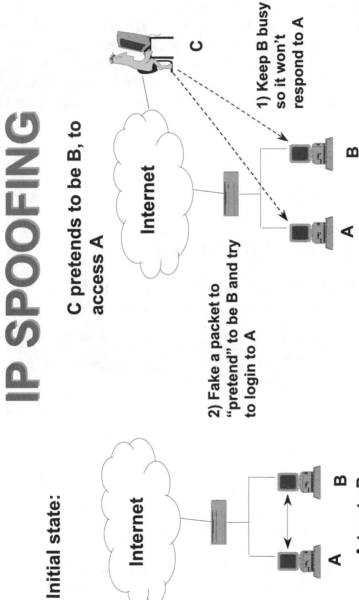

Figure 7–3   IP Spoofing

War-Dialers

Prior to the I-Way, dial-up systems[3] were the predominant method for I-Way robbers and authorized users to gain remote access to the business or government agency computer system. Today, that is still possible; however, it is not as prevalent now that the I-Way exists. Hackers wrote programs in BASIC to find those computers and record their telephone numbers for later attack. This method was made famous by the movie, "War Games."

After identifying a computer system through its dial tone, the hacker then used various other programs or manual guessing to identify a user ID and password that would allow system access. Some systems can still lead the hacker onto an I-Way ramp.

The following is an old program written long ago in BASIC to find those systems for subsequent attack. It is provided for those who long for the simpler "good ol' days" of hacking.[4] The program appears to have been written for an old Hayes modem.

****

```
240 COLOR 7,0,0:CLS:WIDTH 80:KEY OFF:CLEAR
250 LOCATE 11,31:PRINT" Version III of "
260 LOCATE 12,27:COLOR 0,7:PRINT" Wargames Dialer
280 LOCATE 23,27:PRINT "Press any key when ready"
290 Z$=INPUT$(1)
300 OPEN "com2:" AS #1
310 CLS:LOCATE 13,22:PRINT "Do you have a color monitor? (Y/N)"
320 Z$=INPUT$(1):IF Z$="Y" OR Z$="y" THEN COLOR 7,1,1:CLS
330 LOCATE 14,22:PRINT "Would you like instructions? (Y/N)"
340 Z$=INPUT$(1):IF Z$="Y" OR Z$="y" THEN GOSUB 910
350 CLS:LOCATE 14,19:PRINT "Would you like the Modem Speaker Off?
    (Y/N)"
360 A$=INPUT$(1):IF A$="Y" OR A$="y" THEN PRINT #1,"ATMO":A9=1
370 IF A$"Y" THEN PRINT #1,"ATM1":CLOSE
375 REM *********** Sets modem for fast dialing -SK ***************
380 OPEN "com2:" AS #1:PRINT #1,"ATS11=40":CLOSE
390 CLS
400 INPUT "How many number should be scanned (1-10000)";O
410 LOCATE 3,1 :PRINT "Should the successful numbers be recorded to
    disk? (Y/N)"
420 Z$=INPUT$(1):IF Z$="Y" OR Z$="y" THEN A1=1
430 LOCATE 5,1 :PRINT "Would you like a print out of the successful num-
    bers? (Y/N)"
```

440 Z$=INPUT$(1):IF Z$="Y" OR Z$="y" THEN A2=1

450 CLS:IF A2=1 THEN PRINT "Turn printer on."

455 REM ******************* Input Number *******************

460 LOCATE 4,1:PRINT"Input the first three numbers or the area code and the first three numbers."

470 LINE INPUT"->";DIAL$

480 LOCATE 2,1 :PRINT DIAL$;"-"

490 LOCATE 7,1 :INPUT "Input the 4th digit of the number. (xxx) xxx-Xxxx";A

500 LOCATE 2,1:PRINT DIAL$;:PRINT "-";:PRINT USING "#";A

510 LOCATE 10,1 :INPUT "Input the 5th digit of the number. (xxx) xxx-xXxx";B

520 LOCATE 2,1 :PRINT DIAL$;"-";:PRINT USING "#";A;B

530 LOCATE 13,1 :INPUT "Input the 6th digit of the number. (xxx) xxx-xxXx";C

540 LOCATE 2,1 :PRINT DIAL$;"-";:PRINT USING "#";A;B;C

550 LOCATE 16,1 :INPUT "Input the 7th digit of the number. (xxx) xxx-xxxX";D

560 W=5

570 XX=7

580 CLS

590 LOCATE 2,1:PRINT DIAL$;"-";:PRINT USING "#";A;B;C;D:LOCATE 2,34:PRINT" WAITING "

600 IF A<0 OR A>9 OR B<0 OR B>9 OR C<0 OR C>9 OR D<0 OR D>9 THEN CLS:GOTO 490

605 REM ********************* Dialing *************************

610 OPEN "com2:" AS #1:PRINT #1,"ATDT"DIAL$;A;B;C;D

620 T=10

630 FOR X=1 TO 800:NEXT X

640 LOCATE 2,60:PRINT" Time remaining: "T""

650 IF T>0 THEN T=T-1 ELSE 670

660 GOTO 630

665 REM *********** Checking buffer for carrier detect *************

670 L=LOF(1): IF L<230 THEN 790

680 FOR I=1 TO 900:NEXT I:PRINT #1,"+++":FOR J=1 TO 750:NEXT J:PRINT #1,"ATH":LOCATE 2,34:PRINT"NO CARRIER"

690 LET W=W+1

700 LOCATE W,1:PRINT DIAL$;"-";:PRINT USING "#";A;B;C;D

710 IF W>=22 THEN W=5 ELSE 730

```
720 IF W=5 THEN CLS
725 REM ****** Counts how many numbers have been dialed - SK
    ********
730 O1=O1+1:IF O1=O THEN 830
740 D =D + 1
741 IF D=10 THEN D=0:C=C+1
750 IF C=10 THEN C=0:B=B+1
760 IF B=10 THEN B=0:A=A+1
770 CLOSE:GOTO 590
780 GOTO 590
790 LOCATE XX,40:PRINT "computer found at: "DIAL$;"-";:PRINT USING
    "#";A;B;C;D:XX=XX+1
795 REM ************* Saves number on a disk - SK *****************
800 BEEP:IF A1=0 THEN 810 ELSE OPEN "Numbers.Dat" FOR APPEND
    AS #2:PRINT #2,DIAL$;"-";A ;B ;C ;D :CLOSE #2
810 IF A2=1 THEN LPRINT "Computer found at: "DIAL$;"-";:PRINT
    USING "#";A;B;C;D
820 GOTO 680
830 A:0 :B:0 :C:0 :D:0
840 PLAY "mb t100 o4 l32 ecececec"
850 LOCATE 3,24:PRINT O;" NUMBERS HAVE BEEN DIALED"
860 IF A2=1 THEN LPRINT
870 LOCATE 4,31:PRINT "Dialing Complete":IF A2=1 THEN LPRINT"Dial-
    ing Complete"
880 CLOSE
890 END
900 ' The Instructions!-SK
910 CLS:LOCATE 3,1:PRINT "A Wargames Dialer is a program that will scan
    a certain amount of numbers in a"
920 PRINT "range defined by the user (such as the first three numbers in a
    phone#)."
930 PRINT "It scans these numbers for a modem tone, which indicates that
    there is a"
940 PRINT "computer hooked up. The program then stores the number for
    later inquiry."
950 LOCATE 9,1:PRINT "The program will ask you for the amount of num-
    bers to be dialed (Max. 10000)"
960 PRINT "and whether or not you want the numbers are to be recorded
    to a disk file"
```

970 PRINT"(NUMBERS.DAT). The disk file can be accessed by entering
'TYPE NUMBERS.DAT'"
980 PRINT "while in DOS. It will also ask whether or not you have a printer (if you answer"
990 PRINT "'Y' then please turn it on) and whether or not you want the
modem speaker on."
1010 PRINT
1020 PRINT "If you have any questions leave mail for Steven Klein at (201)
994-9620."
1030 LOCATE 23,25:PRINT "(Press any key to continue)"
1040 Z$=INPUT$(1):RETURN

Other Methods, Tools, and Techniques

There are numerous techniques, methods, tactics, and tools available to anyone on the I-Way, as well as other sources such as hacker magazines, computer magazines that discuss I-Way hardware and software vulnerabilities.
The security and law enforcement professional should become familiar with
the basic information provided on the various hacker sites. The techniques
and methods are constantly changing and improving as I-Way security
improves. It continues to be an ongoing challenge for everyone on the I-Way.

SUMMARY

There are many ways to attack systems along the I-Way. Some of the attacks
have been around for some time and only work because the people responsible for the protection of the systems have not instituted the patches or security upgrades. New vulnerabilities are being discovered almost daily and
vendors are quickly (most of the time) coming up with patches to negate the
vulnerabilities. It is a constant, vicious circle.

Many attacks are amateurish and basic while others are very sophisticated. The attackers use a combination of theft, social engineering, and computer manipulation using tools, methods, and techniques found on the
I-Way.

Solutions for protection are available but are not always being used. The
question is why this is the case when so much is known about these attacks
and how to prevent them? Then again, with sex education classes and con-
doms readily available to teenagers, why do teenage girls continue to get

pregnant? The answers to both questions are the same: "I didn't know it would happen to me!"

NOTES

1. There are numerous very good technical papers and books written on the subjects noted. It is not the intention of the authors to provide a technical discussion of the attack methods, but only to provide an awareness of their existence. It is recommended that the reader become more familiar with these attack methods by reading some of the excellent material available on the topics.
2. Information provided from various sources; however, the best summary of these methods was provided by Bellcore's Ed Skoudis.
3. Accessing a computer via a modem by dialing in the computer's telephone number, and having it answered through another modem to the system.
4. The program was received long ago by the authors from some unknown source. Its writers are unknown. It may be that because of their age, their names were removed prior to sharing the program with others or their names were never known.

8

I-Way Robberies!

CHAPTER OBJECTIVE

The objective of this chapter is to provide a series of short summary reports drawn from the public domain, which provide valuable insights into the I-Way incidents that have already happened. These incidents must be understood if one is to appreciate the risks of traveling on the I-Way. It is also necessary to understand the threats since they must be mitigated if one's business or government agency is not to be victimized by the I-Way robbers.

WHAT'S AN I-WAY ROBBERY?

I-Way robberies are those actions taken by miscreants and juvenile delinquents that violate international and national laws, moral standards, and/or ethical standards of a nation or society that involve the I-Way. The I-Way robberies discussed here are alleged to be true and are summaries of actual crimes, incidents, and anecdotes on the I-Way. As noted below, various people have committed these deeds from many parts of the world and for a variety of reasons. All of which leads one to view the I-Way as a big international city where miscreants, honest citizens, businesses, government agencies, security professionals, and law enforcement officers all interact.

WHAT'S AN OOPS?

While driving along the I-Way the authors found that there were some indications of mistakes, and possible interference by government agencies and others that adversely impact users, businesses, and other government agencies. These "Oops" summaries are also provided because many of the difficulties of safely travelling along the I-Way include avoiding the bumps and potholes in the road which sometimes make it seem more of an old country dirt road than a superhighway. In addition, it is important to not lose sight of the fact that there are errors, software bugs, human miscalculations, and upgrades which do not go as planned causing at least as many, if not more, problems on the I-Way than the miscreants. One must be prepared for the "Oops" or "Sh . . . Happens" scenarios.

CATEGORIZING I-WAY ROBBERIES

The I-Way robberies involving actual attacks, incidents, and anecdotes on the I-Way fall into various categories. The security and law enforcement professional should understand the commonality of various methods of attacks so that I-Way security can be established to mitigate them and to be better able to investigate and respond to incidents. In addition, this section provides some very good scenarios that can be used in establishing penetration scenarios to validate the security of Web sites and hosts, as well as information that can be used in employee awareness briefings prior to authorizing employees' access to the I-Way.

Literally thousands of these I-Way robberies have occurred over the years. Several in each category are provided in order to assist in understanding the various attacks that occur daily throughout the world. Some of the stories possibly fall into the "oldies but goodies" category—they are several years old, but they are still valid today. As noted below, these I-Way robberies, incidents, and the like come from all over the world and are reported all over the world.

I-WAY ROBBERIES

I-Way Worm Program: On November 2, 1988, a college student sent a "worm" program through the I-Way which replicated itself and infected I-

Way systems using a certain version of Unix. This program infected thousands of computers on the I-Way for days. The student was identified, prosecuted, and found guilty. This was the first major I-Way crime and one of the most devastating. (Purdue Technical Report CSO-TR-823, 11/29/88)

Masquerading/Trojan Horse: Person(s) unknown have circulated e-mail messages masquerading as being from Microsoft technical support, and claiming to provide a security update to Microsoft Internet Explorer. The message includes an attachment, usually "ie080898," which is actually a Trojan Horse. The result is spam e-mail sent to several I-Way locations. (FBI Advisory, 8/18/98, and CIAC Bulletin I-005C)[1]

Diverting Users/Breach of Trademark and Copyright Laws, Misrepresentation and False Advertising: Some individuals have diverted users from one site to their site or another's site. For example, by placing the words "playboy playboy playboy bunny bunny bunny in the meg-tag of a web site, or writing 'playboy' all over the site, white on white so it isn't visible to readers, Internet search engines will catalogue the site to show up on a 'playboy' search, even if it's a site that sells vegetables." (*Australian Financial Review*, 8/14/98)

Encryption: Two researchers from the University of Berkeley cracked the 64-bit encryption key used for the Groupe Speciale Mobile (GSM) cellular phone standard. There are over 80 million GSM employed phones being used in the world. What is especially interesting is that the last ten digits of the encryption key were zeros, leading some to speculate that this design was intentional to allow eavesdropping on cellular phone calls by government agencies. (*Orange County Register*, 4/14/98)

Oops: On January 23, 1997, AOL subscribers found that they could not retrieve email for 3.5 hours because the AOL engineers made some errors when trying to "boost the service's capacity." (*Orange County Register*, 11/28/97)

Oops: Each night at 11:45 P.M., the I-Way addresses for North America are updated and transmitted throughout the network. Two of those files transmitting the updates became corrupted, which set off alarms. The administrator on duty for Network Solutions Inc. allegedly released the files anyway. This caused many Web sites to be invisible to browsers. (*Orange County Register*, date unknown)

Note: If you are relying on your Web site for conducting business, this "Oops," which is beyond your control, can cost the business millions of dollars in lost revenue—especially if your competitor's site was not affected! So, no matter how secure your Web site is, no matter how much quality control, time, and effort your business has put into electronic commerce, someone, at some time, from some part of the globe may inadvertently ruin your business day! What can you do about such things? Get insurance, plan for such contingencies, and hope it doesn't happen to you.

Oops: Two StrataCom switches developed a problem that spread to 145 other switches across the nation, cutting off customers for approximately 27 hours. Cause: Unknown or they wouldn't say. (*Computerworld*, 4/20/98)

Note: If remote access is vital to your business, ensure that you have backups and an alternate route to your business for your customers.

Social Engineering: A hacker using netaccounts@netscape.net sent out e-mail advising the receivers that they would be given a free communications software program if they e-mailed the sender their user names and passwords. (AGE, Melbourne, Australia, 8/18/98)

Note: No one should ever give his or her password(s) to anyone—not even auditors or security personnel.

Sex Fraud: College students in Malaysia paid a gas station attendant to give them the credit card receipts of the customers. These students then signed the unsuspecting credit card owners up as members of a sex Web site based in a foreign country. In return, the students were paid $5.00US for each new member. (*South China Morning Post*, 8/17/98)

Bank Fraud: A Web site was set up reportedly as the Bank Bumiputra Malaysia. This false Web site asked depositors to give their account numbers and other information to be eligible for a "lucky drawing." (*South China Morning Post*, 8/17/98)

Credit Union Fraud: Hackers charged more than $1 million to the debit cards of credit union members by using a computer to guess the account numbers of the members. (*Washington Post*, 8/15/98)

Politically Motivated Web Page Attack: Hackers allegedly from a group called "Milw0rm" and "Ashtray Lumberjacks" broke into a British Web site, hijacked the sites listed in the ISP's database, and redirected users to its page, which contained antinuclear message and graphics. (*CNETNEWS*.com, 7/6/98)

Political Group Web Site: The Islamic Resistance Aid Committee of Hezbollah has developed a Web site, http://moqawama.org (*Moqawama* is Arabic for resistance), which allows I-Way travelers to communicate with Shiite Moslem fundamentalists. (http://www.infowar.com 2/28/97)

Note: The I-Way is fast becoming a major tool for political groups. It is just a matter of time before some of these groups attack each others' Web sites.

Terrorists' Political Attack: Allegedly, a group known as the "Internet Black Tigers" conducted "suicide e-mail bombings" by trying to swamp the computer systems of Sri Lankan embassies. The group had apparently done so to counter the government's "propaganda sent electronically." (*CNET NEWS*.com, 5/5/98)

Note: This is a simple form of a denial of service attack while at the same time sending their own political messages. The method is simple and cheap. It is surprising that there has not been more of this type of attack, but it will not be surprising to see an increase in the future. Some have classified this as the "first terrorist attack" on the I-Way. That is debatable.

Austrialia's Anti-Porn Legislation: The Australian government announced the formation of a "national framework for regulation of online content" with the purpose of holding ISPs "in breach if they knowingly allow a person to publish material that would be refused publication under the guidelines of the government's Office of Film and Literature Classification or under Australian State or Territory laws." (*Newsbytes News Network*, 7/16/97)

Note: Nice thought; however, how can it be enforced? For ISPs to *knowingly* allow this, they would have to monitor their users' content. ISPs do not want to be the enforcers of government laws—nor do they want to be government censors.

Indonesia to Control I-Way Access: The Minister for Tourism, Post, and Telecommunications, Joop Ave, stated it was a "basic human right to have access to information. . . . We are very much for the free flow of information, but it is quite obvious that there are some limitations. . . . If we talk about pornography, we say no. If we talk about things that will hamper or threaten national security, we will say no. . . . The values of the nation will definitely have bearing upon the application of the Internet. We will not, for example, have 'anything goes' . . . ."

Note: The Minister voices a common concern among many nations. Such nations are in a difficult position, as they consider how to filter sites considered in violation of the nation's laws. It is a very difficult problem: access is needed to compete in the global economic environment so it must be available; access to restricted sites must be denied, but how does one know the sites to filter, except for the obvious (a URL like www.XXXsex.com or newsgroups associated with alt.sex). In addition, the "threat to national security" defined by the government in power usually includes antigovernment statements, which may be very loosely defined by the government. To enforce such laws, I-Way access by all citizens must be monitored. However, monitoring will stifle communication and freedom of speech. Nations will have a difficult, if not impossible, time trying to strike a balance. However, a fair balance is the best one can hope for in some nations.

China's Police Establish Company and Market Anti-Virus Software: China's Jinchen Security and Technology Industry and Commerce Corporation is a police-owned company that produces an anti-virus software product known as *Kill*. The software was developed to defend China's computer networks from local and foreign viruses. The software also is used to find clues in the virus code to assist in finding the creator. Ironically, their software has been pirated! (For more information see http://www.kill.com.cn)(*Reuter*, 7/27/97)

China's Dissenters Use "Political Viruses": After the Tiananmen Square slaughter on June 6, 1989, protesters began attacking the government's computer systems with viruses. One interesting virus asked the computer user whose system was infected to vote for approval or disapproval of Premier Li Peng, whom they held responsible for the slaughter. If the user voted for approval, their system crashed and their files were trashed. Another attack destroyed portions of Deng Xiaoping's draft biography. Subsequently, the writing of viruses was outlawed in China. (*Reuter*, 7/27/97)

Note: China is a good example of another nation struggling with I-Way access and associated freedoms. The future national leaders, the college students, require I-Way access to prepare to lead China into the 21st century. However, these are also the students who are rebelling against their government. If the government limits access, it stifles their knowledge opportunities. If it provides unlimited access, the students can use the I-Way to help in the quest for political freedom. Again, as with Indonesia, Malaysia, Russia, and other nations, governments are trying to find a way to have their cake and eat it too. They may succeed for a while; however, as the I-Way and technology become more powerful, totally wireless, automatically encrypted, and cheaper, the chance of these nations succeeding becomes less and less likely.

United States Intelligence Hackers: The CIA is the subject of complaints by the Japanese and French governments for hacking into their systems to obtain sensitive trade secrets. Now "American intelligence agents" have been accused of hacking into the systems of the European Parliament and European Commission in an attempt to allegedly obtain political and economic secrets to assist in negotiations on the General Agreement on Tariffs and Trade (GATT). (http://www.sunday-times.co.uk/news/pages/Sunday-times/stifgnnws01015.html?youra-c)[2]

Note: The I-Way and other networks provide too easy and too lucrative a target for any government's intelligence agencies to ignore. Economic espionage is a major part of economic warfare just as in the old Industrial Age shooting wars relied on intelligence collection to support planning. Why would we think it should be any different, for as was said several times—only the environment has changed.

Malaysia Arrests I-Way Users for Spreading Rumors: Malaysian police, using the Internal Security Act, arrested people for allegedly spreading rumors of riots in Kuala Lumpur. Initially they can be held for 60 days, subsequently for up to two years without trial. (http://www.infobeat.com/stories/cgi/story.cgi?id=2555508533-ace, 8/21/98)

Note: As with Indonesia, China, and other nations as noted above, Malaysia is struggling with the I-Way's capability of enabling free speech. In this case, it may be considered less a case of freedom of expression and something much closer to a case of yelling "Fire!" in a crowded movie theater. The Malaysian government is very sensitive to talks of discontent and riots after what recently happened in Indonesia.

Cracker Gets More Than 48,000 Passwords: The following was reported by Henry K. Lee, *San Francisco Chronicle*, 8/13/98: ". . . a UC Berkeley Systems Administrator discovered that someone had cracked his password and was using his account—having already successfully cracked over 48,000 passwords from a list of 186,126 encrypted passwords . . . broke into systems at 'a noted Silicon Valley company,' an Indiana ISP, other UC Berkeley systems, Caltech, MIT, and Harvard, having used a Swedish ISP, Telenordia, and coming through computers in England, Denmark, and South Korea. He was finally detected on 29 June 1998."

Note: This is an excellent example of the global problem of hackers where security of the I-Way and its hosts is only as good as its weakest links. In this case, obviously more than one organization was put at risk.

Turkey's Islamist Welfare Party Wins Web Case: The Islamist Welfare Party of Turkey recently won a legal battle to close a Web site in the United States which allegedly had fraudulently masqueraded as the Party's official Web site. The Party's site in Turkey may still be shut down as a "threat to the country's secular constitution and traditions." (http://www.nando.net, 9/26/97)

Note: The point should be quite evident by now that nations are having a difficult time providing freedom of speech and yet ensuring that the government in power stays there.

Lawyers Knocked Off the I-Way for Spamming: In one of the first cases of spamming, a pair of "publicity-hungry" lawyers allegedly sent more than 5,000 Usenet newsgroups unsolicited advertisements. This caused an uproar and triggered a flood of e-mail to the lawyers that knocked them off the I-Way. (*Time*, 12/12/94)

Journalist Subject of Multiple Attacks: A writer for *Newsday* stated that his I-Way access was shut down due to receiving thousands of e-mails. In addition, his telephone was reprogrammed to forward incoming calls to an out-of-state number, and added insult to injury by also adding a message "laced with obscenities." (*Time*, 12/12/94)

Jordanian Intelligence Service on the I-Way: The Jordanian Intelligence service established their own Web site. They said it was a "new policy of openness"; however, some United States information warfare experts believe that it was set up to exploit the I-Way's propaganda potential. The Web site was at http://arab.net/gid. (http://www.dso.com, 2/5/97)

CIA Uses Hacker Technology: It has been reported that the United States CIA has used hacker technology to disrupt international money transfers and other forms of financial activities of Arab businessmen who support the activities of alleged terrorists. (*Washington Post*, 9/14/97)

London Financial Institutions Pay I-Way Extortionists: Miscreants allegedly used logic bombs to extort $400 million as a demonstration of their potential to "destroy" the operations of some London financial institutions. Allegedly, at least one transfer of funds went to Russia. Authorities have denied the story. (*London Times*, 6/2/96)

United States Intelligence Agencies Try to Control I-Way Information Flow: The FBI and National Security Agency successfully lobbied to have a draft of the "Security and Freedom through Encryption Act" that would ban effective encryption systems for United States citizens amended to include violators facing up to five years in prison after January 2000, if the transmission could not be read. (*United Kingdom Guardian*, 9/18/97)

Citibank Attacked by Russian Hacker: In 1994, a Russian successfully penetrated the systems of Citibank and allegedly stole $10 million. Citibank subsequently admitted to a loss of less than $1 million. (*Business Journal of Charlotte*, 10/13/98)

Taiwan Arrests I-Way Users: Taiwan arrested a graduate student who had set up a Web site that instructed its readers how to make bombs out of fireworks. Earlier, they had arrested a Taiwan teenager for operating a Web site, "Firearms Godfather," that advertised the sale of handguns which are prohibited in Taiwan. (http://infowar.com, 10/8/97)

Boy Meets Man on the I-Way: A 12-year-old California boy met a 31-year-old man from Virginia on the I-Way. The boy was reported missing and it was subsequently learned that the man had sent the boy a bus ticket so he could visit. He was subsequently found by police at the man's home. (*Orange County Register*, 10/6/97)

Note: This type of case is not that unusual, with at least several incidents each year. With parents using the computers and the I-Way as their children's "babysitter," coupled with their own lack of literacy vis-à-vis the I-Way, the door is wide open for perverts and other assorted miscreants to prey on children and teenagers.

Hackers Steal Computer Game: Hackers broke into the Web site of "Crack dot Com," a computer game company, and stole the source code of Quake 1.01, as well as their newest game project. The company worried about competitors using that information and source code to assist in their game development. According to the company, "Quake's raw engine value dropped several hundred thousand dollars." (*Wired* Ventures, Inc., 10/8/97)

Man Confesses to Murder on the I-Way: A man, age 29, in an I-Way chat group allegedly confessed to molesting and murdering his 5-year-old daughter in 1995. He was arrested and pled not guilty. (*Orange County Register*, 8/7/98, 7/18/98)

Israeli Hacker and His Students Attack Pentagon Systems: Two students, allegedly tutored by an Israeli hacker, known as "Analyzer," broke into military, government, and university computer systems. They allegedly installed wiretaps to collect passwords. A northern California ISP employee alerted the FBI, who subsequently arrested them. (*Orange County Register*, 7/3/98)

Note: Analyzer reportedly has now been drafted into the Israeli military. With the FBI naming Israel as one of the leading nations involved in economic espionage, one can only speculate what his military job would be.

I-Way Fraud: A Web site offered "free adult images" to those who downloaded "special viewing software." What actually occurred was the victims' telephone lines were disconnected from their provider and rerouted to Moldova, according to the FTC. The Web site owner was getting kickbacks for the rerouting to the foreign telephone company. (*Orange County Register*, date unknown)

China Arrests Software Specialist: China arrested an individual for supplying a pro-democracy Internet magazine with the e-mail addresses of thousands of people. A human rights group cites it as "the world's first prosecution of an Internet user for political reasons." The individual could receive the death sentence or a minimum of ten years in prison. (*Reuters*, Hong Kong, 7/30/98)

Croatia's I-Way Backbone Attacked: Croatian authorities advised that the new I-Way backbone had been attacked by 54 hackers. They believed the attacks came from the United States, and they speculated the miscreants were Serbian sympathizers. (*Los Angeles Times*, 12/24/97)

Note: This is an example of a political attack against a government from outside that nation. When one enters the I-Way, whether the organization is a business, a government agency, or an individual, one is open to global confrontations and attacks.

Attacks against United States DoD Systems: The United States General Accounting Office estimated that the attacks against Pentagon computer systems numbered over 250,000 annually. (*Reuters*, 10/23/97)

Note: This is not surprising because the United States in general and the Department of Defense in particular are global targets. However, the real crime is that the attacks have been successful primarily because the U.S. government has failed to enforce security policy and has not implemented even some of the basic changes required—and available, for free.

University of Minnesota Victim of "Smurf" Attack: The University of Minnesota was attacked using a *smurf denial of service* attack, which is an attack where the victim's I-Way hosts are flooded with replies to false ping packets. The attacker identified the victim's computer as the return address. The university's system was then overwhelmed. The smurf attack caused a "multi-car collision" on the I-Way affecting many other state computer systems.

Note: Such an attack using the "ping" is simple and as noted, denial of service due to networking and I-Way interfaces can cause damage and loss to other than the attacker's target. With so many connections, it is difficult to prepare for such occurrences in advance if one does not know all the I-Way ramps that they travel. This type of denial of service attack happens quite often. It not only causes disruption and information loss but also the possibility of the loss of millions of dollars in revenue to one's business on the I-Way.

Defamation of Character: Person(s) unknown sent e-mail to possibly over one thousand people advising them that "in 48 hours your credit card will be charged $184.80 for three adult movies. . . . If we do not hear from you within 48 hours, we will assume everything is correct and make the charge to your card." The e-mail supplied the telephone number of a Florida businessman (the victim of this scam) and even stated that calls could be made collect. The businessman said he received thousands of calls from all over the world, and he's been defamed as a worldwide porn dealer. He lost not only his reputation but two weeks' worth of work. The alleged miscreant was identified as an individual who was wanted by police and whose boat and car the businessman sold to pay back rent due. (http://www.infowar.com, 8/15/97)

I-Way Vigilantes Against Spam: A group of users blocked I-Way messages posted via UUNet Technologies Inc. because of the amount of spam and sometime pornographic e-mail that was being transmitted. UUNet called it "cyberterrorism" because the group blocked more than 80,000 e-mails in just the first day. (Associated Press, 8/15/97)

Oops! Trading Glitch—Again: The Etrade Group, Inc., trading company was unable to confirm trades made due to computer problems. They halted trading during the last hour of trading on June 11, 1997, also due to computer problems.

"Netizens" as I-Way Vigilantes: Many I-Way travelers are getting upset due to the child porn and other activities taking place on the I-Way. Many have taken it upon themselves to do something about it. For example, a man noted a child molester entered a chat room. He pretended to be a little girl and lured the man into a police trap. A woman whose son had been molested used an online service to catch the perpetrator. A group, patterned after the New York Guardian Angels, Cyberangels, was formed, and also Women Halting Online Abuse (http://whoa.female.com) and Web Police (http://web-police.org).

Note: Most I-Way travelers are aware that law enforcement is either too busy, doesn't understand these issues, or believes it is not under their jurisdiction; therefore, people are taking matters into their own hands. Not only is the I-Way a massive communication tool, it is also a place where "community watch" groups are forming and individuals are becoming more involved as "netizens" to patrol the I-Way and make it safer for children and others.

Major Oops: Teleglobe performed major cable restoration resulting in an outage of 3–15 minutes; periodic interruptions in MAE West service lasting several hours; overloaded BBNPlanet circuit causes periodic problems reaching www.apple.com; "We are having problems in New York right now. The exact nature of the trouble has not been determined. We have no time to fix yet, and are running on our California backup circuit. . . . Service has been restored in New York. The fault appears to have been due to an engineer mistakenly disconnecting one of our circuits . . . ; and finally, "Worldcom" (-NFS=UUNet=Pipex) lost six major ATM trunks from St. Louis, Missouri, to Los Angeles a short while ago. This has disrupted traffic over much of the Internet. Our New York circuit has been repaired but so far we are seeing very little traffic flow across it, presumably because of the Worldcom failure." (http://www.vbc.net, 7/15–17/97)

Note: If an entire business is on the I-Way, some adverse effects may cost millions of dollars in lost revenue and may be beyond the control of the business.

Russian Hacker Pleads Guilty: A Russian hacker pleaded guilty to breaking into Citicorp cash-management systems and stealing money from accounts around the world. (Dow Jones & Co., Inc., 1/25/98)

Note: Russian miscreants are expected to increase in number and are some of the cleverest of the I-Way robbers. Many have ties to Russian organized crime and are a very serious threat to I-Way businesses.

Extortion Attempt Brings Reward Offer: A 10,000 marks ($5,800) reward was offered by a private German bank for a man believed to be between age 25 and 35, who allegedly demanded 1 million marks, after he had already taken 500,000 marks from a customer or customers' account(s). (Agence France-Presse, 1/25/98)

Extortion on Capitol Hill?: Allegedly, forged e-mail messages were sent to United States Senators and Representatives by a person(s) threatening to delete all the computer files on Capitol Hill. The FBI is investigating. (*Orange County Register*, date unknown)

Chaos Computer Club: The hackers of the Chaos Computer Club have allegedly identified a vulnerability in automatic teller machines' magnetic strip cards, and also in Quicken software that allows transferring money between accounts without using the required passwords. The Club members have stated that they will not hack for personal gain. They have been accused of being more of an "IT anarchist's association." (http://www.inforwar.com, 12/2/97)

Arrests for Prostitution Posted on I-Way by Police: The police department of St. Paul, Minnesota, began posting the photos and other information about those that they arrest and charge for being involved in prostitution. This has raised questions of privacy and the posting of such information globally. (C/NET, 10/27/97)

Australian Hacker Hacks the Hand That Fed Him: An Australian hacker quit his job and started a company in competition with his former employer. He allegedly tried to help his own business by crashing his former employer's system, e-mail, and Web services by supposedly changing their configuration. (http://www.infowar.com, 9/23/97)

Hacker E-mail Bombs the United States President and Others: A hacker known as "johnny xchaotic [sic]" has been involved in denial of service attacks against President Clinton, Rush Limbaugh, and others. The attacks were carried out by sending a large amount of e-mail to their accounts. (CNET, Inc. 8/16/96)

Bank in Antigua Alleged to Be Linked to Russian Organized Crime: Antigua government officials stated that a bank soliciting American customers offering 21 percent interest rates on their savings may be linked to Russian organized crime. The two Russian directors disappeared and took with them an estimated $10 million dollars.

Note: Especially when using the global I-Way, one must always remember the old saying: "If it seems too good to be true, it probably is!"

Downloading Software Files and Viruses: "kaos4," a nonresident virus that infects .com and .exe files by increasing the file size by 697 bytes, was found attached to software downloaded from "alt.binaries.pictures.erotica." (*Computerworld*, 8/8/94)

Note: Downloading software, opening attachments, and the like are common methods for getting infected with a virus. In this case, it brings the I-Way closer to real life by merging sex and virus infections.

BMI to Monitor Transmission and Sales of Music on the I-Way: BMI, a music licensing agency, said that it had developed a "Web robot" to keep track of the transmission and sales of music. It allegedly can then use the information in any copyright suits. There are more than 26,000 Web sites that use music, but only a small portion of them have any licensing agreements with BMI. (*Orange County Register*, 10/16/97)

Note: This use of a "Web spy" has greater potential than just music copyright and licensing issues. It can be used or modified for other tracking purposes that may include some serious privacy issues.

Spoofing Internic: An Australian company was alleged to have misled customers by using the name "Internic Software, Inc. (Internic.com)." "Inter-NIC" (Internet Network Information Center—Internic.net) is the controlling agent for commonly used I-Way addresses. The Federal Trade Commission is trying to get the approximately 2000 customers refunds totaling hundreds of thousands of dollars, and forcing the software company to stop using that address. (http://wwwiz.com, 9/97)

Spoofing–AlterNIC Rerouted Internic: An AlterNIC founder was said to have used a hack known as "cache poisoning" to redirect customers to his sight. This was done by exploiting the "helpful hint" field that is sent by a DNS server.

Note: Such rerouting attacks are becoming more common. One should always be alert to such possibilities when accessing Web sites, especially whether the site is actually a .com, .net, .gov, or .org.

Hackers as "Enforcers": A group of about 35 hackers meet on the I-Way through the Internet Relay Chat and through e-mail. The group is allegedly organized to "rid the net of racists and pedophiles." For example, they may come across a pedophile in a chat group. They track him down, notify the I-Way host, and also attempt to deny him use of the I-Way. (http://www.forbes.com, 4/17/98)

Hackers Steal Military Software Programs: A hacking group, calling itself the "Masters of Downloading" bragged about stealing the Defense Information Systems Network Equipment Manager (DEM). The group is allegedly made up of 15 hackers, including eight from the United States, five from Great Britain, and two Russians. According to the hackers, the software remotely manages and monitors the military's telecommunications systems and GPS for its satellites and receivers. The group also has said they have stolen programs that track and communicate with submarines. (*Wired*, 4/21/98 & 4/24/98)

Note: The possibility of this actually occurring cannot be immediately discounted since the United States Department of Defense systems have proven to be continuously vulnerable.

United Kingdom Customs to Scan Hard Disks of Travelers: The United Kingdom announced a new policy of "Computer hard disc scanning by HM Customs and Excise." The purpose is allegedly to scan for pornographic images. The procedures allegedly involve copying the hard disk and then scanning it. The concern is not only one of privacy but also the use that can be made of such information by the country's intelligence service. (owner-isn@sekurity.org0, 8/22/98)

Note: Such actions may be legal; however, the concern of using the information of intelligence collection, planting malicious code, and the violation of any privacy is a cause for great concern. After all, if one nation begins, others will follow. Later, this idea was dropped because it was not practical and also due to mounting political and public outcry.

E-Commerce Marketeers Must Be Careful: An individual has filed a trademark-type application for the phrase "As seen on the Internet." He wants to charge $3000 a year for people to be able to use that phrase. It is speculated that a court battle will be likely. (*Orange County Register*, 7/19/98)

Note: With the increase in electronic commerce and the use of Web sites to advertise, the use of that marketing phrase would be a natural. This is another example of new thinking and new laws—or modifications—that are needed for dealing in this new environment.

Rumors of Hacker Extortions Unfounded: Some have claimed that the numerous stories about high-tech criminals using high-tech weapons to extort millions of dollars from banks and other financial institutions around the world are untrue. The untrue rumors are that over $600 million was extorted from these institutions by threats of using hacking techniques, viruses, and a radio-frequency weapon that would blast high energy beams at computers. This is according to the Defense Evaluation and Research Agency of the United Kingdom of Great Britain. (*TechWeb*, 12/7/97)

"Reformed" Hackers for Hire: Some hackers have begun to attack systems for money. They offer their clients an opportunity to see how well their security is functioning. If the hackers cannot break in, no fee is charged. If they break in, the fee is based on how much they had penetrated the system. (*InfoWar Digest* volume 3, number 3, 3/2/98)

Burmese Use I-Way to Fight Burmese Dictators: Burmese freedom fighters now residing in the United States have formed the Civil Society for Burma (http://www.csburma.org). There is also another site (http://www.fre-burma.org) supported by the Open Society Institute underwritten by George Soros, the financier. Fighting back, the Burmese (Myanmar) government has its own Web site (http://myanmar.com). (*Parade*, 8/23/98)

Note: The great thing about these types of "adversarial sites" is that it gives both advocates and the government in power the use of free speech (something that the Myanmar dictators put people in prison for doing—exercising the right of free speech) to present their side of issues to the global community. The global community can then decide on a position by comparing what each side says. This is a tremendous benefit that could never have been realized except for the I-Way.

Davis Pleads Guilty to Theft of Gillette Trade Secrets: Steven L. Davis pled guilty in Nashville on January 26, 1998, to five counts of theft of Gillette trade secrets. Davis admitted that in 1997 he stole trade secrets concerning a new shaving system and that the losses caused by his conduct were at least $1.5 million. (Boston Business Wire, January 27, 1998)

Note: The fact that a temporary contract employee, Davis, was able to obtain the information concerning the new design of the shaving system and secret them on a single 600 megabyte hard drive is very significant. In the past, detailed drawings and design information would have filled dozens of boxes and attempts to improperly remove them from an organization's premises could have been more easily detected. Preventing someone from removing a paperback book–sized portable external hard drive or removable media (like Zip, Jazz, or Syquest drives) may well be impossible. Organizations need to consider how the internal Intranet and the I-Way have dramatically increased the risks to digital forms of intellectual property and trade secrets and take appropriate measures to manage these risks. The perpetrator here is also alleged to have approached prospective buyers through Internet e-mail, probably using either anonymous re-mailers or e-mail utilities to forge a bogus address to mask his true identity. Once the digital crown jewels are obtained, the act of fencing them can be made much simpler via the I-Way.

Reuters Suspected of Stealing Data: A Connecticut-based unit of Reuters is suspected of trying to illegally obtain proprietary information from rival Bloomberg. Reuter's managers reportedly wanted to obtain information about the "analytics" system used to predict financial trends. The government is investigating whether Reuters Analytics "improperly induced" a consultant to obtain Bloomberg proprietary information. (*ComputerWorld*, 2/9/98, p. 12)

Note: The I-way connection here is quite interesting. The outside consultant may have attempted to penetrate Bloomberg networks and servers via the Internet in order to obtain the targeted information. If proven true, this case could prove to be one of the highest profile "I-Way robberies" to date.

Crackers: We Stole Nuke Data: Three crackers claimed to have penetrated computer systems at India's Bhabha Atomic Research Center, reading e-mails from scientists and deleting files. The crackers identified themselves as savecOre, VeNoMouS, 18, from New Zealand, and JF, 18 from England; they claimed to be members of an organized cracking group called Milw0rm. (2:02pm 3.Jun.98.PDT by James Glave *WIRED NEWS*)

Note: This incident evoked a great deal of interest when first reported. It combines three of the most important lessons for any organization that chooses to be connected to the I-Way. First, the hacker team came from locations outside the national boundaries of the target. Second, they exploited known flaws in the defense of the organization to obtain desired information. Third, their motivations were apparently personal, but the unprecedented global access provided by the I-Way allowed them to follow their individual ethical standards and take actions that they personally felt were acceptable. Expect an unending succession of similar incidents, as well as those undertaken purely for profit, aided and abetted by the ease of access via the I-Way and the all too often shoddy security of targeted organizations.

Hackers Milking Cows: "Swedish hackers sentenced to community service. The well-known Swedish Cyber Thugs, freddie and sober of efnet #999 crew got sentenced to six months community service for hacking several Web pages including macworld.com and macweek.com. The hackers will now serve six months of cow milking on a farm located in the southern parts of Sweden." (http://www.europeiskdebatt.com, 1/7/99)

Note: An interesting sentence and one that for some may be more fun than punishment.

Computer Hacker Gets One Year+ in Prison: A 21-year-old Rhode Island man was sentenced to serve a year and a day in prison for leading a nationwide hacking group known as "Virii." (NewsBit, 1/15/99)

Note: In the past, those found guilty of hacking were given light sentences. However, there appears to be a trend toward longer sentences as the public begins to understand the seriousness of some of the hackers' acts. However, there is also a trend, at least in the United States, for prosecutors and law enforcement personnel at all levels to treat hackers as if they were murderers and rapists. Whether this is done with good intent or intent for more budget and publicity is not known. It is hoped that justice will prevail—balanced justice. One has just to look at the Kevin Mitnick case to see why this is a concern. He is allegedly charged with theft or fraud equal to $80 million. Using such extreme calculations by those in the criminal justice system makes a mockery of the system.

Hackers Arrested in Buryatia: "A group of hackers has been arrested in Buryatia by the department for the struggle against organized crime under the Interior Ministry of the republic with the participation of officers of the Federal Security Service. The criminal group, which included a software specialist, tried to penetrate into secret files of the Ulan Ude telephone exchange, which contain among other things, the classified addresses of officers of law enforcement agencies. A telephone operator of the city information service was also taking part in the hacking attempt. The hackers planned to sell on the 'black market' the information obtained by illegal means. For the first time ever, criminal proceedings were instituted in the republic under Article 272 of the Penal Code, i.e., on charges of 'unauthorized access to computer information.'" (Itar-Tass News Agency, 1/21/99)

Note: Law enforcement and security officers are increasingly becoming targets of these miscreants, to include gangs and organized crime groups. The lack of good information systems security coupled with the massive databases containing information on political figures, law enforcement officers, and others of high visibility is a cause for concern. However, it does not seem that any special precautions are being taken to protect this sensitive information. Hopefully, those responsible won't wait until someone is hurt or killed.

First Cyber-Stalking I-Way Case: A North Hollywood, California, man was charged with stalking under a new state statute relative to cyber-stalking. Allegedly six men over a five-month period had shown up at a woman's home and stated they were answering an online ad and "steamy" e-mails sent in her name that described fantasies of being raped. The North Hollywood man allegedly sent them after being rejected by the woman. Assistant United States Attorney Michael J. Gennaco stated, "This technology has created a whole new class of criminals who would not otherwise have the forbearance to terrorize people face to face. It emboldens them to hide behind computer screens and interfere with other people's lives." (*Los Angeles Times*, 1/22/99)

Note: Gennaco's comment provides an excellent comment that pretty much sums up the entire I-Way robbery topic.

SUMMARY

I-Way robbers use various tricks—sometimes old, sometimes new—to commit their crimes. The issue of accidents still remains one of the greatest challenges to operating an I-Way business. The use of the I-Way by governments is not very different than the use of other tools for controlling others, staying in power, and spying on other nations and individuals. If one is to travel the I-Way as a businessperson, government agency employee, customer, researcher, or in any other profession, one must always be on the lookout for I-Way robbers and be prepared for any contingency.

NOTES

1. See http://ciac.llnl.gov/ciac/bulletins.
2. As stated before, the sites referenced are dynamic and may not contain the information indefinitely.

9

What Caused the I-Way Security Problems?

CHAPTER OBJECTIVE

This chapter will describe the variables that have contributed to the security risks of using the I-Way for both businesses' and government agencies' purposes.

A COMBINATION OF ALL OF THE ABOVE

The question of what has driven us to where we are on the I-Way must be addressed before discussing what can be done to make the I-Way safe for travel by "unarmed civilians." As with most problems these days, the answer is not simple—there probably isn't only one, absolute, true answer—it is a complicated series of interactions of dependent variables. As with dependent variables, changes in one may affect the others either positively or negatively.

For example, more I-Way ramps created more users. More miscreants are attracted to the sites, requiring increased security. Security becomes more sophisticated; therefore, less sophisticated hackers are screened out but those who get in use more sophisticated attack methods. This causes even more sophisticated security so that the potential customers do not decrease.

There are some very specific variables that can be identified, but in doing so, one must always factor in the X variable—the unknown variable. In simpler terms, the X variable is in play and identified when an unplanned, unlikely, and un-thought-of event occurs. Its results are known by the phrase: "S . . . happens!"

We cannot deal with what we do not know, only with what we know. However, we must have contingency plans that factor in the unknown what-ifs. In others words, the reasons for I-Way security problems will be discussed, but we may not address the entire issue because of variable X.

GLOBAL CHANGES

The first and most important message that must be understood, and is only now (due to the Asian and Russian financial crises) beginning to be understood, is this: We must think globally.

Those in the United States, especially, must understand that the map (see Figure 9–1) is the *world*. The United States is not the world and more so than ever before, what happens throughout the world affects the United States—and generally most other countries of the world.

When political changes occur, they may have great impact throughout other nations politically, socially, and economically. There is an increasing role of the United Nations as a global police force. New laws and treaties relative to the I-Way are being discussed and enacted on a worldwide basis.

What the I-Way has helped bring about is more communications between world governments to discuss areas of mutual concern—and those areas of mutual concern in some instances are I-Way related. These global interactions and political decisions are broadcast up and down the I-Way. What appears to be evolving is the I-Way as global nervous system. Just as the human body benefits from the rapid flow of information from each part, the world is benefiting from the increased flow of information via the I-Way. This has caused the world community to react via the I-Way to changes—especially those of a negative nature. Hackers are using the I-Way to voice and display their concerns. As we have seen in the summaries of I-Way attacks, many of these attacks by hackers are for political reasons.

Some examples that clearly are attacks for political purposes are:

♦ The threat of hackers in the People's Republic of China to hold United States firms to blame as coconspirators with the Chinese government to limit the freedom of their citizens

♦ The changing of the United States CIA, NASA, and FBI sites to ones less flattering

Must think globally - not nationally

Figure 9–1 Think globally—not nationally

♦ The changing of the British Labour Party Web site
♦ The changing of many of the Republic of Indonesia Web sites to support independence for East Timor

These are but a few of the many Web site attacks on the I-Way which will undoubtedly increase in the future as more and more people of the world use the I-Way to voice their political views.

This is a remarkable occurrence and one that may often be missed by those who travel the I-Way. The I-Way provides the only true vehicle in the world for any ordinary citizen to voice his or her opinion on any issue in the world from anywhere in the world. Not only that, but it also provides the ability to quickly, through chat groups, e-mail, and Web sites, find others of like opinions and join together as one voice and bring world opinion to bear on political entities to try to force changes. The use of the I-Way concerning the Tiananmen Square slaughter several years ago is an excellent example of average people broadcasting information their government had attempted to restrict.

However, many governments today are trying desperately to control the flow of information. The Russian example of SORM (which entails government monitoring of all I-Way activity which they determine to be of interest) and similar processes in other nations are prime examples of governments that fear the free flow of information. Many other governments want to know what information is flowing in and out of their nations and are also trying to monitor and have access to that I-Way information (e.g., the United States). They are all trying in vain to find some way to control and monitor information.

The issue of I-Way security in this regard is twofold:

♦ Those that represent the government in power who want to monitor and control what information its citizens glean from the I-Way are interested in I-Way security, but for securing their own power.
♦ Those whose voices are silenced by the government in power and those around the world who are their supporters are interested in getting their voices heard and in order to do so, are hacking those Web sites along the I-Way that disagree with them.

Governments are using the I-Way for furthering their political agendas in their information warfare propaganda attacks against their adversaries (e.g., Croatia and Serbia; Israel and Arab nations). Even groups considered as international terrorists by some—Hezbollah, for example—have Web sites to explain their purposes.

So, clashes between governments and citizens backed by their global supporters; clashes among nations of the world; and groups hostile to specific nations, which continue in the old Industrial Age ways, are also now being fought in the new Information Age ways—on the I-Way. All warring factions are concerned with security of their I-Way ramps as well as penetrating those of their adversaries. This will continue. Why should it be any different than it has been since the beginning of the human race? Again, the only true difference is the environment in which these battles take place.

CHANGES IN SOCIETIES

Another concern of both governments and citizens is the changes that are taking place in society—both individual national societies and a new, global society which is forming. One of the major barriers to a global society has always been the language barrier. As more and more documents, e-mail, business, chat rooms, and Web sites proliferate on the I-Way, it appears that English is increasingly becoming the de facto common language. Although language translation software at present is very crude, it has some capability and in the future will likely become significantly more useful. This in itself is an opportunity for societies to gain a better understanding of each other, because a common language or technology which allows better communication can ultimately lead to increased understanding of others—not necessarily agreement, but at least understanding.

However, there are those nations, majorities in some societies, and groups who do not want to see a common language based on English. These interests have attempted to force the use of the national language on I-Way users and Web sites within their domain. For the most part, this has failed because these nations attempt to use Industrial Age thinking and processes in the Information Age. It may be hoped that through the evolution of language translation technologies, society may enjoy the best of both worlds, and all will benefit from improved communications.

The I-Way, the Global Information Infrastructure, is a source of power. We must remember that the GII is a massive international connection of the world's computers, which carries business and personal communications as well as those of the social and government sectors of nations. It is connecting entire cultures, erasing international borders, supporting cyber-economies, establishing new markets, and changing our entire concept of international relations.

In an on-line document, IBM[1] stated it this way:

> When fully realized, the GII will be a vast network consisting of hundreds of thousands of networks. These networks will run our factories, process our financial transactions, organize our work, increase our productivity, instruct us and our children, help physicians and hospitals to care for us, connect us more closely with friends and family wherever they may be, entertain us, and perform a myriad of other services not yet conceived.

Based on the above, and as stated under the prior section, there are those who do not want this to happen. They do not want their cultures subverted by Western nations. Nations like Indonesia and Malaysia with their predominantly Moslem[2] citizens do not want their society corrupted by such things as violent movies, pornography, music glorifying drugs, and the like. In these societies, support groups, religious groups, and governments are working together to filter this type of information from their citizens, while at the same time, those fighting for freedom of expression are fighting to gather that information which they want to see and read. I-Way security is again the method of protecting those who have control in their realm of the I-Way, as well as the target of those who are against those controls or those in control.

ECONOMIC CHANGES

The biggest challenge for governments vis-à-vis the I-Way is maintaining control while gaining the benefits of the I-Way to support their global economic goals. The biggest challenge for businesses is protecting their sensitive and proprietary information that flows along the I-Way, as well as protecting the integrity of their Web sites. This is made much more difficult as nations and businesses work together in this new, global economic environment. This is complicated by the partnerships being formed between businesses in different nations. These expanding global, international businesses' problems are compounded when some firms are partners on some projects but then partner with others who may have been competitors on other projects.

One of the more serious information protection deficiencies is that these international businesses often do not differentiate among these same businesses they have access to as being a competitor and/or partner. Thus, the information that the partner/competitor may access via the I-Way from its partner/competitor is not differentiated. Thus, business employees view these other businesses as partners without discriminating based on the information required under the partnership and the need-to-know principle. In this global economy, where the economic power of a nation is of more value than military power, these security issues have not drawn the attention they needed—until recently. The greatest driver to providing adequate I-Way security is the demand for electronic commerce via the I-Way.

Thus, the driving force to protect the I-Way, from a business viewpoint, is not protecting the information because a security officer said these assets should be protected or the stockholders are demanding it. The driving force is the businesses' customers who have said through polls, e-mail, surveys, and *not* using their money to purchase on the I-Way, that they will not be comfortable doing business, making purchases via the I-Way, until they believe it is secure from miscreants.

This is the driving force—money! For businesses it has always been so. After all, businesses are in business to make money, make a profit. They envision billions of global customers buying their products or services *if* the I-Way can be secured. However, this security must be "non-techie" and invisible to the customer. Anything else limits the businesses' opportunities.

ADVANCEMENTS IN TECHNOLOGY

The most obvious and underlying reason for the lack of security on the I-Way is changes in technology. Such things as decentralization of systems from large mainframes with dumb, diskless terminals maintained by professional information technology staffs gave way to local area networks, dispersed throughout departments and maintained by their own staffs, sometimes on a part-time basis. These changes seem to be occurring exponentially. The explosive growth of this newer, faster, cheaper, and more powerful technology coupled with the exponential growth of the World Wide Web has made the I-Way a major security problem.

I-Way security is always in a catch-up mode, since security has always sat in the back of the bus as the businesses drive the I-Way. Security also went from a centralized approach to one of decentralization. Thus, it changed from being the full-time responsibility of information security professionals in many organizations to the part-time duties of some department staff members. These staff members had little if any training.

I-WAY SECURITY PRIORITY—NEAR THE BOTTOM BUT RISING

As alluded to above and throughout this book, the task and budget for protecting information traveling along the I-Way has been slow in receiving business as well as government support. The United States government, as previously stated, has been one of those whose priority has been to be able to access I-Way traffic instead of supporting its protection using the most state-of-the-art encryption and other tools available. Businesses were not interested in security because it adversely impacted budgets. However, with the use of the I-Way to support electronic commerce, businesses now see where security can help bring in revenue, therefore it is gaining management support. This support will probably increase rapidly as more miscreants take advantage of many businesses' lack of I-Way security. Ironically, these I-Way robbers may do more to increase demand for I-Way security than any other force in the marketplace today.

WHY SECURITY PROBLEMS WILL CONTINUE TO RISE—"BECAUSE THAT'S WHERE THE VICTIMS AND THEIR MONEY ARE"

The attacks will continue to increase as the number of I-Way ramps; Web sites; attackers; electronic commerce transactions; new technology implementations with their new vulnerabilities; and new, sophisticated hacker programs, all converge on the I-Way.

The following chart (Figure 9–2) shows the estimated increase of I-Way hosts:

A recent survey[3] indicated that in January 1998 there were 29,670,000 unique I-Way hosts and six months later there were 36,739,000. The survey also found that the top ten domain names in order were:

- ◆ .com (Commercial)
- ◆ .net (Networks)
- ◆ .edu (Education)
- ◆ .mil (Military)
- ◆ .jp (Japan)
- ◆ .us (United States)
- ◆ .uk (United Kingdom)

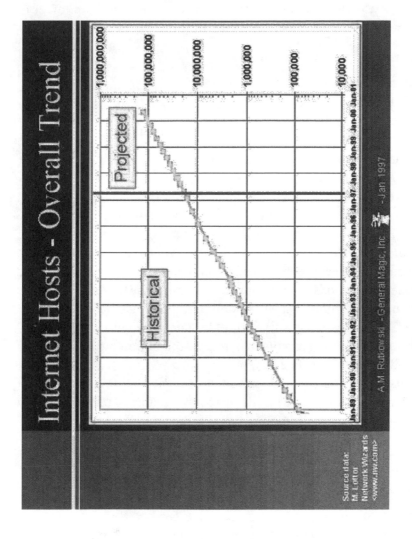

Figure 9–2 Internet Growth (Source: http://www.genmagic.com/Internet/Trends/slide-4.html)

- .de (Germany)
- .ca (Canada)
- .au (Australia)

Another survey,[4] although not an exact science, estimated the number of users on-line as of August 1998 at 131.25 million. By regions, the survey found:

- Africa: 0.80 million
- Asia/Pacific: 22 million
- Europe: 33.25 million
- Middle East: 0.75 million
- Canada and United States: 70 million
- South America: 4.5 million

An August 1998 survey by Relevant Knowledge found that the average I-Way user over 12 years old spent more than eight hours on-line per month. Another survey by NetRatings found that the average user spent over 17 hours a month on-line. The discrepancy, as theorized by NetRatings, was because different methods were employed to calculate the time spent on-line. Whatever the actual number, it will undoubtedly increase.

The *6th eOverview Report* survey by eMarketer in August 1998 estimated that on-line advertising revenue will reach $3.8 billion by the year 2000 and $8.0 billion by the end of 2002.

All this tells us that commercial sites will lead the I-Way surge with businesses spending more on advertising to attract more of the increasingly on-line consumers. This will continue to be fertile ground for the miscreants and those who are trying to mitigate these attacks and protect assets.

SUMMARY

Dependent variables of politics, governments, societies, robustness of security, economic competition, global businesses, number of users, number of consumers, and attackers all are interacting on the I-Way. Each change in any of the variables has some impact on the safety of the I-Way. I-Way security appears to be gaining ground in importance; however, that does not necessarily translate into more or better security. For now, all the interactions of the variables indicate that the I-Way robbers can still commit their crimes, drive away to their hideouts, and not worry about being found, or if found, prosecuted.[5]

NOTES

1. *Understanding the Global Information Infrastructure, IBM Living in the Canadian Information Society* (see http://CAN.IBM.com).
2. The religion, Islam, is a great religion based on the Koran. The practice of that religion by the vast majority of Moslems throughout the world should not be confused with the terrorists who use it as an excuse for criminal conduct.
3. Nua Internet Surveys, http://www.nua.ie/surveys.
4. Nua Survey, http://www.nua.ie/surveys.
5. This is referring to the international criminals, not the juvenile delinquents within a nation who are less sophisticated in covering their tracks and who are caught and prosecuted by that nation.

10

Basic I-Way Protection

CHAPTER OBJECTIVE

The objective of this chapter is to provide an overview of the basic I-Way protection techniques and technologies that are essential to safe travel on the I-Way for businesses and/or government agencies. It will also address some of the fundamental issues that should be considered for secure operation of the Web servers and the intranets that many organizations are creating.

AN I-WAY PROTECTION PROCESS APPROACH

The I-Way protection program must be based on a systems approach (see Figure 10–1). That system or process must consider all basic factors from intrusion detection to recovery.

HOW TO PROTECT AN ORGANIZATION AGAINST I-WAY ROBBERS

Protection begins with the creation of a comprehensive plan for safeguarding your organization against the risks arising from connectivity with the I-Way. The program design phase is based on methods the authors have employed to help a variety of organizations ranging from banks, aerospace, and defense companies to high-technology manufacturers and pharmaceutical organizations. As with any planning process, the recommended

Improve Survivability By Extending Focus

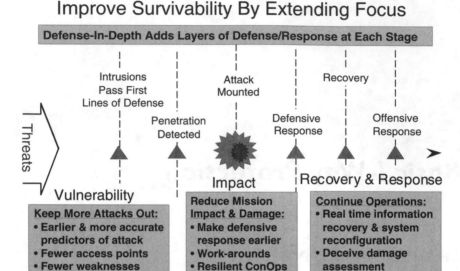

Figure 10–1 An Example of a Systems Protection Approach

approach should be modified and tailored to most closely approximate your organizational priorities and unique culture and business operations.

I-WAY PROTECTION PROGRAM DESIGN

It is important to understand the basic computer, technology, and information protection concepts used today if we are to successfully protect the information and the systems used to process, store, and transmit that information on the I-Way. This information, coupled with a basic knowledge of computers, will assist in better understanding the methods used to mitigate or prevent I-Way robberies.

Basic I-Way protection concepts require that we balance ease of use, costs, capability, flexibility, performance, and protection requirements. There are three basic principles that form the foundation of any effective I-Way security program. The principles are:

1. Access control
2. Individual accountability
3. Audit trails

CIA NEEDED ON THE I-WAY

The objective of any I-Way protection program, whether for an Internet Service Provider, individual Web site operators, or the manager responsible for safeguarding an overall corporate organization is to provide *CIA*:

- ◆ Confidentiality
- ◆ Integrity
- ◆ Assurances

Confidentiality means that the information is protected and only given to those who have the need to know that information to perform their duties. *Integrity* means the information can be relied on to be accurate and the systems, both hardware and software, can be relied on to perform as expected and in accordance with their specifications and documentation. *Assurances* means that the information and systems are available to perform when they are needed.

The I-Way security program is separated into several basic functions. They are:

- ◆ Physical security—Those barriers made up of locks, personal badges, and badge and biometric access control devices.
- ◆ Personnel security—Those processes and controls in place to ensure that people of integrity, without criminal record or drug abuse, are employed.
- ◆ Administrative security—Those processes and controls such as I-Way security policies, procedures, and awareness and training programs.
- ◆ Communications security—The protection of information transmissions, e.g., encryption.
- ◆ Operations—Those processes and controls related to normal, day-to-day operations on the I-Way ramps, system configuration, and system maintenance.
- ◆ Risk management—The formal analyses to identify threats, vulnerabilities, risks, and I-Way security cost-benefits.

I-WAY PROTECTION REQUIRES AN ISSO

In order to protect a business or government agency on the I-Way, a professional who is responsible for the I-Way related information and information systems protection/security program is required. That person is called the I-Way Information Systems Security Officer (IISSO).[1] This position could be a separate position depending on the importance of the I-Way to the employer, or it could be incorporated into the regular ISSO job responsibilities.

The responsibilities of the information systems security officer's position can be summarized as follows: Administer an innovative I-Way information systems security program that minimizes I-Way security risks with the least impact on costs and schedules, while meeting all company and customer requirements.

Responsibilities include:

♦ Managing People: Includes professional integrity building and maintaining relationships, dealing with changes, communicating, developing people, influence, teamwork, work environment, and performance management
♦ Managing the Business of I-Way InfoSec: Consists of commitment to results, customer/supplier focus, decision making, managing resources, planning and organizing, problem solving, strategic thinking, judgment, personal accountability, and ownership
♦ Managing I-Way InfoSec Processes: Includes project planning and implementation, quality persistence, system perspective, and job knowledge

Goals and Objectives

♦ To administer an innovative I-Way information systems security program that minimizes risks with the least impact on business costs and schedules, while meeting all requirements
♦ Enhance the quality, efficiency, and effectiveness of the organization on the I-Way
♦ Identify potential I-Way problem areas and mitigate them before customers identify them
♦ Enhance the company's ability to attract customers through the I-Way because of the ability to efficiently and effectively protect their information and privacy
♦ Establish the organization as an I-Way information systems security leader in the industry.

Strategic Plan

It is important to develop and implement a strategic plan when establishing an I-Way and I-Way information security program. That includes defining the purpose of the I-Way, information security, or systems security program. The program should have as its purpose at least the following focus:

- ◆ Minimize the probability of I-Way security vulnerabilities
- ◆ Minimize the damage if an I-Way ramp vulnerability is exploited
- ◆ Provide methods to efficiently and effectively recover from the damage

Planning considerations include:

    Customer requirements/reasonable expectations
    Good business practices
    Quality management
- ◆ Innovative ideas

The primary objective of the overall I-Way protection program is to:

- ◆ Minimize risks to organization systems and information
- ◆ Minimize impact on costs
- ◆ Minimize impact on schedules
- ◆ Assist in meeting contractual requirements
- ◆ Assist in meeting noncontractual requirements
    Build a comprehensive I-Way systems security environment
    Respond flexibly to changing needs
    Support multiple customers' information protection priorities
    Incorporate new technologies as needed
- ◆ Assist in attracting new customers and retaining current customers through a secure I-Way ramp

The manager responsible for the I-Way protection program must maximize the use of available resources, use team concepts, and apply risk management concepts to achieve objectives.

Tactical Plan

The I-Way information security IISSO should also develop a tactical plan or annual operating plan for I-Way protection. This should include:

♦ Gaining an understanding of current environment, culture, and philosophy by reviewing applicable directives to include:
1. Human Resources
2. Computing
3. Security
4. Auditing
♦ Identifying key team members to include:
1. Human Resources
2. Computing
3. Security
4. Auditing
5. Legal, or other areas unique to the organization
♦ Forming action teams to:
1. Evaluate the current I-Way and I-Way ramp environments
2. Recommend and coordinate changes
3. Identify new processes
4. Support implementation of changes
♦ Action teams should look at developing and/or improving:
1. I-Way policies and procedures
2. I-Way ramp protection awareness program
3. I-Way related systems security documentation
4. I-Way risk assessments/risk analyses

The I-Way risk management process must identify areas of major interest to executive management and customers. The assessments could be qualitative, quantitative, or a combination of both. They should result in a formal report to management complete with recommendations, costs, and benefits. Profits and potential impacts, both positive and adverse, of effective/ineffective I-Way security on the organization's public relations must be considered when making recommendations. The reports should also include an identification of areas that need improvement and areas that are performing well. The approach must be from a business point of view, and include:

1. I-Way threats: Manmade or natural occurrences that can cause adverse effects to systems and information when combined with specific vulnerabilities
2. I-Way vulnerabilities: Weaknesses that allow specific threats to cause adverse effects to I-Way–related systems and information

   3. I-Way risks: The chances that a specific threat can take advantage
      of a specific vulnerability to cause adverse effects to systems and
      information

I-Way security verifications and validations must be part of the program and
should include:

   1. Security in place where needed
   2. Security systems active
   3. Cost-effective security

New technology products should be evaluated for risks and cost-effectiveness.

The Tactical Plan Outline

The plan should define the complete vision of an effective I-Way information
systems security environment that has been optimized for the I-Way; define
the current information systems and I-Way security environment; and identify the differences. Project plans should be developed and implemented to
get from where the organization is currently to where it should be.

Information Systems Security Organization

There is continuous debate as to where in the management structure the I-
Way information systems security responsibility/organization should be
located. Regardless of its reporting structure, it should include developing,
implementing, maintaining, and administering a company-wide I-Way information systems security program to include all plans, policies, procedures,
assessments, and authorization necessary to ensure the protection of customers' and the company's systems and information.

    Operations of the I-Way information security organization should
include:

- All functions and work routinely accomplished during the course of
  conducting the organization's security business
- System access administration and controls to include the direct use and
  control of systems access software, monitoring their use, and identifying access violations
- Analyses of access violations to identify patterns and trends that may
  indicate an increased risk to systems and/or information

♦ Computer crime and abuse inquiries (investigations) conducted where indications of intent to damage, destroy, modify, or release to unauthorized persons information of value

♦ Disaster recovery/contingency planning to include directing the development and coordination of a company-wide program to mitigate the possibility of loss of systems and information, and assure their rapid recovery in the event of an emergency or disaster

♦ Awareness program established and administered to all system users to make them aware of the information systems security policies and procedures that must be followed to adequately protect systems and information

♦ Systems' hardware, firmware, and software evaluated for impact on the security systems and information; where applicable, risk assessments conducted and the results reported to management for risk decisions

♦ Systems compliance inspections, tests, and evaluations conducted to ensure that all users and systems are in compliance with security policies and procedures

♦ Projects initiated where improvements or other changes will be accomplished and where that effort has an objective and will take longer than 30 days, beginning and ending dates

♦ Budget and administration function to include:
   1. Budget: Both capital and operational
   2. Personnel: Ensure the organization is staffed to authorized levels with information systems security professionals to include training, career development, and performance reviews

Measurements

Consider what products and/or services are produced. How does management know when the security organization has done its job? What is currently measured? Why? Who are the internal and external customers of the security organization? How does the company know there is a security presence, adequacy, and compliance?

Measurement determinations include:

1. What should be measured?
2. Why should it be measured?
3. When should it be measured?
4. How should it be measured?

5. Where should it be measured?
6. Who should measure it?

Measurement categories include:

1. Schedule
2. Productivity—how much
3. Cost
4. Performance—how well
5. Planning
6. Justification of head count
7. Justification of budget
8. Briefings to management
9. Briefing of customers
10. Briefing of visitors / employees

Year-end evaluations are also crucial. On an annual basis the security group should assess: What was well done? What did not work so well and why? What didn't get done that should have been accomplished? Why was it not accomplished? What training was accomplished? Were there any noteworthy productivity gains? Were there any budget problems?

THE I-WAY PROTECTION PROGRAM

I-Way protection should be integrated into the business or government agency's overall information security program. There are unique threats, vulnerabilities, and risks associated with the on- and off-ramps. To most people, the need for an I-Way protection program seems obvious, vis-à-vis hackers and economic espionage agents. However, that program must also take into consideration the use, abuse, and misuse of the I-Way by employees. Their use of the I-Way for other than business purposes results in lost productivity and potential lawsuits. For example: Imagine a male employee accessing pornography at work and a female employee walks by and sees it. Some believe that this falls into the category of sexual harassment and the company would then be liable and sued by the female employee.

Approximately a year ago, *PC World* magazine conducted a survey[2] of "top executives of 200 companies" and found that one out of every five employees had been disciplined for unauthorized use of their I-Way ramp. The survey found that the most common offense was relative to the accessing of pornographic Web sites. This was followed by using the company's I-Way ramp to shop online, visiting chat rooms, gambling online, and the unauthorized downloading of software. All of these would violate policies and procedures in most companies, may even be illegal, and/or result in lawsuits.

As part of an I-Way protection program, those systems that access the I-Way should provide a warning screen as part of the I-Way access. The following is an example of a possible warning screen.[3]

"Use of the system and access to the Internet must be solely for company business by authorized personnel only. If you are not an approved, authorized user as defined by the company, you are not authorized access to this system nor any other system through this system. This system may be monitored, intercepted, read, recorded, copied, or captured in any manner deemed appropriate by company personnel. There is no right to privacy and any information that may be of evidentiary value may be given to security or law enforcement personnel at the discretion of the company. The accessing of this system by default constitutes an expressed understanding and consent to the above."

To mitigate the risks the following basic recommendations are provided:

Administrative Security

I-Way Policy
There should be a specific policy that sets out the acceptable uses of the I-Way and other management matters. Consider this a convenient mechanism for the business or government agency "rules of the road." The policy should describe how the connection may be used, specify what must not be done and also describe the nature of oversight or monitoring that the local users may expect from the local organization.

I-Way Procedures
Procedures should be in place and tailored to the specific needs of the business or agency organization, providing detailed information as to how to safely use the I-Way as well as comply with the I-Way protection policy.

Training Staff, Users, and Managers
Over decades of information security work it has been established that most people in most businesses and government organizations will conform to the

required level of security compliance once they understand what is expected of them and why it is important to protect both the organization and themselves. I-Way access is no different. Think of how much worse the chaos would be on physical highways if there was no driver's education training for new drivers. In a similar fashion we need to provide some guidelines and directions for the I-Way users.

Training should consist of both generic orientations to the risks of I-Way activities, complemented with a specialized portion dealing with the specific issues, policies and procedures, technology and business secrets unique to the business or government agency. The contents of such training could range from a list of simple do's and don'ts to a full-blown counterintelligence awareness briefing.

Although some may scoff at the need or benefit of threat awareness for average users, it is a very cost-effective and efficient component of the overall I-Way protection program. As the United States National Counterintelligence Center has noted, exploitation of the I-Way to gather both national security and proprietary technical information is the fastest growing means of spying. Given the prevalence of such activities, the untrained user may receive an unsolicited e-mail message or be lured into a revealing discussion in a "chat session." To defeat such efforts, the best protection mechanism is the informed awareness of the average user. Technical measures can supplement this awareness and together the combination is significantly stronger than either would be standing alone.

One of the most efficient methods of accomplishing these tasks is through the use of Web-based training environments. There are products that provide a structured computer-based training environment for employees/users and the capability to track successful completion of the course. Such tools, as well as individually developed company or agency-developed Web sites, provide a convenient platform from which to provide a consistent message to the target population.

I-Way Physical Security

1. Create Standards for I-Way Systems: All hardware, software, and networks connected to the I-Way must be physically secured against tampering, theft, and so forth.
2. Limit Access to Security Systems: The firewall and other sensitive hardware and software security mechanisms must be secure and access limited to only those individuals who are required to maintain the systems.

I-Way Operational Security

The I-Way Is for Business Use Only

All operations, processes, and work through the I-Way must be done only for the benefit of the organization and must not contain any information that identifies vulnerabilities or compromises the organization's competitive advantages.

Monitor and Control I-Way Use

There are many problems that arise from permitting widespread access and use of the I-Way by all or even a majority of employees in a business or government agency. I-Way e-mail, Web accesses, and file transfers all create particular vulnerabilities that must be addressed in the effort to manage risks. However, every effort to manage the risks of I-Way abuse requires both policy/procedural as well as technological components.

- ◆ Limit on-site use of external Web connectivity to those with a business or operational need, and restrict the options available to average users. The organization should consider limiting external access by employees to those who supply a unique user ID and password. This reduces both the potential for anonymous misuse of the organization's Web connections and also idle time spent randomly "surfing the Net" for personal interests and activities.
- ◆ Create custom e-mail and file transfer filters/logging or use a firewall that provides such features. The custom filter should allow management to identify anyone inappropriately transmitting via e-mail or USENET news postings sensitive documents or materials. Logging the e-mail and file transfers should also identify messages and attachments addressed to designated competitors or other inappropriate destinations. In this area it is critical to consult with legal counsel. The laws are not yet settled and although the technical capability to perform these functions is fairly straightforward, one should ensure the implementation avoids inadvertent violations of relevant laws dealing with any employee expectation of privacy.
- ◆ Web blocking and filtering products exist that can deny access to known pornography sites. Some approach that discourages or prevents access to such sites should be implemented. Well-designed firewall products offer this capability, either included in their own functions or through alliance with other vendors. Typically these blocking systems

work by parsing the URLs (universal resource locators) of Web sites and logging or denying connections to those with explicit language or suggestive indications of the contents—for example, www.sex—.com. The software to deny access typically uses the inclusion of "sex" or other suspect character strings in the URL as a trigger. The filtering software often also uses lists of sites developed by the vendor, which are known to contain graphic and/or potentially offensive content. Such blocking, although never perfect, is an effective method of reducing the risk of unauthorized activities. The software largely prevents individual employees from abusing their access privileges to download illegal child pornography and other offensive materials. Positive efforts to prevent such abuses may be very useful in defending the organization against charges that it tolerated or perhaps even encouraged a "hostile workplace environment." As litigation against organizations for sexual harassment has become more common, it is prudent to consider such technical measures to reduce the potential for employees to claim they were by harassed or offended by coworkers' misuse of the I-Way.

♦ Although there may be some concern on behalf of legitimate users that filtering or blocking tools may impact their legitimate access to relevant business information, in practice the systems work reasonably well and can be adapted to the specific needs of the various businesses or government agencies. For example, consider an employee at a pharmaceutical organization whose product lines or duties may require access to topics such as sexually transmitted diseases. In the case of a site with such materials, there is a good chance the access will be denied by the blocking program. Establishing a "waiver" system whereby legitimate sites that are inappropriately blocked may be opened for access, perhaps using an e-mail–based request to the firewall operations team, allows legitimate access to such sites. Such flexibility should address any problems of overly restrictive filtering.

Web blocking/filtering utilities and many firewalls offer convenient categories of activity reporting. For example, if activity reporting shows that 20 percent or more of Web accesses are to sports sites, management may elect to eliminate such access or to limit availability through the organization's network to hours before and after normal working time. This has the dual benefit of limiting employee's ability to unproductively surf the Net and also helps reduce the waste of the organization's network bandwidth on nonessential services. Conversely, if activity reporting demonstrates significant business use of an external information or service provider, it may provide justification for purchase of an on-site mirror of the information of that resource.

Firewalls

In the world of I-Way commerce the term *firewall* is tossed around as if everyone understands both the technology and its capabilities. Additionally, security departments may find that information technology groups with a smug comment that "we already have a firewall" often dismiss security and protection concerns. The attitude seems to be that as long as there is a firewall nothing can happen! But what is a firewall, why would an organization need one, and what can it do?

A firewall is a specialized computer system designed to protect the I-Way connections of a business or government agency. A firewall system could be compared to a fortified bunker with a robot guard stationed at the virtual perimeter to an organization. This security checkpoint has the job of verifying the authorization of specific persons to enter or depart a facility by checking credentials, and of verifying that bulk transmissions, both inbound and outbound, are properly documented as to the contents and destination.

Like a guard, a firewall has a set of operating instructions that describe what is permitted and under what circumstances. However, like a robot, it is only as good as the programming it receives in making decisions. Although well fortified against a wide range of known threats, the firewall is a fixed point that could potentially be circumvented by savvy intruders who find alternate paths around or through the checkpoint.

In simple terms, a firewall consists of a combination of sophisticated software and dedicated hardware (typically a large UNIX server or a high-end Windows-NT system) connected in a way so as to force all network traffic through the single checkpoint. At this checkpoint, user IDs and requested services are compared to a list of approved users and services and access is denied if not permitted. In very large organizations there may be multiple firewalls operated in support of a specific location or organizational element.

The firewall filters communications based on the user, the protocol, and potentially the address of the user. Its basic purpose is to enforce organizational security policies. It is also a source of audit trails, tracking the activities of individual users, typically by network address.

The firewall may also restrict user I-Way activity or even prevent access altogether, provide a record of Web accesses, and other significant transmissions to or from the site. Many organizations have implemented what is described as Virtual Private Networks (VPNs). VPNs use firewalls at organization locations connected to the I-Way and create an *encrypted tunnel* to provide point-to-point secure communications. Organizations gain the benefit of reduced communications costs because they can use the I-Way to replace expensive dedicated lines between locations.

Firewalls can authenticate identity of individual users' IDs and passwords before they enter or depart the organization's network. They may also check e-mail message attachments to verify that they are free of viruses and addressed to an authorized destination. They also commonly determine whether the specific access point into the organizational network (port) and requested services are available.

Since every primary firewall is by definition connected to the global I-Way, they are prospective targets for every I-Way robber who has the requisite knowledge/skills and motive to attempt a penetration. Therefore, firewalls deserve careful attention to include all of the following:

♦ Planning: Apply a formal risk management process when making decisions involving the installation and configuration of the firewall to balance the business needs against the security risks. Just because a few power users request the latest, coolest application does not mean the firewall should have ports opened without serious consideration of the increased vulnerability this creates. In a sense, opening a port is like removing a brick in the wall. If too many bricks are removed, the security provided by the wall will be compromised.

♦ Superior Maintenance: Any upgrades or patches affecting either the firewall product itself or the underlying operating system must be installed as soon as possible, preferably within 24 hours or less. This is especially important when the patches are recommended in a security advisory from a Computer Emergency Response Team (CERT) or other reputable sources, such as the firewall vendor. It is critical to understand that when a security advisory is published or distributed by a CERT, the vulnerability that is identified may have been in use for days, weeks, months, or perhaps even years by the I-Way robbers! The advisory itself will also likely trigger increased exploitation of the vulnerability as members of the underground who had not previously been aware of the specific exploit now add it to their bag of tricks.

♦ Firewall Vendor Communication: Stay in close communication with the firewall vendor. Request that the vendor provide current information concerning threats and vulnerabilities affecting the I-Way, firewalls, and specific information affecting the security of your I-Way on-ramp.

♦ Security and law enforcement professionals must understand that firewalls are like castle walls; they can be penetrated or neutralized through effective application of appropriate attack tools and techniques. Firewalls are not a panacea, they can be and frequently are penetrated by sophisticated intruders, especially when they have not been properly maintained or when too many ports have been opened and not resealed. The firewall security paradigm also assumes there is a well-defined organizational perimeter to be defended. However, it is often no longer clear where one organization begins and another ends. We are observing the evolution of *extranets*, in which vendors and suppliers of organizations are joined electronically through use of I-Way technologies. Given this increased level of complexity, new security models are required and it is not clear whether the firewall paradigm alone can effectively accommodate these changes. New technologies like JAVA and ActiveX also carry with them the potential (through rogue applets) to circumvent or neutralize firewall-based protection measures. The upshot of all this is very clear: do not trust the firewall by itself to provide absolute security for your I-Way connection. Another way to say it is that a firewall is essential, but not sufficient by itself to fully protect a business's or government agency's on- and off-ramp. A well-designed and implemented firewall must be complemented by other protective measures.

Computer Forensics

Since the crimes associated with the I-Way will, by definition, include digital environments, every organization needs the capability to gather relevant evidence and intelligence from computers and other systems. Some of this information is available through the audit trails in the firewall and other key systems. However, if there is an insider involved, the best evidence of the crime may well be hidden on the suspect's individual microcomputer. In most cases finding this evidence and preserving its evidentiary value will require the use of very specialized utility programs, techniques, and trained people. Working together, these resources search systems for relevant information and evidence of information crimes. Computer forensics is a very significant resource and can play a substantial role in the prosecution of the criminals, since most of them have no idea how many places may contain fragments of files proving their malfeasance.

Intrusion Detection Software

The servers that contain the most valuable information and assets of the organization should have special utility software installed that can detect unauthorized activity. Pattern recognition and other tools exist for Unix and NT operating systems. Although no product at present offers complete assurance that it can detect every attack against critical systems, they are becoming quite useful. As part of a comprehensive protection program, they offer the digital equivalent of a surveillance camera which can monitor specific systems or environments and alert systems security staff when suspicious or dangerous circumstances arise. These tools are expected to improve substantially in the near term and as the functionality improves they will become more useful.

Compartmentalize Internal Networks

If organizational networks are designed and built with only ease of access and sustained connectivity in mind they will not be secure. This is a serious oversight, as information remains an asset that can be lost, yet remain visibly within the control of the owner, for the I-Way robber may take only a digital duplicate. In many businesses and government agencies the internal I-Way is poorly patrolled and the only protection is focused against outsiders. The apparent assumption is that criminals exist only outside the virtual perimeter of the business or government agency, an assumption that can be a costly error. Once past the "robot guard" of the firewall and inside, I-Way robbers are often relatively free to roam the cyber corridors of the enterprise, "shaking doorknobs" seeking systems and databases protected by trivial passwords or other inviting targets.

Businesses and government agencies should adopt a strategy of defense in depth and implement multiple layers of protection to avoid a situation that has been described as the "hard shell and a soft chewy center." Multiple layers of protection are even more important if there is an extranet linking organizations. The participants in an extranet should take steps to ensure that business partners and other participants establish and maintain a reasonable degree of security and control over their own areas before linking to them.

A good way to protect the organization's internal I-Way is to use functionality available in the routers to create internal compartments. Enhanced network security may be achieved with the use of access control features of routers to deny access to one or more internal compartments. Alternatively, some firewall products are optimized for the role of internal network protection. These measures may delay and confuse I-Way robbers and increase the possibility they will be detected and neutralized before they can succeed in their plan.

Enhanced Authentication

Every business and government agency connected to the I-Way should consider implementing an enhanced authentication technology. Such enhanced technologies may include physical tokens (smart cards), software-based tokens, digital certificates, or biometrics. Each of these technologies has advantages and disadvantages and there is no one best solution that works well for every organization. The most important benefit of enhanced authentication is that it can defeat sniffers on network segments since the password and user ID combination is typically good for only a single session. They may also provide an extension to the fixed passwords used in most databases and other applications. The important benefit of enhanced authentication technologies is that they prevent an I-Way robber from using a stolen password and user ID to masquerade as an individual and to misuse access privileges.

In the near term, tokens and smart cards are likely to be used for enhanced authentication since they are already widely implemented. However, over time the convenience of biometrics may well win out if vendors can reduce the price for systems to levels equivalent to alternatives. After all, it is impossible to forget to bring your thumbprint to work.

Utilize Application and Database Security Features

Every major database provides access controls and audit logs to manage the activities of users. However, features and capability are of no use if systems administrators are not required to use them. Businesses and government agencies should ensure that every system environment that is connected to the internal I-Way and that contains significant information employs the available features to manage access and activity. For systems that contain the "crown jewels," the organization may benefit from both enhanced authentication as well as encryption.

Communication

All sensitive, private, and proprietary information must be encrypted when traveling the I-Way. This means individual e-mail messages, as well as all attachments that contain such information, must be protected using encryption when they transit the I-Way.

Organizations that have not yet deployed cryptography to protect sensitive information and critical systems will need to do so in the near term. Virtual Private Networks, which use encryption to tunnel through the unsecured I-Way, are a harbinger of things to come. Expect widespread adoption of robust encryption systems in commercial organizations to be a key feature of the early 21st century. The design and deployment of a public key infrastructure to provide a management framework are essential to achieve both enhanced protection and effective use of cryptography. Single user editions of products like PGP (pretty good privacy), although robust enough for personal protection, do not provide the integration of tools and recovery utilities that is essential in a large organization.

The primary reason that cryptography will be essential is that it provides the greatest degree of protection. Unlike file and system access controls that may be bypassed through exploitation of operating system bugs, well-designed cryptographic security protects at the file level and may require incredible computer power to defeat.

Testing and Evaluation
The I-Way on- and off-ramps, firewalls, and Web security should be continuously tested to ensure that they work as expected and required. I-Ways by their nature tend to be dynamic; thus what is perfectly functional one day may be completely ineffective the next due to changes introduced to accommodate some new function or capability demanded by the business.

Continuous testing of firewalls using the latest vulnerability testing tools and other methods and techniques found on hacker and information security sites is vital. The continuous testing is essential to ensure that the firewall is working as expected and required. The importance of regular systematic and realistic testing cannot be overemphasized. The I-Way is constantly changing and evolving and it is essential to ensure that the protection remains effective in spite of the development of new methods of attack.

I-Way Risk Management
There should be a process in place to conduct formal risk assessment any time that the system on- and off-ramps, firewalls, hardware, software, or anything else significant is changed. The risk management process should ensure that new vulnerabilities are not introduced. The process should also ensure that significant risks are known and that an informed decision is made to balance risk and business benefits.

SUMMARY

Basic I-Way protection must be an integral part of the overall information security program of the business or government agency. I-Way protection should address the following areas: Administration, Physical Security, Operations, Communication Security, Test and Evaluation, Risk Management.

Special attention must be paid to the I-Way on- and off-ramps and their protection through firewalls. Protecting Web sites both inside and outside the firewall is also vital. To ensure the continuous protection of I-Way travelers there should be constant testing and evaluation of protection mechanisms. There should be a balance between the benefits to the business or government agency through I-Way enabled processes and the potential risks involved in using the I-Way.

NOTES

1. See *Information Systems Security Officer's Guide*, Boston: Butterworth-Heinemann, 1998.
2. Newsbytes, Oct. 3, 1997.
3. The actual words used should be coordinated with the company's legal staff to ensure it is worded in such a manner as to be enforceable vis-à-vis any potential disciplinary action for violations. It may also help mitigate potential lawsuits.

11

Driving the I-Way into the 21st Century

CHAPTER OBJECTIVE

Now that we have looked at the past and the present, let's look at the possible future and the environment where computer and technology crimes and frauds of the future will breed along the I-Way, as well as their challenges to security and law enforcement professionals.

GLOBAL CHANGES

The global changes brought on by the I-Way will continue to impact, in both a positive and negative manner, the interactions of nations, as well as their very existence. The rapid changes brought on, in part, by the I-Way will cause increased communications on a global scale. Nations will be torn apart with ever-increasing chaos and rapid disintegration into factions who will use the I-Way to communicate their grievances, desires, and try to build a world consensus in their favor to force governments to allow more freedom to these factions, as well as dissolving portions of these nations into smaller nations. The nations will use the I-Way to justify their controls and government policies. The breakup of the Soviet Union and the old Yugoslavia are just two examples of what other nations may have to look forward to in the 21st century, e.g., Indonesia.

The "economic domino" effect that has taken place throughout the world validates the interlinking and interdependencies of nations. With the expansion of I-Way commerce, these dependencies will play a more crucial role in the global order. Economic espionage will continue to grow in support of a nation's objective of becoming an economic power.

Asia's economic woes will lessen and the Asian nations will gain renewed strength as the dominant economic region of the world, led by China. The financial and intellectual resources of Singapore (Chinese), the intellectual resources and technology of Taiwan (Chinese), integrated with the cheap labor, natural resources of China, including the financial power of Hong Kong, will ensure the domination of China as a global economic power above and beyond national borders.

Ethnic violence will continue to grow on a global basis due to religion and race. For example, in Indonesia the Chinese make up only about four percent of the population but control more than 70 percent of the wealth. Thus, the Chinese in Indonesia became a scapegoat for the Indonesian economic woes. Factions, ethnic groups, and religious groups will increase their presence on the I-Way and sub-I-Ways. Some of these I-Ways will be closed, encrypted links to be used only by those within the selected group.

This can also be easily seen by looking at the nation of Yugoslavia before and after its disintegration into warring factions based partly on religion. Such chaos is expected to continue, if not grow. The impact on the duties and responsibilities of the security and law enforcement professionals is obvious. There will be more need of their services for higher priorities than I-Way robberies, thus increasing the opportunities for I-Way robberies.

Governments will continue to use the Industrial Age legislative processes in vain attempts to control those portions of the I-Way that impact their nations. They will continue to fail, albeit some small successes may occur here and there. As commerce along the I-Way increases, governments will not be able to avoid the temptation of taxing the I-Way commerce, as well as passing other legislation to control the I-Way. However, this will lead to serious disagreements among nations. Some nations will integrate the I-Way environment into the normal course of commerce throughout their nation while others will treat it as a unique environment and make new laws that are specific to the I-Way. Regardless, the laws will be used to support the individual nations in their quest for global and economic power—or at least equality with the more advanced nations of the world.

The issue of privacy (or the lack thereof) will continue to be discussed on one hand while government intelligence and security agencies heighten their I-Way monitoring activities. Unfortunately, privacy issues will continue to run contrary to the needs of businesses and government agencies, thus they will be given no more than lip service so that businesses can grow uninhibited by personal privacy of the individual I-Way travelers and governments can maintain their power and control. This will be supported by nations who see such I-Way commerce as the basis for strengthening their global economic power.

Encryption will continue to become more sophisticated while the issue of key management overhead costs and prohibitions of exporting of effective encryption methods will continue to be debated on a global scale. Nations' security agencies will require and continue to obtain access to encrypted communications via key escrow and back doors, but on a massive scale. There will be attempts to outlaw all encryption that does not meet a nation's standards. Nations without sophisticated technology will require that technology in order to allow I-Way communications to transit their nation. Others will prohibit any encryption under the banner of "national security interests." Their concern, and excuse, will be the use of encryption by factions whose purpose is to bring down the current government.

These vulnerabilities will be exploited by other nations and I-Way robbers who will become more sophisticated in decrypting communications due to more and more sophisticated computers and massive chaining of computers to break encrypted messages.

Copyright violations on the I-Way will continue unabated with more and more information being made available on a massive scale. Thus, the "software police" and others will be so overwhelmed that they will only attempt to investigate and prosecute those cases that provide good public relations for the agency and are violations on a massive scale. These issues will continue to be a concern of only a few of the most mature Information Age nations such as the United States and the United Kingdom. Other nations, including the rest of the European Union, East European nations, and those in Asia, South America, and Africa, will provide only token assistance. This will be done in order to rapidly and as cheaply as possible bring their nations into the Information Age through the use of "free" copyrighted information.

Political factions with common causes (e.g., Save the Whales) will become more active in denying the use of the I-Way and Web sites of those businesses or government agencies whose actions are contrary to those of the factions.

Information warfare will play an increased role in 21st-century warfare. Civilized nations today have little tolerance for violence, human death, and suffering. The use of computers and networks to fight the information wars

of the future will become more common as they offer cheap, rapid, and powerful weapons of mass destruction. Electronic and computer weapons to
destroy an adversary's information infrastructure, and thus their economic
power, will take on more importance. The use of the I-Way by military forces
and techno-terrorists will continue to increase as a nation's adversaries
become more dependent on information systems and the I-Way for their
political and economic power.

The roles of the military, security, and law enforcement professionals
will become more important than ever before. They will be used extensive-
ly to support the governments in power to maintain that power. The military
soldiers will become more technologically sophisticated and the revolution
in military affairs will continue to increase the military's dependence on technology, thus also making it more vulnerable to its nation's adversaries who
exploit information warfare.

SOCIAL CHANGES

The people of all the nations who have I-Way on- and off-ramps will become
more sophisticated in the use of the I-Way. They will have ever-increasing
amounts of information at their disposal, allowing them to become more
knowledgeable on global matters. They also will become more aware of those
throughout the world who have similar and different views. The I-Way as a
massive, personal communications pipeline will provide the means for people to communicate globally as never before. Such massive one-on-one communications will be the driving force that will affect governments,
businesses, and societies to such an extent that the governments and businesses will develop extremely sophisticated techniques to influence these
I-Way communicators on a global scale.

The I-Way will also become one of the primary education vehicles,
replacing many of today's Industrial Age school systems. Already, colleges
and universities are offering courses and degrees through I-Way access. This
will allow individuals to obtain degrees from universities and colleges located in different nations of the world. The I-Way as a global learning center will
not come without challenges from those in the educational systems and their
unions who see such endeavors as a threat to their power and their bureau-
cracies. However, their delaying tactics will be just that, delaying the
inevitable. Security and law enforcement professionals will be able to enroll
in courses and learn from the best in their profession no matter where that

professor may reside. Security and law enforcement professionals will be able to obtain degrees from the best criminal justice and criminology institutes of the world. Furthermore, they will be able to take these courses based on their schedule. "Papers" will be transmitted via e-mail, and tests will be conducted through secure channels where the students' identification will be confirmed. Specialized technology-related institutes will take on a more legitimate role as educational institutions and dominate the educational institutions of today.

TECHNOLOGICAL ADVANCEMENTS

It is obvious that the technological trends to make microprocessors—and everything that they are used in—smaller, more powerful, and cheaper, will continue. This, coupled with the ever-increasing bandwidth, multimedia, and personal communications systems, will provide for a micro-portability previously only dreamed of and shown in science fiction movies. The need to have such devices in order to work, shop, and access information will require that everyone be guaranteed such a system as an inherent right as a citizen of an Information Age nation. Without such devices, the government will be depriving the citizens of everything from due process to the right to work. The I-Way, which still seems a novelty in so many ways, will be in truth one of the mainstream methods of working and communicating.

The development of more sophisticated systems able to understand and react to normal human speech will become commonplace. This technology will be a major breakthrough that will allow previously computer illiterate individuals to use the power of computers, networks, and the I-Way to work, play, and communicate. This will allow poor and uneducated people who could otherwise neither afford a computer, nor learn how to use one, to become better educated and valuable members of societies with less effort.

Enhanced technology will continue to support the drive to global telemedicine where the best specialists in the world will be in a position to medically assist anyone, anywhere, at any time. However, with this enhanced use of the I-Way will come tele-medicine murders. These will be accomplished by changing medical test results, the automated dosages of prescription drugs, changing blood types in the patient's database, and denying tele-medicine services. At some point in the not too distant future, security and law enforcement specialists will be involved in conducting murder investigations where the crime scene will be the I-Way itself.

The future will also bring us biological computers. It is rumored that some are looking at using electrically charged amoebas or other methods that can allow a direct interface with the human brain! Such incredibly advanced computers could perhaps store the entire history of the human race on a single chip. Who will determine what is contained in that history? What are the social ramifications of such dramatic extensions to personal information access? What happens if a criminal or a terrorist embeds a virus, logic bomb, or other malicious software in a computer extension attached to your brain? Some security and law enforcement professionals may require a degree in a field of medicine in order to successfully perform their duties vis-à-vis telemedicine security and criminal investigations.

The wireless age is already upon us and with it the increased use of technology allowing mobile electronic communications from any place on earth to anywhere else. As the growth of networks continues worldwide, it will bring with it more threats from sophisticated international criminals. Such threats will include an increased use of jamming techniques as a denial of service, to commit electronic extortion, or to adversely impact a competitor's ability to perform electronic commerce on the I-Way. As more forms of public communication come to rely on the I-Way, we expect more sophisticated eavesdropping techniques will arise, which will allow I-Way robbers, businesses, and government agencies to invade personal privacy to their respective ends. The increasing use of the many I-Way telephone and video teleconference systems, which are vulnerable to eavesdropping, will make this more common.

INCREASE IN I-WAY ROBBERIES DUE TO INCREASED I-WAY COMMERCE

I-Way crime will rise dramatically as electronic commerce (electronic business) increases over the years. The following estimates[1] are provided so that the reader understands that with this much money in the system, it is too good a target to ignore (1997 compared to 2001):

- Financial services: $1.2 billion to an estimated$5 billion
- Apparel and footwear: $92 million to an estimated $514 million
- PC hardware and software: $863 million to an estimated $3 billion
- Event ticket sales: $79 million to an estimated $2 billion
- Entertainment: $298 to an estimated $2.7 billion

♦ Travel: $654 million to an estimated $7.4 billion
♦ Books and music: $156 million to an estimated $1.1 billion
♦ Business-to-business sales: $8 billion to an estimated $183 billion

Electronic commerce is already on the I-Way and the I-Way is too large for the I-Way robbers to ignore. Billions of dollars through millions of transactions will be conducted each year. To have electronic commerce, one must have sellers, customers, and infrastructure to transfer goods, services, and money securely. Security will continue to be enhanced, thus providing reasonable, cheap, simple transaction security. This will happen exponentially and cause a rapid expansion of the I-Way for electronic business.

In the future, money will not be physical, but logical. It will consist of electronic combinations of "0's" and "1's." In the United States, Wells Fargo Bank in conjunction with a company called CyberCash Inc., in Reston, Virginia, is beginning a pilot project to provide merchants with secure credit card and debit card transactions. This and other pilot projects under way are expected to ultimately lead to a global system of electronic cash, sometimes referred to as *e-cash*. The evolution of electronic cash systems may facilitate new forms of money laundering and completely untraceable payments to I-Way robbers and terrorists for their services.

I-Way robbers have already become more sophisticated as computers have become more sophisticated. Threats to these valuable business and public assets are increasing while the public demands more time spent pursuing violent crimes, allowing less time to be spent pursuing these crimes.

The enactment of international laws will lag behind the technology and the I-Way robberies making it extremely difficult to identify, apprehend, and prosecute I-Way robbers across national boundaries. Some successes will of course occur, as in the international fight against child pornography. However, the more sophisticated, financially based I-Way robberies will grow in number due to the lack of the capabilities of security professionals to protect against them and the lack of capabilities of the law enforcement professionals to investigate and apprehend them.

SECURITY AND LAW ENFORCEMENT

Law enforcement's response to the rapid evolution of the I-Way robbers has been relatively slow. In large part this is because of the prevalence of other, some say more serious, crimes in such nations as the United States. So, the public's priority has been to use the limited, budgeted resources for fighting gangs, drugs, and violent crimes. Computer and high-technology crimes and frauds are considered victimless on many occasions, and thus receive a low priority. This priority order will continue for the foreseeable future.

Law enforcement efforts to forge an effective response to the proliferation of I-Way crimes will continue to be thwarted by the international criminals, international law inadequacies, lack of jurisdiction, lack of budget, and lack of skills. Use of highly skilled private consultants by law enforcement agencies is likely to increase as they will find it very difficult to recruit, train, equip, and especially to retain such staff in their organizations. One can see this happening now when even the FBI is working with hackers to catch hackers. The knowledge and skills required to be effective in patrolling the I-Way are in great demand in the private sector and can be expected to result in experienced investigative staff abandoning public sector wages and working environments for the more lucrative opportunities in private industry.

Perhaps there also will be the evolution of authorized "bounty hunters" chartered by appropriate law enforcement agencies or perhaps even international agencies to pursue, apprehend, or "neutralize" in some other fashion the activities of the more capable I-Way robbers. The relentless pursuit of the James gang by the Pinkerton detectives in the 1880s may play itself out in a modern evolution along the I-Way.

Businesses will continue to expand their use of outside consultants to meet their technology security and investigative needs. In the realm of large, multinational corporate enterprises, the cost of employing sophisticated private patrol services to ensure the businesses' I-Way on- and off-ramps are protected will be seen as merely a cost of doing business in the Information Age. However, small and medium-size organizations will be significantly challenged to provide adequate security for their I-Way connected systems, but a failure to do so may well subject them to ruinous losses. One wonders if there will be anyone who will be affordable and available to protect small businesses.

What appears to be developing is a situation where national law enforcement agencies will be capable of confronting the I-Way robbers on a selective basis involving high dollar incidents, but the local police may well find themselves lacking jurisdiction and resources to contribute much to the prevention or investigation of I-Way crimes, other than the local, teenage hacker. On the other side, the I-Way robbers stand to benefit from a vast increase in lucrative targets as more organizations exploit the I-Way for commercial purposes. The criminals will continue to benefit from new and more sophisticated tools and technologies for compromising the valuable assets of those targets. Lastly, the I-Way robbers will be able to select their physical base of operations from any I-Way connected location on earth, and shift it as necessary to take advantage of lax domestic laws proscribing their activities or to maximize the benefits of a cozy relationship with a corrupt local regime.

SUMMARY

The I-Way of the 21st century will continue its rapid growth and expansion on a global scale. It will play a major role in changing nations, societies, business, and technology, as well as the role of security and law enforcement professionals. By looking at current trends, one can see many indications of the changes yet to come. At the same time, security and law enforcement professionals can be sure of one thing: They and their professions must also rapidly change, or they will cease to have employment in their chosen profession. Furthermore, their profession will require more technical skills than ever before.

FINAL COMMENTS

In the beginning of this book the authors dedicated this book in part to "all the hackers, phreakers, crackers, nuts, weirdos, and associated other human beings who surf, spam, use, misuse, and abuse the I-way. Because of their crazy personalities, criminal conduct, and all-around blatant disregard for rules, laws, and government controls, they have made all our lives more interesting, our work more challenging, and our economy growing."

As George Washington said: "Government is not reason; it is not eloquence. It is force. And force, like fire, is a dangerous servant and a fearful master." Maybe a little craziness isn't so bad if it helps keep the force confined.

Isn't it ironic that those "crazies" out there on the I-Way want no government controls? They want freedom of information, freedom to speak, say, and do as they please on the I-Way. They fight the governments and others trying to control the I-Ways, while at the same time they are the very people who are adding fuel to the "fire" of government control. These are the same people who give all governments and others the excuse for placing more controls, more legislation, more rules, and more monitoring, which adversely impacts what these people allegedly stand for. They may be the cause of their own undoing—and maybe the undoing of the rest of us also.

NOTES

1. "Our Annual Report on Information Technology, Doing Business in the Internet age," *BusinessWeek*, June 22, 1998.

Appendix A
ISI Swiss Army Knife Reference: Sources of Information and Security/Audit Tools

(Reprinted with permission by Ken Cutler of MIS Training Institute.)

SECURITY ARCHITECTURE, STANDARDS, AND REQUIREMENTS

1. Canadian Trusted Computer Product Evaluation Criteria (CTCPEC); Canadian Security Establishment; April 1992
2. Commercial International Security Requirements (CISR); I-4/Ken Cutler, Fred Jones; April 1992; contact MIS Training Institute; 508-879-7999
3. The Common Criteria for Information Technology Security (CC) - Version 1.0; http://www.itsec.gov.uk/, http://csrc.ncsl.nist.gov/; January 31, 1996
4. A Code of Practice for Information Security Management; British Standards Institution; 389 Cheswick High Rd., London W4 4AL United Kingdom; September 1993; 44-181-996-9000
5. Developing a Security Architecture; Handbook of Information Security Management-1994-95 Yearbook; Ken Cutler; Warren, Gorham, & Lamont (Auerbach); 1995
6. IBM Security Architecture - Securing the Open Client/Server Distributed Enterprise; IBM; SC28-8135-01; 1995

7. Information Technology Security Evaluation Criteria (ITSEC) V1.2; CEC, Directorate XIII/F, SOG-IS Secretariat, TR61 02/28 Rue de la Loi, 200, B-1049 Brussels; June 1991
8. Minimum Security Functionality Requirements for Multi-User Operating Systems - Issue 1 (Draft); National Institute of Standards and Technology; January 1992 (also available in machine readable form on NIST Security Clearinghouse)
9. NIST Computer Security Publications; Government Printing Office; (202-783-3238/Voice) - also see NIST Security Clearinghouse (http://csrc.ncsl.nist.gov); for a list of NIST security publications, look for NIST Publication List 91
10. Security in Open Systems; NIST Special Publication 800-7; 1994 (see NIST BBS)
11. Trusted Computer System Evaluation Criteria (TCSEC - "Orange Book" & Others); National Computer Security Center (NCSC); (301-766-8729/Voice) - also see NIST Security Clearinghouse

GENERAL SECURITY/AUDIT REFERENCE AND PRODUCT SELECTION

1. Computer Security Basics; Deborah Russell, G.T. Gangemi, Sr.; O'Reilly & Associates; 1991
2. Computer Security for Dummies; Peter Davis & Barry Lewis; IDG; 1996
3. Computer Security Handbook; Richard H. Baker; McGraw-Hill; 1991
4. Computers at Risk - Safe Computing in the Information Age; National Research Council, National Academy Press, 1991; (To Order by Phone: 800-624-6242)
5. Computer Security Reference Book; K.M. Jackson, J. Hruska, D.B. Parker; Butterworth-Heinemann; 1992
6. COBIT: Control Objectives for Information and Related Technology; Information Systems Audit & Control Foundation; 1996; 847-253-1545
7. Datapro Reports on Information Security; 800-328-2776
8. Data Security Management; Warren, Gorham, & Lamont (Auerbach)
9. Designing Controls into Computerized Systems; Jerry Fitzgerald; (Jerry Fitzgerald Associates 415-591-5676); also available through ISACA
10. EDPACS; Warren, Gorham, & Lamont (Auerbach)
11. EDP Auditing; Warren, Gorham, & Lamont (Auerbach)

12. Handbook of EDP Auditing; Warren, Gorham, & Lamont; 1985 (and annual supplements)
13. Handbook of Information Security Management; Warren, Gorham, & Lamont (Auerbach); 1993 and later supplements
14. Information Security Magazine; ICSA Publications
15. Information Systems Security Officer's Guide; Dr. Gerald Kovacich; Butterworth-Heinemann; 1998
16. International Information Integrity Institute (I-4); SRI International
17. Secure Computing Magazine (formerly Infosecurity News); West Coast Publishing

PBX SECURITY AND TOLL FRAUD

1. PBX Security; David Crowell; The EDP Auditor Journal; Volume II, 1993
2. Private Branch Exchange (PBX) Security Guideline; NIST Computer Systems Laboratory; NIST/GCR-93-635; September 7, 1993
3. Protecting Your Telephone Systems; Steve Purdy; Infosecurity News; July/August 1993
4. Taking a Hard Look at Toll Fraud Protection Services; Network World; June 8, 1992
5. Voice-Mail Security; Marc Robbins; Infosecurity News; July/August 1993

LAN/PC SECURITY AND MANAGEMENT

General

1. Dvorak's Guide to PC Telecommunications; John Dvorak; Osborne McGraw-Hill; 1994 (info on telecommunication and shareware)
2. Handbook of Networking & Connectivity; Gary R. McClain; AP Professional; 1994
3. LAN Times Buyers Directory; Steve Elder, Editor; 801-342-6812
4. McGraw-Hill LAN Communications Handbook; Fred Simonds; McGraw-Hill; 1994
5. Network Security: Data and Voice Communications; Fred Simonds; McGraw-Hill; 1996

6. Network Security Secrets; David Stang & Sylvia Moon; IDG Books Worldwide, Inc.; 1993 (includes software)
7. Norman Data Defense Systems Virus Reports; David Stang; 703-573-8802 (US); 47-32-81-34-90 (Europe)
8. Password Pluckers for Sale; Robert Kane; Infosecurity News; May/June 1993
9. Seeking Security (several articles); Byte Magazine; May 1993
10. Software Publishers Association; http://www.spa.org
11. Using Networks; Frank Derfler; QUE; 1998
12. Virus Bulletin; Virus Bulletin Ltd; 21 The Quadrant, Abingdon, Oxfordshire, OX14 3YS, England; 44-01235-555139

Banyan Vines

1. Banyan Vines; The Professional Reference; Jim Krochmal; New Riders Publishing; 1994

Novell Netware

1. Building and Auditing a Trusted Network Environment with NetWare 4; Novell Application Notes - Vol. 5, Number 4; Novell, Inc.; April 1994
2. Documenting Your Network (NetWare); Steve Kalman; Network Administrator; Nov/Dec 1994
3. Internetworking with NetWare TCP/IP; Karanjit Siyan, et al.; New Riders Publishing; 1996
4. LAN Desktop Guide to Security; Ed Sawicki; SAMS; 1992
5. Managing NDS with NWADMIN; Linda Boyer; NetWare Connection; October, 1996
6. NetWare 4.11 and IntraNetWare; Sandy Stevens; NetWare Connection; October, 1996
7. NetWare Connection Magazine; http://www.NetWare.com/nwc/
8. NetWare LAN Analysis; Laura Chappell; Novell Press/SYBEX; 1993
9. NetWare Security: Configuring and Auditing a Trusted Environment; J. Lamb, S. Jarocki, A. Seijas; Novell, Inc.; 1991
10. NetWare Training Guide: NetWare 4 Administration; Karanjit Siyan; New Riders Publishing; 1994
11. NetWare Training Guide: Managing NetWare Systems, Third Edition (NetWare 3.1x); Debra Niedermiller-Chaffins, Dorothy Cady, & Drew Haywood; New Riders Publishing; 1994

12. Networking with NetWare for Dummies, Fourth Edition; E. Tittel, E. Follis, & J. Gaskin; IDG; 1998
13. Novell's Guide to Integrating NetWare and TCP/IP; Drew Heywood; Novell Press/IDG; 1996
14. Novell's Guide to Integrating UNIX and NetWare Networks; Novell Press/Sybex; 1994
15. Novell's Guide to NetWare 3.12 Networks; Cheryl Currid and Company; Novell Press; 1993
16. Novell's Guide to NetWare 4.0 Networks; Cheryl Currid, Stephen Saxon; Novell Press; 1993
17. Novell's IntraNetWare Administrator's Handbook; Kelley J.P. Lindberg; Novell Press; 1996
18. Using NetWare 4.1; Bill Lawrence, et al.; Que Corporation; 1995

OS/2 LAN Server

1. Connecting with LAN Server 4.0; Barry Nance; Ziff-Davis Press; 1995

Windows NT/Windows 95

1. The Accidental Hacker; Andrey Kruchkov; Windows NT Magazine; February, 1998
2. Essential Windows NT System Administration; Aeleen Frisch; O'Reilly & Associates; 1998
3. Internet Security with Windows NT; Mark Joseph Edwards; Duke Press; 1997
4. "Is NT Secure ?" (entire issue); Windows NT Magazine; October, 1996
5. Microsoft Windows NT 3.5: Guidelines for Security, Audit, & Control; Citibank, NA., Coopers & Lybrand, & Microsoft Corp.; Microsoft Press; 1994
6. Networking Windows NT 3.51; John D. Ruley; Wiley; 1995
7. NT Network Security; Matthew Strebe, Charles Perkins, Michael G. Moncur; Sybex; 1998
8. Platinum Edition - Using Windows 95; Ron Person, et al.; QUE; 1996
9. Securing Windows NT; Robert Hansel; Infosecurity News; September/October 1995
10. Stop Thief; Mark Joseph Edwards; Windows NT Magazine; February, 1998
11. Windows 95 Communications Handbook; Jim Boyce, et al.; QUE; 1996

12. Windows Annoyances; David A. Karp; O'Reilly & Associates; 1997
13. Windows Magazine; www.winmag.com
14. Windows NT in A Nutshell; Eric Pearce; O'Reilly & Associates; 1997
15. Windows NT Magazine; 970-663-4700
16. Windows NT 4.0 Installation & Configuration Handbook; Jim Boyce, et al.; QUE; 1996
17. Windows NT Server Resource Kit - Version 4.0; Microsoft Press; 1996
18. Windows NT Server Resource Kit - Version 4.0, Supplement 1; Microsoft Press; 1997
19. Windows NT Server Resource Kit - Version 4.0, Supplement 2; Microsoft Press; 1997
20. Windows NT Security; Charles Rutstein (NCSA); McGraw-Hill; 1997
21. Windows NT Security Guide; Stephen A. Sutton; Addison-Wesley; 1997
22. Windows NT Security Handbook; Tom Sheldon; Osborne; 1997
23. Windows NT Security: Step by Step; The SANS Institute; 1998 (ntsec@sans.org)
24. Windows NT 4 Server Unleashed; Jason Garms, et al.; Sams Publishing; 1996

UNIX-Windows NT Integration

1. SAMBA - Integrating Unix and Windows; John Blair; SSC; 1998 (includes CD-ROM)
2. Windows NT and Unix Integration; Gene Henriksen; Macmillan Technical Publications; 1998

UNIX-TCP/IP SECURITY AND ADMINISTRATION

AIX

1. AIX RS/6000 System and Administration Guide; James DeRoest; McGraw-Hill; 1995
2. AIX Survival Guide; Andreas Siegert; Addison-Wesley; 1996
3. Audit, Control, and Security Features of the AIX Operating System; Ernst & Young; 1995
4. Elements of AIX Security: R3.1; IBM; GG24-3622-01; 1991
5. Elements of Security: AIX 4.1; IBM; GG24-4433-00; 1994
6. SunExpert Magazine (RS/Magazine Supplement); Computer Publishing Group; 617-641-9101

HP-UX

1. HP-UX: System and Administration Guide; Jay Shah; McGraw-Hill; 1997
2. HP-UX System Security; Hewlett-Packard; Part # B2355-90045; 1992
3. Can You Trust HP-UX?; Ben Klein; Sys Admin Magazine; June 1997

Linux

1. Linux Configuration and Installation, Third Edition; Patrick Volkerding, Kevin Reichard, Eric F. Johnson; MIS:Press; 1997 (includes CD-ROM with LINUX software)
2. Linux: The Complete Reference; Richard Petersen; Osborne McGraw-Hill; 1996 (includes CD-ROM with LINUX, Caldera Lite, Web server, and related UNIX software)
3. Linux Developer's Resource CD-ROM; InfoMagic; 520-526-9565; info@infomagic.com
4. Linux for Dummies - Quick Reference, Second Edition; Phil Hughes; IDG Books; 1998
5. Linux Installation & Getting Started; Matt Welsh; SSC; 1995
6. Linux Journal; SSC; 206-782-7733
7. Linux Network Administrator's Guide; Olaf Kirch; O'Reilly & Associates; 1995
8. Linux Network Toolkit; Paul G. Sery; IDG; 1998 (includes CD-ROM)
9. Linux System Administration; Anne Carasik; M&T (IDG); 1998
10. Linux Web Server Toolkit; Nicholas Wells; IDG; 1998
11. Running Linux; Matt Welsh and Lar Kaufman; O'Reilly & Associates; 1995
12. Sys Admin Magazine; January, 1998 issue; Miller Freeman Publications

Sun Solaris

1. Solaris 2.x System Administrator's Guide; S. Lee Henry, John R. Graham; McGraw-Hill; 1995
2. Solaris 2.x for Managers and Administrators, Second Edition; C. Freeland, Dwight McKay, G.K. Parkinson; Onword Press; 1998
3. Solaris Advanced System Administrator's Guide, Second Edition; Janice Winsor; Macmillan Technical Publishing; 1997
4. Solaris System Administrator's Guide; Janice Winsor; Macmillan Technical Publishing; 1997
5. SunExpert Magazine; Computer Publishing Group; 617-641-9101

General (UNIX-TCP/IP)

1. Audit, Control, and Security Features of the UNIX Operating System; Ernst & Young; 1994
2. Essential (UNIX) System Administration, Second Edition; Aeleen Frisch; O'Reilly & Associates; 1995
3. Improving the Security of Your UNIX System; David Curry; SRI International; 1990
4. Managing NFS and NIS; Hal Stern; O'Reilly & Associates; April 1992
5. Open Computing's Best UNIX Tips Ever; Kenneth H. Rosen, Richard R. Rosinski, & Douglas A. Host; Osborne McGraw-Hill; 1994
6. Practical UNIX and Internet Security; Simon Garfinkel & Gene Spafford; O'Reilly & Associates; 1996
7. "Security"; Sys Admin Magazine (entire issue); August 1998, June 1997, November 1996
8. Sendmail, Second Edition; Brian Costales; O'Reilly & Associates; 1997
9. Sys Admin Magazine; Miller Freeman Publications
10. The UNIX and X Command Compendium - A Dictionary for High-Level Computing; Alan Southerton, Edwin C. Perkins, Jr.; John Wiley; 1994
11. UNIX in a Nutshell; D. Gilly; O'Reilly & Associates; June 1992
12. UNIX Review Magazine; September 1997, November 1996; 415-358-9500
13. UNIX Security; R&D Books (Sys Admin Reference Series); 1997
14. UNIX Security; S. Kapilow & G. Wilson; EDPACS; December 1989
15. UNIX System Security; R. Farrow; Addison-Wesley; 1991
16. UNIX System Security - A Guide for Users and System Administrators; D. Curry; Addison-Wesley; May 1992
17. The UNIX Audit; Using UNIX to Audit UNIX; Michael G. Grottola; McGraw-Hill; 1993

DEC VAX/VMS SECURITY

1. Security Concepts for the DECnet VAX Environment; Allen Lum; Data Security Management; Auerbach Publishers; 1990
2. Security for VAX Systems; Digital Equipment Corporation; EC-G0027-31; 1989
3. VAX/VMS (Several Articles); The EDP Auditor Journal; Volume I, 1993

NETWORK SECURITY AND CRYPTOGRAPHY

1. Applied Cryptography: Protocols, Algorithms, and Source Code in C; Bruce Schneier; John Wiley & Sons; 1997
2. Compression and Encryption; Dr. Dobb's Journal; January 1996
3. Data and Computer Communications - Fifth Edition; William Stallings; Prentice-Hall; 1997
4. E-Mail Security; How to Keep Your Electronic Messages Private; Bruce Schneier; John Wiley & Sons; 1995
5. Extranet Design and Implementation; Peter Loshin; Network Press/SYBEX; 1997
6. Hacker Proof: The Ultimate Guide to Network Security; Lars Klander; Jamsa Press; 1997
7. IBM Cryptographic Concepts and Facilities; IBM; GC22-9063
8. Internet Cryptography; Richard E. Smith; Addison-Wesley; 1997
9. Mastering Network Security; Chris Brenton; Sybex/Network Press; 1999
10. Maximum Security, Second Edition; Anonymous; Sams.net Publishing; 1998
11. Network and Internetwork Security; William Stallings; Prentice-Hall; 1995
12. Network Security: Private Communications in a Public World; Charlie Kaufman, Redia Perlman, Mike Spenciner; Prentice-Hall; 1995
13. The Official PGP User's Guide; Philip R. Zimmermann; The MIT Press; 1995
14. Picking Packets; Lenny Liebmann; Infosecurity News;September/October 1995
15. Understanding Digital Signatures; Gail Grant; CommerceNet Press; 1998

REMOTE ACCESS/VIRTUAL PRIVATE NETWORK SECURITY

1. Building and Managing Virtual Private Networks; Dave Kosiur; Wiley; 1998
2. Fast Connections in Small Packages; Les Freed; PC Magazine; January 20, 1998

3. Guarding the Flank with Radius & TACACS; Dan Backman; Network Computing; February 1, 1998
4. Is RAS Safe?; Zubair Ahmad; Windows NT Magazine; December, 1997
5. Reining In Remote Access; William Dutcher; PC Week; August 11, 1997
6. Remote Access Security; Paul Funk; NetWare Connection; November 1996
7. TACACS, RADIUS Secure Servers; William Dutcher; PC Week; October 20, 1997
8. Unlocking Virtual Private Networks; Mike Fratto; Network Computing; November 1,1997
9. A Virtual Private Affair; Mike Hurwicz; Byte; July 1997
10. Virtual Private Networks; Charlie Scott, Paul Wolfe, & Mike Erwin; O'Reilly; 1998
11. Virtual Private Network: Do You Need One?; Internet Security Advisor; Winter 1998 (Vol.1 No.4)
12. VPN Growing Pains - Remote access: VPN vs. dial-up; Networld World; December 8, 1997
13. Windows NT Magazine; August 1997 (numerous articles on RAS, PPTP, Steelhead)
14. Your Own Private Internet; David Hafke; Windows Magazine; February 1, 1998

USE AND SECURITY OF THE INTERNET

General Information and User Guides

1. Boardwatch Magazine; 8500 W. Bowles Ave., Suite 210, Littleton, CO 80123; 303-973-6038; subscriptions@boardwatch.com
2. Dr. Bob's Painless Guide to The Internet; Bob Rankin; No Starch Press; 1996
3. Internet Standards and Protocols; Dilip C. Naik; Microsoft Press; 1998
4. Internet World Magazine; PO Box 713, Mt. Morris, IL 61054; info@mecklermedia.com
5. Official Microsoft Internet Explorer 4 Book; Bryan Pfaffenberger; Microsoft Press; 1997
6. Official Netscape Communicator 4 Book; Phil James; Ventana; 1997
7. Official Netscape Navigator 4.0 (Windows Edition); Phil James; Netscape Press; 1997

8. The Internet for Dummies, Fourth Edition; John R. Levine, Carol Baroudi, & Margaret Levine Young; IDG Books; 1997
9. The Internet for Dummies Quick Reference, Third Edition; John R. Levine, Margaret Levine Young, & Arnold Reinhold; IDG Books; 1997
10. The Internet Tool Kit; Nancy Cedeno; Sybex; 1995
11. The Internet Unleashed; SAM Publishing; 1994, 1995 (includes software)
12. The Whole Internet - User's Guide & Catalog, Second Edition; E. Krol; O'Reilly & Associates; April 1994
13. Using Netscape 3: Special Edition; Mark R. Brown; QUE; 1996 (includes licensed copy of Netscape Navigator 3 - US version)

Technical TCP/IP Network Administration

1. Cisco IOS Network Security; Cisco Press/Macmillan Technical Publishing; 1998
2. Cisco TCP/IP Routing Professional Reference; Chris Lewis; McGraw-Hill; 1997
3. DNS and BIND, Second Edition; Paul Albitz & Cricket Lui; O'Reilly & Associates; 1997
4. The Essential Guide to TCP/IP Commands; Martin Arick; John Wiley & Sons; 1996
5. Getting Connected - The Internet at 56K and Up; Kevin Dowd; O'Reilly & Associates; 1996
6. Internetworking with TCP/IP, Volume I, Third Edition; Douglas Comer; Prentice-Hall; 1995
7. IPv6: The New Internet; Christian Huitema; Prentice-Hall; 1995
8. Managing IP Networks with Cisco Routers; Scott M. Ballew; O'Reilly & Associates; 1997
9. Networking Personal Computers with TCP/IP; Craig Hunt; O'Reilly & Associates; 1995
10. Practical Internetworking with TCP/IP and UNIX; Smoot Carl-Mitchell & John S. Quarterman; Addison-Wesley; 1994
11. TCP/IP for Dummies, Second Edition; Marshall Wilensky & Candace Leiden; IDG Books; 1997
12. TCP/IP Network Administration; C. Hunt; O'Reilly & Associates - Second Edition; 1997
13. TCP/IP: A Survival Guide for Users; Frank Derfler & Steve Rigney; MIS Press; 1998

PERL—Practical Extraction and Report Language

1. Discover PERL 5; Naba Barkakati; IDG Books; 1997 (included CD-ROM)
2. PERL 5 How To; Mike Glover, Aidan Humphries, Ed Weiss; Waite Group Press; 1996 (includes CD-ROM with PERL interpreter and sample applications)

USE AND SECURITY OF THE INTERNET

Internet Security—General

1. Actually Useful Internet Security Techniques; Larry J. Hughes, Jr.; New Riders Publishing; 1995
2. E-Mail Security; Bruce Schneier; John Wiley & Sons; 1995
3. Hazards of Hooking Up; Al Berg; LAN Times; June 17,1996
4. Implementing Internet Security; William Stallings, Peter Stephenson, & Others; New Riders Publishing; 1995
5. Internet Besieged; Dorothy Denning, Peter Denning, et al; Addison-Wesley; 1998
6. Internet Security for Business; Terry Bernstein, Anish Bhimani, Eugene Schultz, Carol Siegel; John Wiley & Sons; 1996
7. Internet Security: Guide to Web Protection; A Supplement to Infosecurity News; July/August 1996
8. Internet Security - Professional Reference; Numerous Authors; New Riders Publishing; 1996 (includes CD-ROM with security & audit software tools)
9. Internet Security Secrets; John Vacca; IDG Books; 1996
10. Internet Security with Windows NT; Mark Joseph Edwards; Duke Press; 1997
11. Network (In)Security Through IP Packet Filtering; D. Brent Chapman; Proceedings of the Third USENIX UNIX Symposium; September 1992 (also available on NIST BBS)
12. Practical UNIX and Internet Security; Simon Garfinkel & Gene Spafford; O'Reilly & Associates; 1996
13. Protecting Networks with SATAN; Martin Freiss; O'Reilly; 1998

Internet Security—Firewalls

1. Building Internet Firewalls; D. Brent Chapman & Elizabeth D. Zwicky; O'Reilly & Associates; 1995
2. Firewalls Complete; Marcus Goncalves; McGraw-Hill; 1998 (includes CD-ROM with demo versions of major firewall products)
3. Firewalls: Defending the Front Line; Kevin Tolly, John Curtis, & Elke Passarge; LAN Times; June 17,1996
4. Firewalls & Internet Security - Repelling the Wiley Hacker; Bill Cheswick & Steve Bellovin; Addison-Wesley; 1994
5. Great Walls of Fire (Firewall Security); Linda Boyer; NetWare Connection; January 1997
6. Internet Firewalls & Network Security, Second Edition; Karanjit Siyan; New Riders Publishing; 1996
7. Keeping Your Site Comfortably Secure: An Introduction to Internet Firewalls; NIST Special Publication 800-10
8. Kicking Firewall Tires; Char Sample; Network Magazine; March 1998

World Wide Web Administration and Security

1. ActiveX Demystified; David Chappell, David S. Linthicum; Byte Magazine; September, 1997
2. Apache Server for Dummies; Ken A.L. Coar; IDG Books; 1998
3. Bots and Other Internet Beasties; Joseph Williams; SAMS.net Publishing; 1996
4. Building Web Commerce Sites; Ed Tittle, et. al; IDG Books; 1997
5. Digital Cash: Commerce on the Net; Peter Wayner; Academic Press; 1996
6. Extranet Design and Implementation; Peter Loshin; Network Press/SYBEX; 1997
7. Hooked on Java; Arthur van Hoff, Sami Shaio, Orca Starbuck; Addison-Wesley; 1996
8. How to Set Up and Maintain a World Wide Web Site; Lincoln D. Stein; Addison-Wesley; 1995
9. Intranet Working; George Eckel; New Riders Publishing; 1996
10. Java and Web-Executable Object Security; Michael Shoffner, Merlin Hughes; Dr. Dobb's Journal; November 1996

11. Java Security; Gary McGraw & Ed Felten; John Wiley & Sons; 1997
12. The Lotus Domino Server: Integrating Lotus Notes 4.6 With the Internet; Steve Londergran; M&T Books; 1997
13. Lotus Notes & Domino Network Design; John Lamb, Peter Lew; McGraw-Hill;1997
14. Microsoft FrontPage 98; Laura Lemay; SAMS.net; 1997
15. Netscape Server Survival Guide; David Gulbransen; SAMS.net Publishing; 1996
16. Protect Your Privacy on the Internet; Bryan Pfaffenberger; John Wiley & Sons; 1997
17. Using Netscape Communicator; Peter Kent; Que Corporation; 1997
18. Using Netscape 3; Mark R. Brown; Que Corporation; 1996
19. Webmaster in A Nutshell; Stephen Spainbour & Valerie Quercia; O'Reilly; 1996
20. Webmaster's Handbook; John M. Fisher; Prima Publishing; 1996
21. Webmaster's Professional Reference; Loren Buhle, et al.; New Riders Publishing; 1996
22. Web Security; Lincoln Stein; Addison-Wesley; 1998
23. Web Security: A Matter of Trust; Word Wide Web Journal - Volume 2, Issue 3; O'Reilly & Associates; Summer 1997
24. Web Security & Commerce; Simson Garfinkel, Eugene Spafford; O'Reilly & Associates; 1997
25. Web Security Source Book; Avi Ruben, Dan Geer, Marcus J. Ranum; John Wiley & Sons; 1997
26. Web Site Administrator's Survival Guide; Jerry Ablan, Scott Yanoff; SAMS.net Publishing; 1996
27. Windows NT 4 Web Development; Sanjaya Hettihewa; Sams.net; 1996
28. Your Personal Net; Michael Wolff; Wolff New Media; 1996 (free updates at http://www.ypn.com)

IBM LARGE NETWORK SYSTEM SECURITY

1. IBM Security Architecture - Securing the Open Client/Server Distributed Enterprise; IBM; SC28-8135-01; 1995
2. Introduction to System and Network Security: Considerations, Options, and Techniques; IBM, 1990, GG24-3451-01
3. MVS/ESA Planning: Security; IBM, 1990, GC28-1801-0
4. IBM Cryptographic Concepts and Facilities; IBM; GC22-9063

OPEN, DISTRIBUTED SYSTEMS SECURITY AND MANAGEMENT

1. Client/Server Architecture; Alex Berson; McGraw-Hill, Inc.; 1992
2. Client/Server Computing; Dawna Travis Dewire; McGraw-Hill; 1993
3. DCE Security Programming; Wei Hu; O'Reilly & Associates, Inc.; 1995
4. DCE: Unifying Your Network Fabric; Eric Hall; Network Computing; November 1, 1996
5. Distributed CICS; Richard Schreiber, William R. Ogden; Wiley-QED; 1994
6. Distributed Computing (Byte Special Report); Byte Magazine; June 1994
7. IBM Security Architecture - Securing the Open Client/Server Distributed Enterprise; IBM; SC28-8135-01; 1995
8. Essential Client/Server Survival Guide, Second Edition; R. Orfali, D. Harkey, J. Edwards; Van Nostrand Reinhold; 1996
9. Implementing Kerberos in Distributed Systems; Handbook of Information Security Management - 1994-95 Yearbook; Ray Kaplan, Joe Kavara, Glen Zorn; Auerbach; 1995
10. LAN Times Guide to Interoperability; Tom Sheldon; Osborne McGraw-Hill; 1994
11. LAN Times Guide to SQL; J.R. Groff & P.N. Weinberg; Osborne McGraw-Hill; 1994
12. Limitations of the Kerberos Authentication System; S. Bellovin & M. Merritt; USENIX - Winter '91 - Dallas, TX (also printed in Computer Communications Review; Oct. '91)
13. Mastering Oracle7 & Client/Server Computing; S. Bobrowski; SYBEX; 1994
14. Multivendor Networking; Dr. Andres Fortino, Jerry Golick; McGraw-Hill; 1996 (includes CD-ROM)
15. Network and Distributed Systems Management; Morris Sloman (Principal Editor); Addison-Wesley; 1994
16. Network and Internetwork Security: Principles and Practice; William Stallings; Prentice Hall; 1995
17. Network Security Policy; Terry L. Jeffries; NetWare Connection; January 1997
18. OLTP Handbook; Gary McClain; McGraw-Hill; 1993
19. Oracle DBA Handbook - 7.3 Edition; Kevin Loney; Osborne McGraw-Hill; 1994

20. Powerbuilder for Dummies; Jason Coombs, Ted Coombs; IDG; 1995
21. Securing Client/Server Applications; Peter T. Davis; McGraw-Hill; 1996
22. Security in a Client/Server Environment; P. Teplitzy; Information Systems Security; Auerbach Publishers; Summer 1993
23. Security in Distributed Computing; Glen Bruce, Rob Dempsey; Prentice Hall; 1997
24. Security Issues in the Database Language SQL; NIST Special Publication 800-8; August 1993; Government Printing Office (also available on NIST BBS)
25. The Guide to SQL Server (Second Edition); Aloke Nath; Addison-Wesley; 1995
26. Sybase Developers Guide; Daniel J. Worden; SYBEX; 1994
27. Understanding DCE; W. Rosenberry, D. Kenney, & G. Fisher; O'Reilly & Associates; September 1992

COMPUTER CRIME, HACKERS, AND VIRUSES

1. 2600 Magazine; 516-751-2600; http://www.2600.com
2. American Eagle Publications; 520-367-1621
3. Backlisted! 411 Magazine; 310-596-4673
4. Computer Crime - A Crime Fighter's Handbook; David Icove, Karl Seger, & William VonStorch; O'Reilly & Associates; 1995
5. Computer Hacking: Detection & Protection; Imtiaz Malik; Sigma Press; 1996
6. Computer Viruses; Deloitte Haskins & Sells (Deloitte & Touche); 1989 (PC's, MVS, UNIX)
7. Computers Under Attack; Peter J. Denning; ACM Press, 1990
8. The Cuckoo's Egg; Clifford Stoll; Doubleday; 1989
9. Cyberpunk; Katie Hafner and John Markoff; Simon & Schuster; 1991
10. The Hacker Crackdown; Bruce Sterling; Bantam Books; 1992
11. The Little Black Book of Viruses; Mark Ludwig; American Eagle Publications; 1991 (reprinted 1995)
12. Maximum Security - 2nd Edition; Anonymous; sams.net; 1998
13. Secrets of A Super Hacker by the Knightmare; Dennis Fiery; Loompanics Unlimited; 1994
14. Security Insiders Report; 11567 Grove St. N, Seminole, FL 33708; (813-393-6600)

15. Spectacular Computer Crimes; Buck Bloombecker; Dow Jones-Irwin; 1990
16. Terminal Compromise; Wynn Schwartau; Inter-Pact Press; 1991; (813-393-6600)
17. Terminal Delinquents; Jack Hitt & Paul Tough; Esquire, December 1990
18. Virus Factbook; NCSA; 1992; (717-258-1816)
19. Virus, They Wrote; Corey Sandler; PC Computing; September 1994
20. VSUM Virus Index (Software); Patricia Hoffman; updated monthly; available on McAfee BBS, EXEC-PC, and others
21. Wire Pirates (Internet Security); Paul Wallach; Scientific American; March 1994

BROWSING AND TCP/IP UTILITY PROGRAMS

Browsing Tools

1. MOSAIC: http://www.ncsa.uiuc.edu/
2. NETSCAPE: http://www.netscape.com/
3. CHAMELEON: http://www.netmanage.com/
   Dialup version included with many book/software bundles, including Internet for Windows for Dummies Starter Kit, and Internet Unleashed
4. MICROSOFT INTERNET EXPLORER: http://www.microsoft.com/
5. LYNX: ftp://ftp2.cc.ukans.edu (text-based browser)

Lists of TCP/IP Software

1. Browser Watches:
   ♦ http://www.webcompare.com/ (Browsers and Web Servers)
   ♦ http://www.ski.mskcc.org/browserwatch/browsers.html
     (Tools Analysis by Dave J. Garaffa)
2. List of WinSock Software (w/Reviews by Forrest Stroud): http://cws-apps.texas.net/
3. Comparison of DOS/Windows TCP/IP Software:
   ♦ ftp://ftp.cac.psu.edu/pub/dos/info/tcpip.packages (also see USENET group: comp.protocols.tcp-ip.ibmpc)
4. The Internet Tool Kit; Nancy Cedeno; Sybex; 1995
   Numerous other Winsock and Internet related tools are discussed

SOURCES OF SECURITY AND AUDIT TOOLS (PUBLIC DOMAIN/SHAREWARE)

COPS (www.ciac.org)

courtney (www.ciac.org)

crack, cracklib (www.ciac.org)

dig (www.ciac.org)

ethload/ethdump (ftp.cc.utexas.edu)

fremont (www.ciac.org)

gabriel (www.ciac.org)

gobbler (ftp.wustl.edu)

ISS freeware (www.ciac.org)

Kerberos (athena-dist.mit.edu)

linux (www.linux.org)

logsurfer (www.art.dfn.de/eng/team/wl/logsurf)

L0phtCrack (www.l0pht.com)

merlin (www.ciac.org)

mscan (www.rootshell.com)

NAT: NetBIOS Audit Tool (www.securenetworks.com)

npasswd, passwd+ (www.ciac.org)

NetScan tools (www.shareware.com)

NTFSDOS (www.sysinternals.com)

OPIE (www.ciac.org)

PERL (ftp.netlabs.com, ftp.cis.ufl.edu)

PGP (net-dist.mit.edu)

ptscan (www.blueglobe.com)

Saint network security scanner (www.wwdsi.com/saint)

SATAN (www.ciac.org), Satan - Patched for Linux (www.sunsite. unc.edu/pub/Linux/system/network/admin/satan-1.1.1.linux.fixed2.tgz)

SHADOW Intrusion Detection (www.nswc.navy.mil/ISSEC/CID)

S/KEY, logdaemon (www.ciac.org)

SOCKS (www.ciac.org)

SSH (ftp.cs.hut.fi/pub/ssh)

stel (ftp.dsi.umin.it)

strobe (bundled with ISS 1.3 - www.iss.net)

sudo (ftp.cs.colorado.edu/pub/sysadmin/sudo)

swatch (www.ciac.org)

tcpdump (www.ciar.org)

TCP Wrapper, tripwire (www.ciac.org)

Texas A&M Toolkit/Tiger Scripts (www.ciac.org)

thief, toneloc wargames dialers (ftp.paranoia.com)

tripwire (www.ciac.org)

Webtrends Security Scanner - formerly asmodeus (www.webtrends.com)

winsock & related utilities (ftp.coast.net/SimTel, www.shareware.com)

winzip (www.winzip.com)

WS_Ping Pro Pack (www.ipswitch.com)

xidle (www.wins.uva.nl/pub/solaris)

XScreensaver (http://138.253.42.172/hppd/hpux/X11/Desktop)

INTERNET SECURITY AND AUDIT RESOURCES

Web Sites—General Internet Information

http://www.ietf.cnri.reston.va.us/home.html (Internet Engineering Task Force)

http://www.w3.org (WWW3 Consortium)

http://www.commerce.net (CommerceNet)

http://info.cern.ch/hypertext/DataSources/WWW/Servers.html (list of WWW servers) http://www.openmarket.com/info/internet-index/current.html (Internet Facts)

http://www.cic.ohio-state.edu/hypertext/faq/usenet/FAQ-List.html (List of FAQ)

http://www.boardwatch.com/ (Boardwatch Magazine Online)

http://www.internic.net/ (directories of Internet users and resources)

http://info.webcrawler.com/mark/projects/robots/robots.html (Internet Robots)

http://tile.net/listserv/ (searchable index of Internet mailing lists)

http://www.law.vill.edu/ (list of U.S. government WWW servers)

http://www.cc.gatech.edu/gvu/user_surveys (Georgia Tech. Web-user surveys)

http://www.umich.edu/~sgupta/hermes/survey3 (analysis charts of Georgia Tech. GVU surveys)

http://www.dejanews.com (Newsgroup Q&A - use in lieu of newsgroup subscription)

Web Sites for Auditors

http://www.acl.com/audit.html (Audit Central)

http://www.aol.com/auditnet/karlhome.html (Jim Kaplan's listing of Web sites for auditors)

http://www.auditserve.com/ (Technical Research Center for Control Professionals)

http://www.bitwise.net/iawww/ (Internal Audit Web Page)

http://www.rutgers.edu/Accounting/raw/iia/ (Institute of Internal Auditors)

http://www.isaca.org/ (Information Systems Audit and Control Association)

http://www.misti.com/ (MIS Training Institute)

http://www.netaxs.com/~edoig/ASAP_index.html (publicly shared audit programs) http://www.tc.pw.com/tc/217e.htm (Price Waterhouse Expert Assistance for Audit Planning)

Web Sites—Hackers

http://www.2600.com (home of famous hacker periodical)

http://www.hackerz.com/ (Hacker Site with numerous links to other hacker sites)

http://www.mcs.net/~candyman/under.html (Underground WWW server)

http://www.fc.net/phrack.html (Phrack Magazine)

http://www/l0pht.com/ (Lopht Heavy Industries Hacking magazine)

http://www.nmrc.org/ (Nomad Mobile Research Center - Hacker Tutorials and Tools)

http://www.rootshell.com/ (Well Indexed Hacker Tutorials and Tools)

http://www.warforge.com (Hacker Trojan Horse Software - Back Orifice, NetBus, & others)

http://207.98.195.250/ (Rhino9 Network Scanners - Ogre, Legion, Hacker Tutorials)

http://www.unitedcouncil.org/ (Links to Hacker Newsgroups)

Web Sites—Assorted Security Resources

http://www.alw.nih.gov/Security/security.html (National Institutes of Health - Computer Security)

http://www.securiteam.com (extensive security vulnerability & tool information)

http://www.ers.ibm.com/security-links/index.html (Extensive security links)

http://www.nsi.org/ (National Security Institute - security legislation, security mgmt)

http://www.infoworld.com/security/ (Security Watch)

http://www.securityserver.com/ (Gateway to Information Security) http://www.Security-Online.com/ (Security Online)

http://www.simon-net.com (Security Information Management Online Network - Simon '97)

http://www.iss.net/ (Unix & Windows NT information & tools - commercial)

http://www.cert.org/ (CERT security bulletins, checklists, security tools, VIRUS-L)

http://www.cs.purdue.edu/coast/coast.html (extensive security archives/mirror site)

http://www.ciac.org (Dept. of Energy CERT - extensive security bulletins & tools)

http://www.first.org/ (numerous generic and government related security documents)

http://www.issa-intl.org/ (Information Systems Security Association)

http://www.misti.com/ (MIS Training Institute/Information Security Institute)

http://csrc.ncsl.nist.gov/ (NIST Information Security Clearing House)

http://www.telstra.com.au/Info/security.html (security reference index)

Web Sites—Netware Security

http://www.nwconnection.com/ (NetWare Connection magazine archives)

http://www.novell.com/ (NetWare software and support information)

Web Sites—UNIX Security

http://www.alw.nih.gov/Security/security.html (UNIX security information)

http://www.geek-girl.com/bugtraq/archives.html (UNIX/Bugtraq archives)

http://www.stokely.com/unix.sysadm.resources/shareware.www.html (Vast UNIX resources) http://ciac.llnl.gov/ciac/ (CIAC security bulletins, UNIX-TCP/IP security tools)

http://www.lat.com/ (Los Alamos security repository, Gabriel, UNIX-TCP/IP security resources)

http://auk.uwaterloo.ca/aixgroup/ (AIX FAQs and other information)

http://www.austin.IBM.com/ (RS/6000 AIX security & other topics)

Web Sites—Windows NT Security

http://www.ntshop.net/, www.ntsecurity.net/ (Windows NT security information & tools)

http://www.somarsoft.com/ (Windows NT security information & tools)

http://www.telemark.net/~randallg/ntsecure.htm (Windows NT Web server security issues)

http://www.ntresearch.com/ (Windows NT security checklist)

http://www.iss.net/vd/ntfaq.html (Windows NT vulnerabilities database)

http://www.trustedsystems.com/ (Windows NT security checklist, security audit tools & white papers)

http://www.ntbugtraq.com/ (Windows NT Bugtraq archives)

http://www.microsoft.com/security/ (Security fixes and information for Microsoft products)

http://www.txdirect.net/~wall/ntlinks.htm (Bill Wall's Windows NT Links)

Web Sites—Internet, WWW, and Electronic Commerce Security

http://www.isr.net (Internet Security Review - Online Edition)

http://www.epic.com (Electronic Privacy Information Center)

http://www.winmag.com/flanga/bt97/bt810.htm (Web Browser Security w/Security Tests) http://www.bsdi.com/server/doc/web-info.html (information on WWW security)

http://www.sophist.demon.co.uk/ping/index.html ("Ping of Death" Web Page)

http://www.genome.wi.mit.edu/WWW/faqs/www-security-faq.html (WWW Security FAQ)

http://www-ns.rutgers.edu/www-security/reference.html   (Rutgers WWW Security Reference page)

http://www.zurich.ibm.ch/Technology/Security/sirene/outside-world/ecommerce.html (List of sites with information about secure electronic commerce)

http://www.proper.com/www/server-chart.html (comparison of WWW servers)

http://www.webcompare.com/ (comparison of WWW servers)

http://www.netcraft.co.uk (monthly survey of international WWW server installed base)

Web Sites—Active Web Page Security

http://www.axent.com/swat (references and examples of security vulnerabilities)

http://hoohoo.ncsa.uiuc.edu/docs/tutorials/includes.html (SSI Security)

http://www.webcom/~webcom/help/inc/include.shtml (SSI Security)

http://www.primus.com/staff/paulp/cgi-security (CGI Security)

http://hoohoo.ncsa.uiuc.edu/cgi/security.html (CGI Security)

http://www.perl.com/perl/news/latro-announce.html (PERL Interpreter Probe/Locator "latrodectus cyberneticus")

http://www.rstcorp.com/javasecurity/links.htm (JAVA Security)

http://www.javasoft.com/sfaq/ (JAVA Security)

http://www.cs.princeton.edu/sip/pub/secure.html (JAVA Security)

http://www.math.gatech.edu/~mladue/Hostile/HostileApplets.html (JAVA Security) http://whenever.cs.berkeley.edu/graffiti (JAVA Security)

http://microsoft.com/intdev/security/ (ActiveX Security)

http://www1.halcyon.com/mclain/ActiveX/Exploder/FAQ.htm (ActiveX Security)

http://www.security.org.il/security/iebugs.html (ActiveX Security)

http://web.mit.edu/crioux/www/ie/index.html (ActiveX Security)

http://www.osf.org/~loverso/javascript (Javascript Security)

http://www.netscape.com/newsref/std/cookies_spec.html (Cookies Security)

http://www.currents.net/cookies.html (Cookies Security)

http://www.illuminatus.com/cookie/ (Cookies Security)

http://www.research.digital.com/nsl/formtest/stats-by-test/Netscape/Cookie.html (Cookies Security)

http://info.webcrawler.com/mak/projects/robots/robots.html (Web robots security)

Web Sites—Firewall Security

http://www.clark.net/pub/mjr/pubs/fwfaq (Marcus Ranum Firewall FAQ)

http://www.zeuros.co.uk (Rotherwick Firewall Resources)

http://lists.gnac.com (GreatCircle Firewalls Digest archives)

http://www.nwconnection.com/ (Jan '97 issue - excellent technical tutorial on firewalls)

http://www.cisco.com (Cisco Web Site - numerous how-to's FAQ on router security)

http://www.icsa.com/ (International Computer Security Association - firewall certification)

Web Sites—Software Repositories

http://www.ddj.com/ (Dr. Dobb's Journal software repository)

http://www.shareware.com (shareware/freeware software repository -

Windows & non-Windows systems)

http://www.download.com (shareware/freeware software repository - Windows systems)

http://www.tucows.com (international shareware/freeware software repository - Windows systems)

Web Sites—Linux

http://www.linux.org/ (Linux page)

http://www.aoy.com/Linux/Security/ (Linux Security page)

http://www.cs.texas.edu/users/kharker/linux-laptop (Ken Harker's Linux Laptop site)

http://members.ping.at/theofilu/netscape.html (Linux-Netscape Help Page)

http://www.redhat.com (commercial & freeware Linux software resources)

http://www.suse.de (commercial & freeware Linux software resources)

http://sunsite.unc.edu/pub/Linux/system/network/admin/ (extensive freeware repository)

Web Sites—Year 2000 (Y2K)

http://www.vear2000.com (Peter de Jager Y2K Site)

http://y2klinks.com (Hub of Year 2000 Millennium Resource Site Ring)

http://www.zdnet.com/zdy2k/ (Ziff Davis Y2K Site)

http://www.compinfo.co.uk/y2k.htm (UK Y2K Site)

Web Sites—Information Warfare

http://www.infowar.com (Winn Schwartau Information Warfare Site)

http://www.au.af.mil/own/sandt/iw-hmpg.html (Information Warfare Links)

http://www.psycom.net/iwar.1.html (Institute for the Advanced Study of Information Warfare) http://www.fas.org/irp/wwwinfo.html#infowar (Federation of American Scientists (FAS) Intelligence Resource Program)

http://www.rand.org/publications/RRR/RRR.fall95.cyber/ (Rand Research Review)
http://www.aia.af.mil/aialink/homepages/afiwc/index.htm (Air Force Information Warfare Center)

http://www.leglnet.com/libr-inwa.htm (Information Warfare Law Library)

FTP Sites—Miscellaneous

ftp://athena-dist.mit.edu (Kerberos software & references)

ftp://ciac.llnl.gov (CIAC security bulletins, UNIX-TCP/IP security tools)

ftp://coast.cs.purdue.edu (security tools & references)

ftp://crvax.sri.com (RISKS Digest)

ftp://csrc.ncsl.nist.gov (NIST security FTP server)

ftp://decuac.dec.com (routers, firewalls, & UNIX tools)

ftp://ds.internic.net (primary Internet RFC repository)

ftp://ftp.auscert.org.au (Australian CERT - UNIX/Internet security)

ftp://ftp.bellcore.com (numerous UNIX & TCP/IP security resources)

ftp://ftp.cisco.com (routers and firewalls)

ftp://ftp.coast.net (vast archive of PC software including Internet/Winsock tools)

ftp://ftp.eff.org (Computer Underground Digest)

ftp://ftp.informatik.uni-hamburg.de (virus information - UNIX & other)

ftp://ftp.nisc.sri.com (Internet usage statistics, DNS registry list)

ftp://ftp.ripe.net (regional InterNIC for Europe)

ftp://ftp.sunet.se (numerous UNIX & TCP/IP security resources)

ftp://ftp.sura.net (numerous UNIX & TCP/IP security resources) ftp://ftp.uu.net (numerous UNIX & TCP/IP security resources; USENIX)

ftp://info.cert.org (security bulletins, checklists, security tools, VIRUS-L)

ftp://nasirc.nasa.gov (NASA security bulletins)

ftp://net.tamu.edu (firewalls & UNIX security tools)

ftp://nisca.acs.ohio-state.edu (firewalls)

ftp://nist.ncsl.nist.gov (NIST BBS - security bulletins & numerous security/audit references)

ftp://research.att.com (firewalls)

ftp://rs.internic.net (Internet registration services - 703-742-4777)

ftp://theta.iis.utokyo.ac.jp:/pub1/security (security tools & information)

ftp://tis.com (firewalls, crypto product list, other security tools & information)

ftp://ftp.win.tue.nl (numerous UNIX & TCP/IP security tools & references, including SATAN)

Security Mailing Lists/Email Servers

aixserv@austin.ibm.com (AIX bulletins including security)

bugtraq-request@crimelab.com (UNIX security exposures)

cert-advisory-request@cert.org (security bulletins)

docserver@csrc.ncsl.nist.gov (NIST document mail server)

majordomo@8lgm.org (subscribe 8lgm-list: "Eight Little Green Men" UNIX security exposures, hacker exploit scripts)

majordomo@alive.ampr.ab.ca (HACK-L: hacker alerts)

majordomo@lists.gnac.com (subscribe firewalls-digest: Brent Chapman's firewalls digest)

majordomo@iss.net (subscribe ntsecurity-digest: Windows NT Security digest) mailserv@ds.internic.net (primary Internet RFC repository)

risks-request@CSL.SRI.COM (RISKS digest)

listserv@lehigh.edu (SUB valert-L: urgent virus warnings)

Security/Audit Related Usenet Groups

alt.2600

alt.business.internal-audit

alt.crackers

alt.hackers

alt.security

alt.security.pgp

alt.security.ripem

comp.protocols.kerberos

comp.risks

comp.security.announce

comp.security.misc

comp.security.unix

comp.unix.admin

comp.unix.wizards

comp.virus

info.pem.dev

misc.security

sci.crypt

For a full list of USENET newsgroups & FAQs:
ftp://rtfm.mit.edu or e-mail to: mailserv@rtfm.mit.edu

INTERNET SECURITY AND AUDIT RESOURCES— USEFUL INTERNET RFCS

General

RFC1118   Hitchhiker's Guide to the Internet
RFC1147   FYI on Network Management Tools
RFC1359   Connecting to the Internet
RFC1392   Internet User's Glossary
RFC1402   There's gold in them thar networks!...
RFC1700   Well-Known Ports (TCP/IP Applications 7)
RFC1883   Internet Protocol, Version 6 (IPv6)
RFC1855   Netiquette Guidelines

Security

RFC1038   Draft Revised IP Security Option
RFC1108   U.S. Department of Defense Security Options for the Internet Protocol
RFC1244   Site Security Handbook (replaced by RCF 2196)
RFC1281   Guidelines for the Secure Operation of the Internet
RFC1319   The MD2 Message-Digest Algorithm
RFC1320   The MD4 Message-Digest Algorithm
RFC1321   The MD5 Message-Digest Algorithm
RFC1334   PPP Authentication Protocols
RFC1352   SNMP Security Protocols
RFC1355   Privacy and Accuracy Issues in Network Information Center
RFC1411   Telnet Authentication: Kerberos Version 4
RFC1412   Telnet Authentication: SPX
RFC1416   Telnet Authentication Option
RFC1422   Privacy Enhancement for Internet Electronic Mail - Part I
RFC1423   Privacy Enhancement for Internet Electronic Mail - Part II
RFC1424   Privacy Enhancement for Internet Electronic Mail - Part III
RFC1446   Security Protocols for Version 2 of the Simple Network Management Protocol (SNMPv2)
RFC1455   Physical Link Security Type of Service
RFC1457   Security Label Framework for the Internet
RFC1472   The Definitions of Managed Objects for the Security Protocols of the Point-to-Point Protocol
RFC1492   An Access Control Protocol, Sometimes Called TACACS

RFC1507   DASS - Distributed Authentication Security Service
RFC1508   Generic Security Service Application Program Interface
RFC1509   Generic Security Service API : C-bindings
RFC1510   The Kerberos Network Authentication Service (V5)
RFC1511   Common Authentication Technology Overview
RFC1535   A Security Problem and Proposed Correction With Widely Deployed DNS Software
RFC1579   Firewall-Friendly FTP
RFC1636   Report of IAB Workshop on Security in the Internet Architecture
RFC1675   Security Concerns for IPng
RFC1704   On Internet Authentication
RFC1710   Simple Internet Protocol Plus White Paper
RFC1731   IMAP4 Authentication Mechanisms
RFC1734   POP3 Authentication Command
RFC1750   Randomness Recommendations for Security
RFC1751   A Convention for Human-Readable 128-bit Keys
RFC1760   The S/KEY One-Time Password System
RFC1805   Location-Independent Data/Software Integrity Protocol
RFC1810   Report on MD5 Performance
RFC1824   The Exponential Security System (TESS): An Identity-Based Cryptographic Protocol for Authenticated Key-Exchange
RFC1825   Security Architecture for the Internet Protocol
RFC1826   IP Authentication Header
RFC1827   IP Encapsulating Security Payload
RFC1828   IP Authentication Using Keyed MD5
RFC1829   The ESP DES-CBC Transform
RFC1847   Security Multiparts for MIME
RFC1848   MIME Object Security Services
RFC1851   The ESP Triple DES Transform
RFC1852   IP Authentication Using Keyed SHA
RFC1853   IP in IP Tunneling
RFC1858   Security Considerations for IP Fragment Filtering
RFC1864   The Content-MD5 Header Field
RFC1875   UNINETT PCA Policy Statements
RFC1898   CyberCash Credit Card Protocol Version 0.8
RFC1910   User-based Security Model for SNMPv2
RFC1928   SOCKS Protocol Version 5
RFC1929   Username/Password Authentication for SOCKS V5

RFC1938   A One-Time Password System
RFC1948   Defending Against Sequence Number Attacks
RFC1949   Scalable Multicast Key Distribution
RFC1961   GSS-API Authentication Method for SOCKS Version 5
RFC1968   The PPP Encryption Control Protocol (ECP)
RFC1969   The PPP DES Encryption Protocol (DESE)
RFC2196   Site Security Handbook (replaces RFC 1244)

How to Get RFCs

Send e-mail to: mailserv@ds.internic.net
<message>
document-by-name rfcXXXX   [XXXX:RFC]

COMMERCIAL INTERNET PROVIDERS

United States

1. America Online; 800-827-6364
2. AT&T WorldNet; 800-400-1447
3. Compuserve; 800-336-6823, 614-529-1340
4. Holonet; 510-704-0160
5. IBM Global Network; 800-455-5056
6. Microsoft Network; 800-426-9400
7. Netcom; 800-501-8649
8. Pipeline; 717-770-1700, 703-904-9115
9. Prodigy; 800-PRODIGY
10. PSI; 800-827-7482
11. UUNET Technologies; 800-488-6384

NOTE: U.S. providers listed above may also offer international POPs.

United Kingdom

1. Compuserve; 0800-289378
2. Delphi; 01223-566950
3. Demon; 0181-349-0063
4. Direct Connection; 0181-3170100

5. Eunet; 01227-266466
6. GreenNet; 0171-7131941
7. Pipex; 01223-250120

Canada

1. Hookup Communications; 905-847-8000 (voice)
2. UUNET Canada; 416-368-6621 (voice)
3. UUNorth; 416-225-8649

For an expanded lists of Internet service providers:

1. Via E-mail:
   ◆ info-deli-server@netcom.com ("Send PDIAL" in subject)
2. Via Web Page Browsing:
   ◆ http://dixie.tagsys.com/Provider/ListOfLists.html
   ◆ http://www.internic.net/infoguide.html
   ◆ http://www.isoc.org/~bgreene/nsp-index.html
   ◆ http://www.teleport.com/~cci/directories/pocia.html
   ◆ http://www.thelist.com

PROFESSIONAL AND TRADE ORGANIZATIONS

Contingency Planning

1. Association of Contingency Planners (ACP); ACP National Headquarters, PO Box 341, Brigham City, UT 84302-0341; Phone: 800-445-4ACP
2. Disaster Recovery Institute; 1810 Craig Road #213; St. Louis, MO 63146; Phone: 314-434-2272
3. International Disaster Recovery Association (IRDA); c/o BWT Associates; PO Box 515, Turnpike Station; Shrewsbury, MA 01545; Phone: 508-845-2585
4. Mid-Atlantic Disaster Recovery Association (Eastern PA, Southern NJ, DE, MD, DC, & VA); c/o Sunny Bolander (410-528-2541), Walt Helgerman (301-657-5034)
5. Survive!; P.O. Box 1614, Mt. Laurel, NJ; Phone: 609-778-5702

IBM Systems

1. IBM Users Groups (GUIDE/SHARE); Phone: 312-822-0932

Information Security

1. Computer Security Institute (CSI); 600 Harrison St., San Francisco, CA 94107; Phone: 415-905-2378
2. Information Security Institute; 310 Wrights Circle - Suite A; Seneca, SC 29678; Phone: 864-882-8666
3. Information Systems Security Association (ISSA); ISSA Headquarters, c/o Technical Enterprises, Inc., 7044 S. 13th St., Milwaukee, WI 53154; Phone: 414-768-8000
4. International Information Systems Security Certification Consortium (IISSCC, Inc.); c/o Rick Koenig, Suite 100, Parkview Office Tower, Worcester, MA 01609; Phone: 508-842-7329
5. International Information Integrity Institute (I-4); SRI International; Phone: 415-859-4729
6. International Computer Security Association (ICSA); 10 South Courthouse Ave., Carlisle, PA 17013; Phone: 717-258-1816

Information Systems Auditing

1. Information Systems Audit And Control Association (ISACA); ISACA International Headquarters; 3701 Algonquin Road, Suite 1010; Rolling Meadows, IL 60008; Phone: 708-253-1545
2. The Institute of Internal Auditors (IIA); 249 Maitland Ave., Altamonte Springs, FL 32701; Phone: 407-830-7600
3. MIS Training Institute; 498 Concord St., Framingham, MA 01702; Phone: 508-879-7999

Novell Netware

1. Novell Users International; 800-453-1267 x-1267

Open Systems

1. Open Group (formerly Open Software Foundation - OSF); OSF (chapter meetings): Security SIG meetings - locations and dates TBD; c/o Paul Metz (603-472-2991/617-621-8778) or Jim Schindler re: Security SIG (408-447-4600)

Records Management

1. Association of Records Managers and Administrators (ARMA); ARMA International, 4200 Somerset, Suite 215, Prairie Village, KS 66208; Phone: 913-341-3808

UNIX/TCP-IP

1. UniForum; 2910 Tasman Drive, #201, Santa Clara, CA 95054; Phone: 800-255-5620, 408-986-1645
2. USENIX Association; PO Box 2299; Berkeley, CA 94710; Phone: 510-528-8649

Appendix B
Attachment 4-2: State Statutes

OFFENSES DEFINED IN STATE STATUTES[1]

Unauthorized Access:
Alabama, Alaska, Arizona, Arkansas, California, Colorado, Connecticut, Delaware, Florida, Georgia, Hawaii, Idaho, Illinois, Indiana, Iowa, Kansas, Kentucky, Maryland, Michigan, Minnesota, Missouri, Montana, Nebraska, New Hampshire, New Jersey, New Mexico, New York, North Carolina, North Dakota, Oklahoma, Oregon, Pennsylvania, Rhode Island, South Dakota, Tennessee, Texas, Utah, Virginia, Washington, Wisconsin, and Wyoming.

Computer Fraud:
Arizona, Arkansas, California, Colorado, Florida, Georgia, Hawaii, Idaho, Illinois, Kansas, Kentucky, Louisiana, Michigan, Minnesota, Mississippi, Nevada, New Jersey, New Mexico, North Carolina, North Dakota, Oklahoma, Oregon, Pennsylvania, Rhode Island, South Carolina, South Dakota, Tennessee, Utah, Virginia, Wisconsin, and Wyoming.

Against Computer Users:
Florida, Louisiana, Mississippi, Missouri, North Carolina, and Wyoming.

Against Computer Systems:
Alabama, Arizona, Arkansas, California, Colorado, Connecticut, Delaware, Florida, Georgia, Hawaii, Idaho, Illinois, Iowa, Kansas, Kentucky, Louisiana, Michigan, Minnesota, Mississippi, Missouri, Montana, Nevada, New Hampshire, New Jersey, New Mexico, North Carolina, Oklahoma, Oregon, Penn-

sylvania, Rhode Island, South Carolina, South Dakota, Tennessee, Texas, Utah, Virginia, Washington, Wisconsin, and Wyoming.

Interruption of Services:
California, Connecticut, Delaware, Illinois, Nebraska, Nevada, New Hampshire, Oregon
Pennsylvania, Utah, Virginia, Wisconsin, and Wyoming.

Tampering:
Illinois, Indiana, Missouri, New Jersey, and New York.

Misuse of Information:
Connecticut, Delaware, Kentucky, New Hampshire, New Jersey, Pennsylvania, and South Dakota.

Theft of Services:
Alabama, Alaska, California, Connecticut, Delaware, Iowa, Maine, Massachusetts, Minnesota, Nebraska, New Hampshire, Ohio, Oregon, Virginia, and Wisconsin.

Venue:
Arkansas, California, Connecticut, Delaware, Georgia, Kentucky, Mississippi, New Hampshire, New Jersey, South Carolina, South Dakota, Tennessee, and Virginia.

Affirmative Defense:
California, Connecticut, New Hampshire, New York, and Texas.

Civil Remedy Provided:
Arkansas, California, Delaware, Missouri, New Jersey, Virginia, and Wisconsin.

NOTES

1. Information taken from various Department of Justice documents.

References and
Recommended Reading

Aburdene, Patricia, and John Naisbitt. *Megatrends 2000*. New York: Avon Books, 1990.

Anonymous. *A Hacker's Guide to Protecting Your Internet Site and Network, Maximum Security*. Indianapolis, IN: Sams.net Publishing, 1997.

Banks, Michael A. *How to Protect Yourself in Cyberspace: Web Psychos, Stalkers and Pranksters*. Scottsdale, AZ: The Coriolis Group, Inc., 1997.

Bellovin, Steven M., and William R. Cheswick. *Firewalls and Internet Security*. New York: Addison-Wesley, 1994.

Bequai, August. *Techno-Crimes: The Computerization of Crime and Terrorism*. Lexington, MA: D.C. Heath and Co., 1987.

Breton, Thierry, and Denis Beneich. *Softwar*. New York: Holt, Rinehart and Winston, 1984.

Burger, Ralf. *Computer Viruses: A High-Tech Disease*. 3rd Edition. Grand Rapids, MI: Abacus, 1989.

Carroll, John M. *Computer Security*. London: Butterworth, 1977.

Cheswick, William R., and Steven M. Bellovin. *Firewalls and Internet Security: Repelling the Wily Hacker*. Reading, MA: Addison-Wesley, 1994.

Clark, Franklin, and Ken Diliberto. *Investigating Computer Crime*. Boca Raton: CRC Press, Inc., 1996.

Computer Viruses: Proceedings of an Invitational Symposium, October 10-11,

1988. Deloitte Haskins & Sells, Co-sponsored with Information Systems Security Association.

DeMaio, Harry B. *Information Protection and Other Unnatural Acts: Every Manager's Guide to Keeping Vital Computer Data Safe and Sound.* New York: Amacom, 1992.

Edwards, Mark J. *Internet Security with Windows NT.* Loveland: Duke Press, 1998.

Felten, Edward W., and Gary McGraw. *Java Security.* New York: John Wiley & Son, 1997.

Fernandez, E.B., et al. *The Systems Programming Series: Database Security and Integrity.* International Business Machines Corporation, 1981.

Fialka, John J. *War by Other Means: Economic Espionage in America.* New York: W.W. Norton & Company, 1997.

Fites, Philip, and Martin P. J. Kratz. *Information Systems Security: A Practitioner's Reference.* New York: Van Nostrand Reinhold, 1993.

FitzGerald, Jerry. *Business Data Communications.* Canada: John Wiley & Sons, 1984.

Garfinkel, Simson, and Gene Spafford. *Practical UNIX Security.* O'Reilly & Associates, Inc., 1991.

Government Accounting Office. *Information Superhighway: An Overview of Technology Challenges.* GAO-AIMD 95-23.

Gurbani, Vijay K., and Uday O. Pabrai. *Internet & TCP/IP Network Security.* New York: McGraw-Hill, 1996.

Hafner, Katie, and John Markoff. *Cyberpunk: Outlaws and Hackers on the Computer Frontier.* New York: Touchstone, 1992.

Handbook of Information Security Management, 1994-95 Yearbook. Edited by Zella G. Ruthberg and Harold F. Tipton. Boston, MA: Auerbach Publications, 1994.

Hsiao, David K., et al. *Computer Security.* New York: Academic Press, 1979.

Icove, David, et al. *Computer Crime: A Crimefighter's Handbook.* Sebastopol, CA: O'Reilly & Associates, Inc., 1995.

Kabay, Michel E. *The NCSA Guide to Enterprise Security: Protecting Information Assets.* New York: McGraw-Hill, 1996.

Kenney, John P., and Harry W. More. *Principles of Investigation.* 2nd Edition. St. Paul, MN: West Publishing Co., 1994.

Knightmare, The. *Secrets of A Super Hacker.* Port Townsend, WA: Loompanics Unlimited, 1994.

Kovacich, Gerald L. "Hackers: From Curiosity to Crime." The Association of Certified Fraud Examiners. "The White Paper" magazine, Vol. 17, No. 4, Aug-Sep 1993, p. 9.

Kovacich, Gerald L. *The Information Systems Security Officer's Guide.* Boston: Butterworth-Heinemann, 1998.

Landreth, Bill. *The Cracker: Out of The Inner Circle: A Hacker's Guide to Computer Security.* Bellevue, WA: Microsoft Press, 1985.

Leibholz, Stephen W., and Louis D. Wilson. *Users' Guide to Computer Crime: Its Commission, Detection and Prevention.* Radnor, PA: Chilton Book Company, 1974.

Levy, Steven. *Hackers: Heroes of the Computer Revolution.* New York: Anchor Press, 1984.

Mair, William C., et al. *Computer Control & Audit.* 3rd Edition. New York: Touche Ross & Co., 1981.

Martin, James. *Security Accuracy and Privacy in Computer Systems.* Englewood Cliffs, NJ: Prentice-Hall, 1973.

McGraw, Gary, and Edward W. Felten. *Java Security: Hostile Applets, Holes, and Antidotes. What Every Netscape and Internet Explorer User Needs to Know.* New York: John Wiley & Sons, 1997.

Melvern Linda, Nick Anning, and David Hebditch. *Techno-Bandits.* Boston: Houghton Mifflin, 1984.

Naisbitt, John. *Megatrends.* New York: Warner Books, 1982.

Naisbitt, John. *Megatrends Asia.* New York: Simon and Schuster, 1996.

National Research Council. *Computers at Risk: Safe Computing In the Information Age.* Washington, D.C.: National Academy Press, 1991.

"Nations Band Together Against Cybercrime," Reuters, 10 Dec. 1997.

Norman, Adrian R.D. *Computer Insecurity*. New York: Chapman and Hall, 1983.

Ohmae, Kenichi. *The Mind of the Strategist*. Middlesex, England: Penguin Books, 1982.

Parker, Donn B. *Computer Security Management*. Reston, VA: Reston Publishing Company, 1981.

Parker, Donn B. *Crime by Computer: Startling New Kinds of Million-Dollar Fraud, Theft, Larceny, & Embezzlement*. New York: Charles Scribner's Sons, 1976.

Platt, Charles. *Anarchy Online: Net Crime, Net Sex*. New York: Harper Paperbacks, 1996.

Roberts, Ralph. *Computer Viruses*. Greensboro, NC: Compute! Publications, Inc., 1988.

Rose, Lance. *Netlaw: Your Rights in the Online World*. Berkeley, CA: Osborne McGraw-Hill, 1995.

Schwartau, Winn. *Information Warfare: Cyberterrorism: Protecting Your Personal Security in the Electronic Age*. 2nd Edition. New York: Thunder's Mouth Press, 1996.

Schwartau, Winn. *Information Warfare: Chaos on the Electronic Superhighway*. New York: Thunder's Mouth Press, 1994.

Schwartau, Winn. *Time Based Security*. Seminole, FL: Inter-Pact Press, 1999.

Schweizer, Peter. *Friendly Spies: How America's Allies Are Using Economic Espionage to Steal Our Secrets*. New York: Atlantic Monthly Press, 1993.

Shaffer, Steven L., and Alan R. Simon. *Network Security*. Cambridge, MA: AP Professional, 1994.

Stang, David J., and Sylvia Moon. *Network Security Secrets*. San Mateo, CA: IDG Books Worldwide, Inc., 1993.

Steele, Guy L., Jr., et al. *The Hacker's Dictionary*. New York: Harper & Row, 1983.

Sterling, Bruce. *The Hacker Crackdown: Law and Disorder on the Electronic Frontier*. New York: Bantam Books, 1992.

Stoll, Clifford. *The Cuckoo's Egg*. New York: Doubleday, 1989.

Toffler, Alvin. *Future Shock*. New York: Bantam Books, 1971.

Toffler, Alvin. *The Third Wave*. New York: Bantam Books, 1980.

Toffler, Alvin. *Powershift*. New York: Bantam Books, 1990.

Toffler, Alvin, and Heidi Toffler. *War and Anti-War*. Boston: Little, Brown, 1993.

Toffler, Alvin, and Heidi Toffler. *Creating a New World Civilization*. Atlanta: Turner Publishing, Inc., 1994.

Walker, Bruce J., and Ian F. Blake. *Computer Security and Protection Structures*. Stroudsburg, PA: Dowden, Hutchinson & Ross, Inc., 1977.

Wood, Charles Cresson. *Information Security Policies Made Easy*. Sausalito, CA.: Self-Published, 1994.

MAGAZINES

InfoSecurity. Published monthly by the International Computer Security Association, 106 Access Road, Norwood, MA, 02062, USA.

Information Security. Published by West Coast Publishing, 161 Worcester Road, Suit 201, Framingham, MA, 01701, USA.

Computers & Security. Published by Elsevier Technology, P.O. Box 150, Kidlington, Oxford, OX5 1AS, UK.

WEB SITES

Associations

http://www.gocsi.com

http://www.acfe.org

http://www.asis.com

http://www.icsa.com

Hackers

http://www.2600.com

http://www.unitedcouncil.org

http://www.phrack.com

http://www.underground.org

http://Lopht.com

Information Systems Security

http://www.infosecuritymag.com

http://www.securitymanagement.com

http://www.issa.org

http://www.icsa.com

http://www.ics2.org

http://www.securityinfo.com

http://www.crypto.com

http://www.cs.purdue.edu/coast/coast.html

http://www.telstra.com.au/info/security.html

http://www.nsi.org/compsec.html

http://www.iss.net/vd/library.html

http://www.ntbugtraq.com

http://www.tno.nl/instit/fel/intern/wkinsec.html

http://www.cs.purdue.edu/coast/hotlist

http://java.sun.com/security

http://spam.abuse.net

http://cs-www.ncsl.nist.gov

http://www.ncsa.com

http://www.rootshell.com

http://www.microsoft.com/ie/security

http://www.netscape.com/assist/security

Auditing

http://www.isaca.org

http://www.iia.org

Government

http://www.piperinfo.com/~piper/state/states.html

http://www.ustreas.gov

http://www.usdoj.gov

http://www.fbi.gov

http://www.ifs.univie.ac.at.~uncjin/uncjin.html

Law Enforcement

http://www.ncjrs.org

http://www.nlectc.org

http://police.sas.ab.ca

http://wings.buffalo.edu/student-life/

Public-Safety/Other

http://innotts.co/~mick2mc/ukpolice.html

http://www.lookup.com/Homepages/91900/home.html

Law

http://www.law.indiana.edu/law/lawindex.html

http://www.internetlawyer.com

http://law.house.gov

http://www.americandream.com

http://www.ilpf.org

http://www.discovery.org/iltfrls.html

Terrorism

http://interlog.com/~vabiro

http://www.site.gmu/~cdibona

http://www.tezcat.com/~top/terrorist

http://www.xensei.com/users/humcom/police.htm

CERTs

http://www.auscert.org.au

http://www.cert.org

http://ciac.llnl.gov

http://www.assist.mil

http://fedcirc.llnl.gov

http://www.first.org

http://www.cert.dfn.de/eng/dfncert

http://www-naisirc.nasa.gov/nasa/index.html

http://www.cert.dfn.de/eng/csir/europe/certs.html

About the Authors

WILLIAM C. BONI, MBA
E-mail: bboni@gte.net

Mr. William C. Boni leads Pricewaterhouse Coopers Information Protection practice, which helps organizations safeguard their most important assets: trade secrets and proprietary information. Over the past 22 years Bill has helped a variety of organizations design and implement cost-effective programs to protect both tangible and intangible assets. Prior to joining PricewaterhouseCoopers, Bill worked as the Director of Information Protection Services for Amgen, the world's largest and most successful biotechnology company. He designed the company's overall program to protect critical information, intellectual property, and trade secrets against a wide range of threats. He also implemented programs to safeguard the company's global network and computer systems. Other assignments in his distinguished career include work as a U.S. Army counter-intelligence officer; federal agent and investigator; investigator and security consultant with Kroll Associates; Vice President of Information Security for a major regional bank; and program security officer for "Star Wars" projects with defense technology companies such as Hughes Aircraft and Rockwell.

Bill has been quoted by leading print publications such as the *Wall Street Journal, U.S. News & World Report,* and the Los Angeles *Times.* He has also appeared on both "Prime Time Live" and CNN "Television News" discussing espionage directed against American high technology corporations. He is a member of the American Society of Industrial Security Standing Committee on Protecting Proprietary Information; the Society of Competitive Intelligence Professionals; and the Information Systems Audit & Control Association.

DR. GERALD L. KOVACICH, CFE, CPP, CISSP

E-mail: kovacich11@home.com

Dr. Gerald L. Kovacich graduated from the University of Maryland with a bachelor's degree in history and politics, with emphasis in Asia; the University of Northern Colorado with a master's degree in social science with emphasis in public administration; Golden Gate University with a master's degree in telecommunications management; the DOD Language Institute (Chinese Mandarin); and August Vollmer University with a doctorate degree in criminology. He is also a Certified Fraud Examiner, Certified Protection Professional, and a Certified Information Systems Security Professional.

Dr. Kovacich has over 36 years of industrial security, investigations, information systems security, and information warfare experience in both government and business. He has worked for numerous technology-based international corporations as an ISSO; security, audit, and investigations manager; and consultant. He has also developed and managed several internationally based InfoSec programs for Fortune 500 corporations and managed several information systems security organizations, providing service and support for their information warfare products and services.

Dr. Kovacich has taught both graduate and undergraduate courses in criminal justice, technology crimes investigations, and security for Los Angeles City College, DeAnza College, Golden Gate University, and August Vollmer University. He has also lectured internationally, and presented workshops on these topics for national and international conferences as well as written numerous published articles on high-tech crime investigations, information systems security, and information warfare, both nationally and internationally.

Dr. Kovacich is currently living on an island in Washington state where he continues to write, lecture, and conduct research relative to information systems protection, information warfare defensive and offensive operations, and high-tech crime.

Index